EXPLORATIONS IN RHETORIC

Studies in Honor of
Douglas Ehninger

DOUGLAS WAGNER EHNINGER (1913-1979)

EXPLORATIONS IN RHETORIC

Studies in Honor of
Douglas Ehninger

Ray E. McKerrow, Editor
University of Maine—Orono

Editorial Committee:

James R. Irvine
Colorado State University
Donovan Ochs
University of Iowa
Michael Osborn
Memphis State University
Marilyn J. VanGraber
Diogenes Associates

SCOTT, FORESMAN AND COMPANY GLENVIEW, ILLINOIS

Dallas, Tex. Oakland, N.J. Palo Alto, Ca. Tucker, Ga. London

Library of Congress Cataloging in Publication Data
Main entry under title:

Explorations in rhetoric.

  Includes bibliographical references and index.
  1. Rhetoric—Addresses, essays, lectures.
2. Ehninger, Douglas. I. Ehninger, Douglas.
II. McKerrow, Ray E.
PN175.E96   808   81-9244
ISBN 0-673-15518-8   AACR2

CONTENTS

ACKNOWLEDGMENTS

The "Dedication" and "Introduction" explain the genesis of *Explorations in Rhetoric* and preview its examination of rhetoric's conceptual, historical, and technical dimensions. On behalf of the editorial committee, I wish to express appreciation to each of the authors for their unique and illuminating contributions to this exploration.

As editor, I am deeply grateful for the diligence and dedication of members of the editorial committee. From the initial review stages through final revisions of the essays, their editorial skills and advice, as well as their sense of timing in providing encouragement when I was most in need, will long be remembered. Several other scholars also were instrumental in selecting and reviewing essays at various stages of development, and to them we express appreciation: Gerard Hauser, Pennsylvania State University; Daniel O'Keefe, University of Illinois; Richard Leo Enos, Carnegie-Mellon University; Walter R. Fisher, University of Southern California; James Golden, Ohio State University; and Pat Burnes, Erling Skorpen, and Virginia Steinhoff, all from the University of Maine—Orono. The wise counsel and support provided by Flo Beth Ehninger and by Samuel L. Becker, Chairman of the Department of Communication and Theatre Arts at the University of Iowa, have been valuable to me and the committee. In addition, the support granted this project by the administration and the Department of Speech Communication at the University of Maine—Orono has been instrumental in bringing this volume to fruition.

The editorial staff at Scott, Foresman and Company also is deserving of recognition. Jo Ann Johnson, who worked closely with Douglas Ehninger, as well as Richard Welna, Barbara Muller, and Lynn Friedman have been more than generous with their time and energy in shepherding this project through to completion. Scott, Foresman and Company's cooperation in undertaking the publication of this *festschrift* is deeply appreciated. Their decision is a reflection of their commitment to the speech communication discipline and is, in itself, a fitting tribute to the person this volume honors.

RAY E. MCKERROW

DEDICATION

Explorations in Rhetoric is dedicated to Douglas Wagner Ehninger (1913–79). While many dedications are "in memory of," this volume represents something qualitatively different. In our minds and hearts the work is less "in memory of" than "because of" Douglas Ehninger.

When the project was initiated, "in memory of" was certainly far from our minds. Doug was still very much among us—prodding, directing, encouraging, criticizing, and always watching. That he is not present to see the volume completed is a regrettable accident of fate. We expected him to be our most vigorous critic! We expected, also, to hear him announce gruffly that no one should dedicate a book to him, a comment which would have been in keeping with his character. Thus, it was appropriate for Bruce Gronbeck, in presenting Doug's widow with the Speech Communication Association's first posthumous Distinguished Service Award, to remark that Doug "would have blushed" to accept it for himself. He would have blushed. Indeed, we rather anticipated that response when he accepted this completed volume, a volume written "because of" his continuing contribution to the speech communication discipline.

When speaking of a professional colleague we wish to honor, our encomia usually divide into well-established categories. We address our comments to the institutions he attended and the institutions whose faculties he graced; we speak of his publication, scholarship, and service to the profession. And, we speak of his lasting contribution to those fortunate enough to have interacted with him as teacher and friend.

We dedicate *Explorations in Rhetoric* to Douglas Ehninger because of the fine institutions which he represented and to which he contributed as both student and faculty member. Northwestern, Ohio State, Virginia, Florida, and Iowa are all pleased to claim him. As a student he became part of the traditions at Northwestern and Ohio State, and as a faculty member he helped build enduring traditions at Florida and Iowa.

His colleagues and students in the South will remember Douglas Ehninger as a debate coach of some considerable repute. The contribution he made in his never-ending love/hate relationship with forensics and its tradition is attributable to many qualities of mind and spirit, but two are worthy of note: his penchant for studying theory as

This dedication was written by MARILYN J. VANGRABER, *who is President, Diogenes Associates, Burlington, Vermont.*

well as perfecting practice and his equally memorable habit of devoting total energy and concentration to whatever he was doing. Even though most of his Iowa students heard frequent disparaging references to his "twenty wasted years" in debate, the positive and pervasive influence of those years on his career and personality is readily apparent. Indeed, all of his writing and teaching demonstrated the thorough preparation, incisive analysis, clear organization, and professional approach that he learned from and taught in debate. Douglas Ehninger was indelibly marked by debate, and in turn imbued colleagues and students with an appreciation for the positive virtues of such training and discipline.

We dedicate *Explorations in Rhetoric* to Douglas Ehninger because of his publication and scholarship. Ehninger's published monographs and books have been fundamental fare in virtually every communication curriculum in the nation, with some of the more popular items being translated into French and Spanish for use abroad. A number of the monographs have been reprinted in so many places that reading certain collections produces a kind of déjà vu.

It is no accident that this collection of studies, too, should contain references to Doug's published efforts. His "Campbell, Blair, and Whately: Old Friends in a New Light," "On Systems of Rhetoric," and "Argument as Method: Its Nature, Its Limitations and Its Uses," stand as eloquent testimony to the pervasiveness of his contribution in each of the dimensions of rhetoric.

Publication, while frequently confused with scholarship, is not the same thing. Scholarship is research, study, investigation, and examination. It is the product and demonstration of curiosity and criticism, of evaluation and judgment. Scholarship is the exercise of discipline and consistency, and of that most favorite of Ehninger god-terms, "rigor." Sometimes, scholarship culminates in publication. Always, it contributes to the continued growth and development of the scholar. Douglas Ehninger was a scholar.

His love of scholarly activity was a continual motivating force during the varied phases of his academic career. His tenure as a debate coach was both respectable and successful, but it was not enough. He moved on to an exhaustive and estimable study of the systemic features of eighteenth-century rhetorics and rhetoricians. Although he might profess to be bored, this was an area to which he and his students continually returned, each time to find something helpful in their quest for knowledge about the principles and practices of rhetoric. Ehninger became a well-known and respected "expert" in this period; however, for his probing intellect, the eighteenth century also was not enough.

For at least the last fifteen years of his life, Ehninger immersed himself in the study of an impressive array of contributors to his never

quite completed vision of contemporary rhetorical thought. Philosophers, psychologists, and linguists jostled for ideational position with
journalists, dramatists, and historians. No one thinker or discipline was
too far removed from the mainstream to be considered, and he reveled
(quietly and off-handedly, of course) in the straightfaced presentation
of some esoteric find to a class of "advanced" graduate students who
thought they already knew everything.

While his study was wide, it was not compensatingly shallow. He
was not persuaded, for example, that Kenneth Burke's contribution
was all that earth-shattering. Nonetheless, he did what a lot of
self-styled Burkeans never did: he read Burke. Scholars do that,
usually before they make a judgment for good or ill.

Even to the end, Ehninger was doing the things a scholar does:
reading, studying, analyzing, synthesizing. He was at his best when
pulling disparate pieces of a puzzle together and, in the clear, analytic
style that was his trademark, setting forth his conclusions for others to
judge. In the process, good pieces that did not fit one particular puzzle
were not discarded; they were set aside for another time, another place,
another puzzle.

We dedicate *Explorations in Rhetoric* to Douglas Ehninger because
of his service to the profession. The Speech Communication
Association justifiably recognized his contributions with its Distinguished Service Award. During his career, Ehninger served as editor of
Speech Monographs and as associate editor of the *Quarterly Journal of
Speech*. He was president of SCA during what Gronbeck referred to as
"particularly troubled times," and as president and member continually sought to improve its status and its service. Other institutions and
individuals have equally good reasons to recognize him. He involved
himself in his profession; he devoted himself to his profession; he was a
thorough and total professional.

Having given all these good reasons for dedicating *Explorations in
Rhetoric* to Douglas Ehninger, I now turn to what is the most important
reason: the impact he had on his students, the way they were changed,
shaped, and directed; ultimately, his effect on who and what they
became. It is no accident that the contributors to this volume were all
Doug's students. We designed it that way, deliberately and purpose-
fully. We intended the design to say that our study and apprenticeship
with Ehninger had ineradicable meaning for us. Because of that
meaning, we are writing a book and putting his name on it.

The impact an individual has on his students is an amalgam of
many things: personality, ideas, values, behavior, and a collection of
even more intangible factors. Ehninger's personality certainly *had*
impact on his students. He could be alternately sensitive and
contentious, open and abrupt, talkative and taciturn. He could be

remarkably tolerant of one student's inept reporting, and caustically *in*tolerant of the next. Sitting next to him at a seminar table could be a warm, shared experience. It also could be like sitting next to a time bomb which just stopped ticking!

As a result, his seminars were not occasions to relax and be taught. They were situations in which students became of necessity the primary instrument of their own education; their peers became secondary instruments; and the "teacher," frequently unobtrusively, did whatever was necessary to keep the process in motion. He seldom lectured, preferring to listen to others do so. He did not "display" his often superior knowledge as many teachers do, preferring to defer to students who had read something "more recently" than he. He did not offer his own opinions and positions to a class, preferring to be asked. Prying an opinion from him, as a matter of fact, frequently required a pretty hefty crowbar, and then the opinion was apt to be prefaced by "I'm probably wrong, but . . . ." What invariably followed was a clear distillation of the central issues under discussion, with crisp demarcations between and among competing ideas and positions.

Ehninger's ideas and values marked us, too, as frequently because we disagreed with them as because we found them acceptable. Many students "discovered" Whately or Toulmin or Perelman or Searle or Polanyi—explored the nature of controversy or the language of discourse, created new ways of looking at motives or invention or speech acts—because they disagreed with Doug and were determined to *prove him wrong*. That you *could* disagree with Ehninger in class, or later in the relative safety of a convention presentation or published essay, was often motivation to launch into a research project. His attention to students extended beyond the classroom. He would make the time, for example, to attend a convention presentation of a student because he had heard that one of his interpretive works was being called into question. No matter how well-reasoned or vigorous the "question," he would congratulate the individual on the clarity of the argument, while reserving judgment on the accuracy of the attack.

In fact, many of us have wondered who saw behind a seemingly frigid facial exterior to the faint smile that lurked there, almost unseen; we also have wondered how many recognized the secret pride he felt in a student's ability to attack and defend an idea or judgment with good data and sharp intelligence. But who detected the smile or the pride is unimportant; the achievemnt was what mattered.

Ehninger's behavior as professional and scholar also shaped his students. Many of them refer to Doug's counsel that good writing needed rigorous rewriting—that is, "blood on the typewriter keys." While it is not uncommon to counsel this behavior, it is uncommon to live it. Many demand rigor from their students' writing; few demand the same from themselves. Some have written more than Douglas Ehninger and some have written better; very few have been as consistently demanding of themselves in their own work. Doug's example personified his counsel, demonstrated its efficacy, and motivated many of us to heed his advice.

As scholar, teacher, counselor, and friend, Doug's influence was the result of his personality, his example, and his expectations. He expected, required, demanded excellence. A student's best effort was acceptable, but only for the present. Growth was not only possible, it was necessary. Improvement in all phases of research and writing was expected. For students, this expectation *became* the "Iowa tradition." Ehninger's place in that tradition is central and enduring.

This book is dedicated to Douglas Wagner Ehninger—to the tradition he represented, the standards he defended, the rigor he demanded. We dedicate it with respect for what he was and with gratitude for what that helped us to become.

MARILYN J. VANGRABER

INTRODUCTION

These essays in honor of Douglas Ehninger form a coherent pattern of development which was certainly not predetermined by the selection committee. With a skillful assist from the editor, they reflect much of the cohesive intellectual life of Professor Ehninger himself, and indicate the degree to which he marked the lives and interests of his students.

The result is that the book has more the character of a symposium than a collection of independent essays. Perhaps even more, the book seems representative of an Ehninger seminar, with its collective quest after ideas and its sense of intellectual adventure.

Douglas Ehninger's intellectual life, and so also those of his students whose essays are printed here, was centered on the subject of rhetorical theory. The first assignment for a novice in Ehninger's seminar classes was to write a short paper defining the nature of

This introduction was written by MICHAEL OSBORN who is Professor and Chairperson, Department of Theatre and Communication Arts, Memphis State University.

rhetoric. Years later, most of us are still working on the assignment, attempting to remove that large "Incomplete" from the record. That challenge elaborates here into the following basic questions:

(1) What first questions should we ask as we set out to build a rhetorical theory?
(2) How shall we proceed to answer them?
(3) What is the nature of that knowledge which rhetoric engenders?

One impulse in contemporary studies has been to seek the deeper, stable structure of relationships implied by the study of speech. Michael McGuire's essay makes the case for the value of such study. The advantage of structuralism is that it points to a resolution of the conflict between the humanist and the scientist. It discovers principles which, in their observational nature, satisfy that scientific stipulation, and in their implicative and suggestive nature, encourage the speculative investigations of the philosopher and humanist. In McGuire's analysis structuralism synthesizes mechanical and empirical models of reality; we can see how these models, though distinct, are also fundamentally related. The ground of their convergence is in language, the nexus of empirical and social reality. Thus we may ask, what are the persistent structures of speech behavior, discoverable within and across rhetorical artifacts, and we may make this the first question on which to build a theory.

Structuralism seems psychologically, almost religiously, satisfying in that it does presuppose a certain fundamental organization within subjects rhetorical. Some may hesitate to grant the act of faith required in accepting such pervasive, meta-real structures outside, inside, or "beneath" rhetorical experience. Research in archetypes, one might say, offers evidence of such structure, but that evidence is surely still limited and tentative. We are, I suspect, in need of further basic research before grounding rhetorical theory on the rock of structuralism. Moreover, structuralist theory seems to carry a heavy freight of determinism. While providing a systematic macrorhetoric, it would seem to deal poorly with the *art* of rhetoric and with the possible uniqueness of the speech encounter. It would seem to provide the critic with poor equipment to assess the quality and ethics of rhetorical performance.

Finally, I am not sure the structuralist metaphor fits well Ehninger's provocative analysis of rhetorical systems. During the lively moments when the systems concept was generating in Ehninger's thinking, it was my impression from day-to-day conversation with him that an organic conception of rhetoric was—initially at least—far more instrumental in his thinking: that is to say, there was a life-force in the conception of rhetoric which had found first a grammatic articulation, then a psychological realization, now a sociological awakening, as this living idea of human communication evolved and grew across time.

Nevertheless, McGuire begins the seminar of this book quite ably. Ehninger would have been gesturing and arguing and diagraming enchanting thought structures on his inevitable blackboard before the discussion of McGuire's essay had concluded.

Michael Calvin McGee adds a certain dialectical quality to the book by urging a materialist approach that would make rhetorical theory strictly derivative from practice. McGee denies that theory should begin with presuppositions such as those which set out in search for structures: he would ask simply, what is the consciousness reflected in the rhetorical practice of each age, and how is that consciousness created? He urges that we reawaken to the Marxist injunction that "it is not consciousness that determines life, but life that determines consciousness." (I can't help the incidental impression that in terms of pedagogy, McGee provides a sophisticated rationale for returning to the formulary tradition of the study of speech models). There are many wonderful moments in this essay, and McGee's epigrammatic, Emersonesque style makes them the more memorable. His statement concerning the larger realization of rhetoric that awakens within the materialist view is eloquent, and there is a rather brilliant realization here of the rhetorical dreamlife of a people, in which "even the dead can participate."

As striking as these moments may be, the overall approach to theory suggested by McGee seems rather narrow, and would result in declaring illegitimate or irrelevant certain traditional theoretical concerns. If we discipline ourselves to a theory derived strictly from observation, limited to generalizations from data, then we have no grounds for introducing standards for qualitative or normative judgment. If one were in an unpleasant mood (and Ehninger could be ruthless in his search after an idea), one might ask, "Whence derive the standards which compel McGee to posit the materialistic approach?" Values which transcend the observable come back to haunt scholarly inquiry, even in the act of observing reality, and always there are the nagging questions, "Can there be a world apart from ideas of the world?" "Can we escape, in the very dawning acts of sensation and perception, selecting what we see and projecting ourselves into the observation?" Where I part company with McGee, and where I believe he parts company with his better self, is in the naturalistic bias that leads him to draw a sharp distinction between idea and reality: "If history matters at all to rhetorical theory, and I am convinced that it does, it is material history, not the history of ideas." I am convinced Ehninger would have been alternately charmed and enraged (and secretly delighted) by this essay, and that the seminar would have to recess to give all a chance to recover from the discussion that would ensue.

Samuel Watson's essay joins and extends the dialectic of the book by synthesizing Michael Polanyi's views concerning human reason. As presented here, Polanyi would deny the supra-personal claims of structuralism, would reject McGee's materialism, and would assert the primacy of ethical concerns in any theory concerning rhetoric. While McGee sees little personal risk in communication, stressing that we assume different roles in communication situations which do not involve the true self, Polanyi argues that because the sense of self is formed rhetorically, we risk that sense of personal identity whenever we join in rhetorical transactions. What formed us may alter us, and the extent to which we are reborn in rhetoric is also the extent to which we die.

While McGee's materialism would stress the collection of "data" as a first task for the building of theory, Polanyi holds that such doctrine gives to "knowledge" more reliability than can actually be justified, while denying judgment and wisdom their proper attention. Polanyi's doctrine of personal knowledge makes it possible to talk about responsibility in communication and even about the existence of evil. Watson summarizes: "Of all animals man alone seeks truth, justice, and beauty, under a firmament of standards which he sets for himself and affirms to be true by submitting to their guidance. At the same time, of all animals man is alone capable of falsehood and evil." For Polanyi the goal of reason, then, even in popular discourse, is not to exemplify structures nor to manifest consciousness, but rather to create meaning and to achieve discoveries. Rhetoric's role is to facilitate this process, much as Bacon found a vital part for rhetoric in the advancement of learning.

To this distinctive other voice introduced into the inquiry by Watson, Richard Cherwitz and James Hikins add the support of John Stuart Mill. For to the obvious questions, "Is personal knowledge really a 'knowledge'?" and, "Is communication justified by the transmission of such knowledge?" Mill would seem to offer a qualified "yes." This conditional affirmation also strengthens the normative direction of Polanyi's thought. For through its process of ethical argumentation, which in *On Liberty* means subjecting a truth-claim to access, defense, and correction, rhetoric transcends personalized knowledge, or at least elevates it to a public and sharable status. Moreover, the system of beliefs materialized and accepted in social reality represents more than mere consensus: through the process of ethical argumentation that system is legitimized, and becomes transmuted into a responsible set of premises for public discourse.

Thus rhetoric has a constructive truth-function, and *On Liberty* can be perceived as a treatise on argumentation in a sense larger than the traditional emphasis on tactics and structure. Rather, the work justifies argument by revealing its function, and in the process also justifies the human liberty to pursue such argument wherever it may take us.

But this knowledge that we receive through argument—is it, as tradition would emphasize, uncertain, contingent, and at best probable? Bruce Gronbeck enters the seminar quest at this point to affirm the possibility of certitude. Premises, he says, can "force" conclusions, can make us *submit* to a demonstration even when we may be initially reluctant.

His essay, which comes to focus on the nature of inference and the conditions under which it occurs, looks upon inference-making as rule-governed behavior which operates under certain sanctions. The most basic form of inference, perceptual inference, which results in claims such as "This is a tree," he finds conclusive but of little interest argumentatively. Yet we need to be wary of such simple declarative statements; their form may disguise value judgments and submerged argumentative structures. "I am a Man," printed on signs carried by striking sanitation workers in Memphis before Martin Luther King was slain, was probably the most powerful rhetorical statement of that extended crisis. Such statements, which seem formally innocent, can function in their settings as strategic depictions. Operating without adjectives or any other sign of rhetorical intent, they can implant themselves as categories of perception and predispose our judgments.

As he pursues his thesis Gronbeck does indeed place argumentative forms within their existential settings. His point is that social expectations evolve which, when satisfied within a specific argument, will constitute the force it exerts upon auditors. Thus the context of an argument provides not just its specific challenge, but the operational standards by which it will be adjudicated. Gronbeck urges that we spend less time trying to extrapolate models of argument from their living milieus and more time examining patterns of rhetorical compulsion created at given moments in public discourse, giving rise to a formidable, even if evanescent, power. What one generation finds argumentatively compelling will become a wonder to the next. Gronbeck's position seems clearly in harmony with McGee's materialism, and would also seem compatible with Polanyi's pluralistic acceptance of the legitimacy of belief-systems as they operate in various societies at various times. Thus the seminar gains resonance from his essay.

The problems of how rhetorical knowledge is generated and of how argument is formed are given historical perspective by Donovan Ochs' reexamination of rhetorical invention as counseled by Cicero.

Ochs is troubled by the mechanical approach to invention taught generally in Roman rhetoric, and by why a man of the rhetorical world like Cicero would have taken such artifice seriously. Ochs goes to the *Topica,* Cicero's last work on rhetoric, for an answer. He finds that in Cicero's treatment the inventional topics no longer remain static "places" or receptacles of thought; rather, they have evolved into a dynamic model of the reasoning process. For the mature Cicero the topics were aimed not at furnishing an argument with commonplaces, but rather at achieving credibility with auditors. The range of application was not predetermined and closed, but rather would be limited only by the speaker's knowledge, imagination, and by the circumstances of the audience and occasion. Thus Cicero forms a bridge to the modern theory of argumentation. Ehninger, who along with his concern for the present had a true antiquarian regard for the past, would have been fascinated. He would have been further taken by the Ciceronian concept of maximal propositions, which are warrants for making inferences. The maximal proposition may also be thought of as an axiom, or as a fundamental "rule" in Gronbeck's terminology, by which the game of argumentation is sanctioned and played on specific occasions. However, Ochs notes, Cicero does not develop a consciousness of such deviations from the sterile doctrine of his day. He is not curious concerning the implication of his views for rhetorical theory. More's the fun for us!

Eric Skopec continues the historical perspective but changes somewhat the focus of the inquiry. His point of departure is more the systems of rhetoric concept Ehninger introduced, applying its precepts to the rhetoric-as-expression emphasis which developed as part of the Romantic movement in the British intellectual environment. Indeed, it is Skopec's contention that systems of rhetoric must be viewed as part of the total environment of ideas in which they gain pre-eminence. In the mind-body dualism which was evidenced in the era considered by Skopec, rhetoric ceased being concerned with invention and arrangement, forms provided more by nature than by art. Rhetoric rather saw to the expression of the emotions through striking language and effective bodily action. So long as such expression was regarded highly, rhetoric was not negatively affected by the basic dualism. But when the romantic view of mind began to fade, and the need and importance of rationality were reasserted, rhetoric found itself cut adrift from the vital intellectual arts and left without significance in new theory.

Yet how are we to account for the reemergence of rhetoric in our time? Skopec, I believe, may overemphasize the role of environment in determining the fate of theory. Can there not be Ideas which persist through time, and which interact with their environments, shaping as well as being shaped? This, I believe, is the view that Ehninger presented, establishing a dialectic between the concept of rhetoric and the times in which it developed. Thus he presented that Idea as pressing towards its fulfillment at any given moment in ways made possible by the intellectual climate. The organic development of a concept of rhetoric might be deflected or delayed, but its essential direction would lie within its own predisposing nature.

If we assume this slightly modified explanation, then we can say that the rhetoric of which Skopec speaks was in a time of pause before the concept of rhetoric would find a vital new opportunity for development. That opportunity would be provided in the sociological awareness which was already dawning in Hegel, who saw the orator as expressing the advancing consciousness of his people. Thus we can see how Skopec's account of rhetoric-as-expression comes into consonance with the macrorhetoric articulated by Ehninger.

Still operating in the historical mode, Ray E. McKerrow asks us to reassess the importance of Richard Whately, who has greatly influenced twentieth-century views of argument, and whose *Elements of Rhetoric* had been introduced by Ehninger in its most recent edition. Whately has been a bone of contention between those who see in him an affirmation of Aristotelian views and others who, following more the systems approach, view him as marked by eighteenth-century thought. While dealing with this controversy, McKerrow also reveals Whately's thoughts on the nature of rhetorical knowledge, thereby relating the essay to the central quest of this book.

Concerning historical position, McKerrow views Whately on his own terms, without the macroscopic bias which would turn Whately either towards the neoclassical school or towards the evolutionary systems concept. From this perspective we see Whately in terms of his realism, nominalism, relativism, and empiricism. It is in terms of relativism that Whately's concept of rhetorical knowledge emerges most interestingly in the context of this book. Such knowledge is distorted in the sense that it reflects the viewer's self-interest in objects of perception, and is further distorted when it is transmitted and selectively received by auditors. Rhetorical knowledge can only be probable, not because of any objective uncertainty among facts in the world (Aristotle's position), but because of the subjective nature of human judgment. Thus rhetorical knowledge expresses our beliefs about things rather than revealing the things themselves, a point of view which would seem to relate to the personal knowledge approach. But in terms of that approach Whately was unable to see the vital, constitutive connection between argument and the sense of self. Thus he could see the technique of argument and even glimpse its nature, but he could not see its human significance.

The James Golden and Josina Makau essay returns the focus to rhetorical knowledge, viewed from the specialized perspective of legal reasoning. The authors propose to study United States Supreme Court deliberations as exemplary of legal reasoning, which they offer in turn, citing Toulmin and Perelman, as a paradigm of practical reasoning. Probably some will object to such concentric assumptions, arguing that we must strain a great deal to make Supreme Court reasoning representative of the great center of practical argumentation. Rather, they will say, such discourse points more towards refined and perfected models of reasoning, its reliance upon precedent through the doctrine of *stare decisis* being at least more similar to the reliance of mathematical reasoning upon the axiom. Moreover, the specialized audience which this essay ably and perceptively describes would make such argument quite uncharacteristic. Perhaps judicial argumentation is a mixed mode which operates on the border between practical and perfected reasoning.

Nevertheless this essay makes a considerable contribution in identifying a four-step process of deliberation which is characteristic of such reasoning. This process should prove of great value for comparative study alone, even if it does not develop a common model for argumentation in general. What it does describe is a mode of deliberation which is highly deductive in nature and form, highly sensitive to the authority of precedent and strongly authoritative in its own presumptions. It is a conservative argument, much governed by rules, and dedicated as much to producing consistency in its own behavior as to providing justice in the particular case.

So-called "problems of the penumbra" produce the urgency and the creative potential of judicial rhetoric. If each case fell neatly into the sphere of a precedent, there would be little need for rhetoric, just as there is little need for rhetoric in logical/mathematical reasoning. Instead, the challenge to judicial argumentation is to make the best match possible between the specific case and the relevant precedents, and to defend and justify this act of interpretation and classification. To the degree that it extends precedents, the resulting decision has the potential to influence public behavior, and to be absorbed eventually within the norms and the "knowledge" of a society.

The audience for judicial reasoning would appear to approach Perelman's concept of the universal audience. As described here, this audience represents a convergence of the real and the ideal, the particular and the universal. While quite exacting in its standards of argument, it also grants unusual authority to the decisions reached through such argument. This concept of audience should prove quite valuable for scholarship in rhetoric. At the point where this highly rule-constrained, conservative, but authoritative rhetoric meets this demanding but compliant audience lies the epistemic function of judicial reasoning. That such rhetoric creates an influential form of public knowledge is undeniable. Legal argumentation need not be paradigmatic to deserve our serious attention.

Ehninger, I know, would have been interested by this essay especially because it touches one of his favorite subjects, debate. I recall his passionate involvement in so many wonderful arguments concerning the nature of debate and I am sure no more could be accomplished in the seminar after the discussion of this essay. Fittingly, it closes the book.

Ehninger would have left this particular meeting of the class highly stimulated, and the argument and discussion would have spilled out after him into the halls and coffee-shops. This book should generate such excitement in our field, and just as in an Ehninger seminar class, should produce fresh discoveries on the morrow.

MICHAEL OSBORN

The Structural Study of Speech

Michael McGuire

One problem attracting the efforts of rhetorician and communication theorist alike is "theory-building" or "modeling"; terms which will be used interchangeably here.[1] Methodological differences between theory-building efforts of the rhetorician and the communication theorist create the impression that two very different purposes or interests are at work, or that two completely different activities are going on. If there is a way to explain that the scientist and humanist (as they have been called)[2] are working toward the same ends with necessarily different but compatible, even cumulative methods, then relationships may be inferred between rhetorical and communication theory which prefigure coherency of research at a more abstract and theoretically interesting level than hypothesis generation and hypothesis testing.[3] Such a discussion, avowedly heuristic, is the topic of this paper: it is my purpose to articulate the case for structuralism and to suggest its applications and implications for the study of speech.[4] First, the perspective *structuralism* will be introduced by explication of its underpinning assumptions.

MICHAEL MCGUIRE *is Associate Professor of Speech Communication at the University of Georgia, and Visiting Associate Professor of Rhetoric at the University of California, Davis.*

Second, structuralism's key distinctions, between empirical and social reality, between *langue* and *parole,* will be explained, and the methods and models advocated by structuralism in light of its distinctions will be set forth. Lastly, structuralist methods will be applied to the study of speech.

THE STRUCTURALIST PERSPECTIVE

Structuralism is a term applied to a growing body of writings in several disciplines: linguistics, anthropology, literary criticism and theory, and psychology, to name a few. Structuralists in all fields proceed from the concept "that the world is made up of relationships rather than things,"[5] and so attempt by analysis to discover formal relations through which elements in a structure or system achieve significance. Structuralism is therefore holistic, arguing that the meaning of any thing, action, or experience cannot be understood apart from the whole, the structure, of which it is a part.[6] Therefore, foremost among structuralism's assumptions relevant to speech is that all human activities and objects "signify beyond themselves."[7] In this sense all social phenomena are *language-like,* and susceptible to analyses of their lexicons (parts or pieces, like words, available in the system) and their grammars (laws or rules which regulate combinations of the pieces available in the system). Claude Lévi-Strauss puts this central issue thus: "The question may be raised whether the different aspects of social life (including even art and religion) cannot only be studied by the methods of, and with the help of concepts similar to those employed in linguistics, but also whether they do not constitute phenomena whose inmost nature is the same as that of language."[8]

The structuralist attempts to isolate the latent "deep structures" of social phenomena; as Piaget says, "Structuralism . . . seeks to explain empirical systems by postulating 'deep' structures from which the former are derivable."[9] These "deep structures" are purely mental or epistemological; like the prototype, grammar, they are not empirically derived, and neither are they products of pure analytical logic. But structuralism is committed to the position that what is simply observable is rarely the whole truth; it treats social relations as a linguist would a surface structure and seeks to explain what deep structure social systems have, and what sort of "grammar" is necessary to derive the surface structures from deep structures. Structuralism is concerned above all with "the strictly human process by which men give meaning to things"; it is therefore a humanism of sorts.[10] But the sort of humanism structuralism represents is the science of man defined as *"homo significans"*: structuralism in Roland Barthes's words, is *"a mode of thought* (or a 'poetics') which seeks less to assign completed meanings to the objects it discovers than *to know how meaning is possible,* at what cost and by what means."[11] Structuralism would not ask *what* Aesop's fable about the fox and the crow means, but rather *how* the fable can have the meaning it does. Questions of archetype and genre abound in structuralist literary criticism, as do models which depict genre traits and are held to be the "grammars" of the various works making up the genre.

Structuralism is essentially scientific because it establishes laws in its domain of inquiry, and demonstrates the existence of universal structures in human thought or signification. These structures "are held to be essentially homologous, subject to transformation from one to another much like algebraic equations. This stance leads to the view that there is a universal manner of structuring which may be genetic."[12] Now, from this point of view, the latent structure, a mental model, is the object of empirical analysis. Lévi-Strauss's work (especially *The Savage Mind*) posits the existence of universal structures of opposition (mainly binary) and grounds them in surface observations, or social facts. Hawkes explains:

> *An analysis of the analogical relationship between the oppositions of "up" and "down," "hot and cold," "raw" and "cooked" will offer insights into the nature of the particular "reality" that each culture perceives.*
>
> *A good example is the opposition between "edible" and "inedible" which all cultures maintain. Obviously the nature of the items placed under either of these two headings will crucially determine the way of life involved, since what is at stake is assent to the same "ordering" of almost the entire material world. "Analogical thought" will move a culture to distinguish a "foreign" culture from itself on this basis, so that the opposition "edible-inedible" will become analogically related to the opposition "native-foreign." This means that "transformations" between the two sets of "similar differences" become possible: "that which is inedible" becomes a metaphor of "that which is foreign." So, one of the persistent English metaphors for the French occurs because frogs' legs, placed under the heading "edible" in France, find themselves under the heading "inedible" in Britain.*[13]

Structural analogs or chains of oppositions are not limited either to the simple binary, antithetical form, or to the realms of practical, natural, or "realistic" thinking. Nowhere is structuring more prevalent than in totemic thought,[14] and totemism has basic analogs to social structure, as Edmund Leach notes:

> *It is a fact of empirical observation that human beings everywhere adopt ritual attitudes towards the animals and plants in their vicinity. Consider,*

for example, the separate . . . rules which govern the behavior of Englishmen towards the creatures which they classify as (1) wild animals, (2) foxes, (3) game, (4) farm animals, (5) pets, (6) vermin. Notice further that if we take the sequence of words: (1a) strangers, (2a) enemies, (3a) friends, (4a) neighbors, (5a) companions, (6a) criminals, the two sets of terms are in some degree homologous.[15]

In these analyses, *what is universal, and empirically derived, is structure, not substance:* there may be no one object universally classified "edible," but the categories "edible-inedible" and their relations to each other and to social perception are universal. The relations are part of social structure, greater as a whole than the sum of the parts.

From the structuralist perspective the making of models of speaking has the purpose of discovering the social structure of speaking. Lévi-Strauss observes, "social relations consist of the raw materials out of which the models making up the social structure are built, while social structure can, by no means, be reduced to the ensemble of the social relations described in a given society."[16] Social structure is a method and outcome for social sciences in general. Usually the method is called *structuralism.*

Certainly structuralism as a method is not wholly precise, but stands somewhere in between factor analysis and Burkean method in terms of its uniformity. Roland Barthes's essay "The Structuralist Activity" speaks to the point:

The goal of all structuralist activity, whether reflective or poetic, is to reconstruct an "object" in such a way as to manifest thereby the rules of functioning (the "functions") of this object. Structuralism is therefore actually a simulacrum of the object, but a directed, interested simulacrum, since the imitated object makes something appear which remained invisible, or if one prefers, unintelligible in the natural object. . . . Structuralism is essentially an activity of imitation, which is also why there is, strictly speaking, no technical difference between structuralism as an intellectual activity on the one hand and literature in particular, art in general on the other: both derive from a mimesis, based not on the analogy of substances (as in so-called realist art), but on the analogy of functions (what Lévi-Strauss calls homology).[17]

The structural study of speech, therefore, will be marked in large measure by the building of models which isolate the unique strategic levels of speaking phenomena, and yet can be compared with models of different strategic levels. The structural study of speech enables comparison of models of different types of speaking, speaking in different cultures, and different social phenomena. Lévi-Strauss elaborates four criteria of models which are structural:

First, the structure exhibits the characteristics of a system. It is made up of several elements, none of which can undergo a change without effecting changes in all the other elements.

Second, for any given model there should be a possibility of ordering a series of transformations resulting in a group of models of the same type.

Third, the above properties make it possible to predict how the model will react if one or more of its elements are submitted to certain modifications.

Finally, the model should be constituted so as to make immediately intelligible all the observed facts.[18]

The interesting question becomes, why choose one or the other kind of model for exhibiting human speaking? Like many other social phenomena, speaking cannot be explained fully by any one model. Lévi-Strauss gives the example of the laws of marriage:

The laws of marriage provide the best illustration. . . . In primitive societies these laws can be expressed in models calling for actual grouping of individuals according to kin or clan; these are mechanical models. *No such distribution exists in our society, where types of marriage are determined by the size of the primary and secondary groups to which prospective mates belong, social fluidity, amount of information, and the like. A satisfactory (though yet untried) attempt to formulate the invariants of our marriage system would therefore have to determine average values—thresholds; it would be a* statistical model.[19]

Yet, as he goes on to point out, whereas a statistical model describes (prescribes, as well) permissible marriages, a mechanical model describes (and prescribes) prohibited marriages. Similarly, Lévi-Strauss notes the possibility of studying suicide on the mechanical (individual's personality, history, social groups, etc.) and statistical (frequency of suicide in a society, in a profession or other group, on a certain day of the week or year, etc.) levels, ultimately making comparisons for types of suicides, societies, and other social phenomena. The structural study of speech embraces realistic diversity regarding methods of constructing models.

The phenomenon of human speech may be studied and modeled statistically or mechanically. If by "human speech" we mean only the production of sound, a mechanical model of vocal apparatus is necessary and sufficient to explain it. On the other hand, when we include "communication" and concepts of meaning, both signs and symbols, then speech becomes much more difficult to model because of these new levels which call for explanations of human perception, language, social settings, and more. Statistical models have been especially popular for the study of group interaction—where frequency counts have been taken—and for the study of message effects on large populations. Mechanical models have been popular for the analysis of discourse and, historically, for prescriptive purposes as well. The *statistical models display empirical reality*—what effect, e.g., *did* occur and was measured; the *mechanical models display social reality*—how discourse achieves meaning. At this point, structuralism's distinctions between empirical and social reality and between mechanical and statistical models command detailed explication.

SOCIAL REALITY VERSUS EMPIRICAL REALITY

The distinction between social reality and empirical reality is problematical in part because the former is one thread in the whole tapestry of the latter, yet is abstracted from and explanatory of the latter. Sometimes the models of social reality are coincidentally accurate or true models of empirical reality; but because empirical verifiability is not the criterion by which social knowledge expressed in models of reality is believed or counted as knowledge, the distinction between reality-defined-empirically and reality-defined-socially remains.[20] For this distinction to be meaningful, particular differences between the properties of empirical and social reality must be established. Structuralism elaborates these particular differences.

Time and Space

The specific character of perceived empirical time is historical, nonreversible, or diachronic; events as empirical phenomena are said to have beginnings and endings. Considered socially, the American Revolution is very much present today, manifest physically in the Constitution, the boundaries of certain states, and other particulars. Moreover, symbols persist after the Revolution (and some new ones are developed based upon it), although their relevance to *empirical reality* is greatly diminished while their relevance to *social reality* remains high, perhaps even increases. These symbols may be used as behavior models for responses to empirically new but socially old (recurrent) problems. Thus the specific character of perceived social time is nonhistorical, reversible, or synchronic.[21]

Empirical space is apprehended as indivisible and continuous, lacking any demonstrable beginning or ending points, separated only by physical laws, for example, such that two material objects may not at the same time occupy the same space. Social space, on the other hand, is measurable and divisible by a variety of preconscious and conscious units of demarcation.²² Social space is divided rather arbitrarily at many levels into nations, states, or regional subunits of those; and more microscopically, space is divided into zones of social distance, personal distance, and intimate distance.²³ That some of these boundaries may coincide with topographical features, as national borders have been rivers or ocean shores, makes them no less arbitrary, as revealed by disputes about how many miles of ocean off one's coast legitimately belong to one's social organization. Although there is variation between cultures with respect to how space is divisible, the structures or concepts of public and private space are widely understood and practiced. Finite and divisible, social space is susceptible to redistribution accomplished by redefinition, whether explicit or tacit.

Langue and Parole

Like many of contemporary structuralism's distinguishing assumptions, the distinction between *langue* and *parole* occurs first in the work of Swiss linguist Ferdinand de Saussure. The inheritor of a tradition which conceived and studied languages as words with attached meanings, subject to observable, historical changes, Saussure argued that language must be studied not only as words and in terms of diachronic time, but also as a relational or structural system and in terms of synchronic time.²⁴ *Langue* refers to the system of language; *parole* refers to speech, or people's use of language.

Saussure uses the analogy of the game of chess to explain the distinction and relationship between *langue* and *parole*. Chess is a system of rules existing separate from and prior to any particular instance of playing chess; paradoxically, the system only becomes concretely, empirically real through the play of individual games which establish a great variety of relations among the pieces.²⁵ Similarly, the system *langue* (language) exists prior to and as determiner of the actual "nature of each manifestation of *parole* [speech], yet it has no concrete existence of its own except in the piecemeal manifestations that speech affords."²⁶ Because *langue* never appears *in toto* at once, it is not observable and not empirically real; it must be inferred from the analysis of *parole*. This inference, as noted earlier, is the model by which structuralist method performs all of its analyses, whether of myth, kinship systems, or visual arts.

Concretization and Abstraction

Empirical reality is given in concrete particulars apprehended through senses which, because they are inherently structuring, introduce the abstraction of homogeneity onto phenomena. Distinctions between *appearance* and *reality* are grounded in the knowledge that human perception does in fact structure data; and the distinction is valid whether one believes the structuring is a distortion, and whether one believes the structuring occurs before, during, or after the momentary state of perceiving. Basically, empirical reality consists of concrete particulars; governing relations between particulars—for example, causation, correlation, subordination—are not necessarily part of empirical reality, even if they may be accurate and testable descriptions.[27]

Social reality consists almost exclusively, if not totally, of structures, relations or abstractions, and is apprehended mainly through cognition. Matter, substance, and the concrete are significant *only* insofar as they are necessary to exemplify relation or structure and *only because of* their relations within the system. Language is a model of one such system, where the relation of the *signifier* "cat" to the animals *signified* is arbitrary, explainable only by a (language) system which is self-regulating, and not "empirically" derived. Paradoxically, in the distinction between *appearance* and *reality,* it is the cognitive, structural invention which is *reality,* and the empirical manifestation which is *appearance.*[28] Relations posited by or as social reality do not have to exist in praxis or be true in order to continue to be posited and to have adherents.

Interface

In what has been said thus far the term *empirical* has been applied rigidly and consistently to natural reality, but has been rendered inapplicable to any model or theory thereof. No doubt some readers find that usage too restrictive, since it suggests there is no such thing as "empirical research" but only research of empirical phenomena or of social phenomena. Further, it may strike some that if social reality is a fact in empirical reality, then the distinction advanced that social reality is structural and empirical reality is not relational cannot hold. It now becomes important to describe the interface of empirical and social realities using the phenomenon of human speech to resolve these problems.

Human speech as an empirical reality is mechanical energy, largely vibration and wind, which we call "sound." Other animal species produce sounds in some of the same ways humans do, but generally exhibit less flexibility of sounding—they make fewer distinguishable sounds. And there is a dimension exclusively possible and almost always present in *human* speech which is nonetheless independent of speech, or even of the ability to vocalize or to hear: language.[29] All members of our species can acquire language; only members of our species can acquire language, presumably because language is genetically a human possibility.[30] Language is not the sounds in the air sent by speaker A to B, and language is not the thought or feeling A tries to communicate to B. *Language is the structure which enables A and B to pair sounds with objects or ideas.*[31] In human speech the nexus of empirical and social reality is the structure language, which links form and content making meaning possible. Language is the social side of human speech by which phonation, simple speech, becomes *speaking*.

Speaking is a social institution, which entails both an established system and an evolution. Theoretically, *speaking*, if it is a social institution, must be controlled by laws analogous to those which regulate other social institutions, e.g., language. In the case of speaking, there are laws of the established, static system, and different laws which govern the evolution; and these laws would be of the nature that the former would be synchronic and relational, the latter diachronic and particular.[32] It therefore stands to reason that a comprehensive explanation of speaking will disclose both empirical and social laws and phenomena. These phenomena are sufficiently different to demand that research use distinguishable and appropriate models. Much progress has been made in the sciences of linguistics and anthropology because of the distinctions elaborated: what remains is to explain how they apply to the study of human speech.

Mechanical and Statistical Models

For all the handwringing and lamenting among speech communication scholars that we lack a paradigm, there has been no demonstration that either (1) there is reason to believe that all aspects of the phenomenon *speaking* can be explained by one kind of thinking; or (2) there is truth in monolithic mentality and folly in multiplicity or diversity. In fact, although Thomas Kuhn's name is invoked as authoritative proof that progress is paradigmatic, it must be remembered that Kuhn's view is not simplistic: he points out that often the destruction of a paradigm is a prerequisite for scientific progress, and he is very clear that no paradigm ever does "explain all the facts with which it can be confronted."[33] Moreover, the sciences Kuhn discusses are studies of phenomena which are manifest in empirical reality alone; phenomena which must be studied as both empirical and social are of a different kind, requiring, perhaps, two or more models for explanation or prediction—even for mere description.

The two kinds of models explained here, *mechanical* and *statistical*, are common to both physical and social science, and are present in research on speech communication, though often only as tacit assumptions.[34] Recently, however, Charles R. Berger provided a particularly lucid essay on "The Covering Law" which, in terms different from those here, explained mechanical and statistical models.[35] Examples and explanations of these models will be given here, and the remainder of this essay will illustrate the usefulness of these models in studying human speech.

Mechanical Models

Mechanical models are on the same scale as phenomena they illustrate. Thus, when a particular mechanical model is reducible to a mathematical formula it takes a form like these:

$$C = 2\pi r \quad \text{or} \quad A = bh,$$

where the circumference of every individual circle is equal to two times π times the circle's radius; the area of every rectangle is equal to the length of its base times the length of its height (expressed in any unit of measurement). The first formula above may be viewed as a definition of π ($\pi = \frac{C}{2r}$), and as tautological in that sense; the second formula, though of the same kind, is not marked by the same defect. These models are "on scale" because their elements stand in the same relation as the elements of the phenomena being modeled and the relationships being expressed. No matter the size or shape, the area of every rectangle equals the product of its base and height.

One may doubt here at the outset whether any phenomena of human speech are sufficiently uniform to be modeled this way. Indeed, most mechanical models of social phenomena seem not reducible to the mathematical precision of $A = bh$. Social phenomena, unlike rectangles, seem susceptible to weak or loose formulation. The model of a language sentence, $S = NP\ VP$ is on scale to all language sentences, but lacks the mathematical precision of the model $A = bh$ for all rectangles, if only because of the possibility of sentences appearing which suppress the NP—for example, "Please go away." The NP "you" is understood but unstated; in geometry, two lines cannot be understood as a rectangle missing two sides. But, however one views the question of the existence of universal, *immutable* imperatives in social reality makes no difference to the validity of mechanical models. In part this is because mechanical models concern synchronic time only, so evolution of the system modeled has no operational value in the model.[36] Secondly, for the entire class of models which are homemade, conscious models of the social reality of speaking, the question "Is it always so?" is not relevant, because that question concerns empirical reality.

Aristotle's *Rhetoric* is an example of a mechanical model (or a series of such models) of speaking. It is, of course, limited in rendering only the structures of public speaking. The Aristotelian genres forensic, deliberative, and epideictic are structurally discrete, divided by time or tense, by the end(s) of speaking, and by the subject or matter.[37] Also, Aristotle's enumeration of "the modes of persuasion," *ethos, logos,* and *pathos,* is a mechanical model; its details are filled in throughout Books I and II in the discussions of human character, passions, and the *topoi* of enthymemes.[38] These mechanical models display and compare the possible social structures of speaking; they do not prescribe or describe the proportional relationships between, say, how much proof in a particular speech is *ethos* and how much *logos.*

Statistical Models

Statistical models are on a different scale from phenomena they illustrate. Thus, when a statistical model is reduced to a formula it takes the form

$$P\ (X,Y)\ =\ r,$$

meaning, "in the long run the proportion of instances of the type X that are also of the type Y is approximately r."[39] Statistical *models* are not, however, the same things as statistical *methods.* One must note that statistical models necessarily concern diachronic time. For example, statements like "The probability of rain today is .50" are based upon numerous observations of days similar to this one in regard to humidity, wind, temperature, and other conditions; such observations themselves require serial time. Diachrony of statistical models has also to do with their scale: even though there is a .50 chance of rain today, there will not be .50 occurrence, for either it will rain or it won't. We may suffer drought for thirty consecutive days of .50 probability of rain. The statement describes an average value. It is a model of empirical reality and a very precise one, because over empirical, diachronic time, it is accurate.

Statistical models which have to do with speaking are no less tied to diachrony and empirical reality. For the most part, statistical models of speaking are *extensive:* based upon samples of larger populations, they are not on scale, and they predict in the same way as the weather forecast above.[40] Consider, for example, the recent article by Gerald Miller, Frank Boster, Michael Roloff and David Seibold on "Compliance Gaining Message Strategies."[41] The essay compares strategies people choose to employ in messages intended to persuade in either interpersonal or noninterpersonal, short- or long-term situations.

Comparisons of mean ratings by 168 people reveal likely and unlikely strategies chosen for each situation. (Oddly, *Threat* was the top-rated choice in long-term interpersonal and in short-term noninterpersonal situations, which reasonably might be expected to be dissimilar.) Comparison of the mean ratings by subjects responding to the role-play situations yields a statistical model, not even of actual frequency, but of reported relative likelihood among choices across situations: an interpersonal weather forecast. It should be noted that the statistical models in the essay measure subjects' ratings of mechanical models given to them (e.g., of Threat, Promise, Altercasting), and elaborate on or revise other mechanical and statistical communication models.

The frequent interdependence of statistical and mechanical models of speaking phenomena is somewhat misleading. That is, statistical models usually generalize categories approaching mechanical models, or test mechanical models. But as Gary Cronkhite and Jo Liska have shown in "A Critique of Factor Analytic Approaches to the Study of Credibility," some widely known, statistically tested mechanical models—i.e., credibility factor names—are not scale models of the same elements, or tested by the same statistical procedures.[42] Structuralists in general, and particularly Claude Lévi-Strauss, discuss mechanical and statistical models in a way which suggests that the former may be especially suited to social reality and the latter to empirical reality. It remains here to review significant mechanical and statistical models from the study of speech to demonstrate the heuristic potential and relevance of the structuralist position. The examples of mechanical models come from rhetorical theory, and the statistical models from communication theory.

RHETORICAL, MECHANICAL MODELS

Rhetorical theory is concerned with the social structure of discourse, its *langue,* which is best revealed by mechanical models in what I am calling the structural study of speech. Douglas Ehninger's essay "On Systems of Rhetoric" perhaps best exemplifies the potential of applying structuralist methodology to historically selected social models of discourse—theories of rhetoric—by isolating both the invariant constituents of rhetorics and their "variable product[s] of need and environment."[43] Ehninger reconstructed classical rhetoric to show that it was "grammatical" or message-centered; he similarly showed late eighteenth-century rhetoric to be "psychological," and he underlined the "social" or "sociological" structure of contemporary rhetoric. Each of these rhetorical systems derives its structural uniqueness from the social reality it models; each represents what worked (and what people wanted to work) in a particular epoch. The notion of a system of language (Saussure's *langue*) from which expressions or utterances *(parole)* are derived is basic to structuralism. To conceive rhetoric in the same way as language in general is an immensely fruitful perspective, and Ehninger first brought to light the need to grasp not only the evolution of rhetorical concepts, but also to analyze and explain rhetorical theories' adequacies as discrete, generative structures or systems.

Two additional mechanical models which illustrate and may be explained by structuralist principles of analysis now may be mentioned. Certainly both are widely familiar and influential. First is Lloyd F. Bitzer's model, "The Rhetorical Situation."[44] In introducing his model Bitzer notes, "There are circumstances of this or that kind of structure which are recognized as ethical, dangerous, or embarrassing. What characteristics, then, are implied when one refers to 'the rhetorical situation' . . . ?"[45] The constituents of Bitzer's model are the now-familiar terms *exigence, constraint,* and *audience,* but the guiding functional principles are the notions *situation* and *fitness,* which envision discourse as precipitated by a situation in reality which *calls for certain kinds of responses* but not others. The reality in which rhetorical situations inhere is not, strictly speaking, empirical reality; it is social reality. In Bitzer's words, the *rhetorical* situation does not equate with the *historical* situation because "some situations . . . persist; this is why it is possible to have a body of truly rhetorical literature. The Gettysburg Address, Burke's Speech to the Electors of Bristol, Socrates' Apology—these are more than historical documents, more than specimens for stylistic or logical analysis. They exist as rhetorical responses *for us* precisely because they speak to situations which persist."[46]

Although Bitzer does not elaborate systematically the causes or nature of persistence through time or rhetorical situations, it is possible to do so profitably here to determine the reality base of truly rhetorical exigencies. The specific property of time in social reality is synchrony or reversibility.[47] The American Revolution as an empirical reality is over and complete; as a social reality it is present now, and even seen in empirical evidence such as our Constitution, the beliefs we have about ourselves, boundaries of certain states, etc. But in a different sense, the *symbols* which persist after the Revolution remain viable although their relevance to empirical reality is diminished. Because their rhetorical value is high these symbols may be used as models for responses to *empirically new but socially old* problems. The structural and functional constituents of rhetorical situations, their exigencies and constraints, can recur because they are creatures of social reality.

The second model is Kenneth Burke's pentad of *Act, Scene, Agent, Agency,* and *Purpose.*[48] These terms identify the constituents of a mechanical model which may be applied to social behavior, including rhetorical situations, as well as to literature, poetry, drama. According to Burke these elements are present in every rhetorical discourse, but the ratios between them, the emphasis placed upon each component, varies with the world-view of the rhetor. If this is the case, then the pentad is nearly a perfect mechanical model because it allows the reconstruction of discourse on perfect scale with the actual discourse in ways that feature the interrelationships between all of the elements. With this mechanical model the critic's task is not mechanistic application, but reconstruction of the ratios between the constituents of the pentad; a simple enumeration of what fits where makes no contribution because no restructuring occurs. What is necessary is the reconstruction of *qualitative* and *quantitative* relationships among the *Act, Scene, Agent, Agency,* and *Purpose;* such a reconstruction would be derived from a mimesis based upon homology—the analogy of functions.

Burke's writings contain other, more particular mechanical models: redemption, identification, and hierarchies are modeled in many of his critical works. In one early work, Burke discusses the locating of "associational clusters" and learning of "what goes with what" which enable a critic "to disclose by objective citation the structure of motivation operating here."[49] For Burke, critical analysis explains "the ways in which a 'symbolic' act is 'representative' " and this principle of representation he expresses in the structural model *synecdoche.*[50] *Synecdoche* is a mechanical model because, like the pentad, it is an on-scale model of the way in which symbolic representation is managed—of the way (to use Burke's example) that Lady Macbeth's washing her hands stands for her guilt.

The dramatistic model advanced by Kenneth Burke, the situational model advanced by Lloyd Bitzer, and the disclosure of structure in systems of rhetoric by Douglas Ehninger all suggest that rhetorical theory is concerned with the making of mechanical models—the study of structure. Concepts in rhetorical theory, from the *topoi* to the speech act, reflect the concern for modeling the structures of social reality. A double structure of rhetoric emerges from an understanding of its restructuring of part of social relations. On one hand, rhetorical theory is generative of practical discourse: rhetorical theories from all periods provide language structures deemed useful for practical discourse. Beneath all the surface variety with regard to, e.g., kinds of evidence or ends of oratory, all rhetorical theories have the grammatical function of providing models or structures of language, although there are differences from theory to theory with regard to what sorts of structures of language are permissible or recommended. On the other hand, exactly because of the tendency for rhetorical theories to specify the spheres of discourse to which they apply, rhetorical theories also structure social institutions by limiting the forms of language recognizable as legitimate for use, and by limiting the social forums available to the would-be rhetor. These two structures, the grammatical and the social, influence each other. The inclusion of pulpit oratory as a social-rhetorical structure is invariably accompanied by the inclusion within the grammatical-rhetorical structure of an explanation of the use of scripture as evidence. The grammatical and social structures of rhetoric thus serve to perpetuate and legitimate one another, and are separable only artificially for pedagogical convenience. Lastly may we note that the models of rhetorical theory are mechanical in nature, as opposed to statistical.

COMMUNICATION, STATISTICAL MODELS

Communication theory is concerned with empirical reality and is marked by the elaboration of statistical models to describe and predict human communicative behavior. This is not to say that all studies in communication theory collect and analyze data into statistical models;[51] nonetheless, the relevance and fruitfulness of statistical models for the study of speech is best exemplified by communication theory. For this discussion of communication theory's statistical models the distinction between the general methods of observation and experimentation should be observed. Models of either the mechanical or the statistical kind are derived from observation; by experimentation a model can be tested to determine how it reacts when changed.[52] The well-designed communication experiment is a test of the empirical truth or accuracy of a model; the well conducted observational-statistical study determines the empirical reality of communication as manifest in observable behavior (which may include self-reports).

An observationally derived statistical model of tremendous complexity is *Cross-Cultural Universals of Affective Meaning,* by Charles Osgood, William May, and Murry Miron.[53] This work computes, factor analyzes, and compares the assignment of the now-familiar meaning dimensions *goodness, potency,* and *activity.* The analysis of data collected by semantic differential measures yields statistical models which show, for example, that more difference exists between cultures' concepts of "the good" than between their concepts of "the bad." That is, subjects attributed "goodness" to more things and with more relative variance than they attributed "badness."

Osgood's development of semantic differential scales as a measuring technique was the result of the attempt to determine what dimensions, and how many, shape human beings' assignment of "meaning" to things and concepts. Osgood assumed a finite field called "semantic space":

> a region of some unknown dimensionality and Euclidean in character. Each semantic scale, defined by a pair of polar adjectives, is assumed to represent a straight line that passes through the origin of this space and a sample of such scales then represents a multi-dimensional space. . . . To define the semantic space with a maximum efficiency we would need to determine that minimum number of orthogonal dimensions or axes . . . which exhausts the dimensionality of the space.[54]

Semantic differential scales locate concepts or things at a point in three dimensional semantic space: "The point in space which serves us as an operational definition of meaning has two essential properties . . . the *quality* and *intensity* of meaning."[55] Intensity is the *mean* rating by subjects of a concept on a scale which represents one quality, e.g., "goodness."

Statistical models built from semantic differential or similar measures are limited in nature. The concept of relative intensity does not apply to any dichotomized variable—whether of meaning, demography, behavior, or any quality. Thus, while we could measure President Carter's relative and average believability (believable/not believable), we could not measure an individual's belief of an assertion in the same way, since one either does or does not believe the claim that, e.g., the world is flat; the Pope is Catholic. It is, of course, possible to determine statistically what percentage of a sample of a population does believe such a claim, or stands on either end of a dichotomized variable.

A number of studies have tried to test (and build) experimentally a statistical model of credibility. I refer to the studies by Berlo, Lemert, and Mertz,[56] and by James McCroskey,[57] though many more could be cited.[58] One powerful argument which has supported experimental and statistical studies in this and other areas is the notion that they are independently verifiable and cumulative through replication. Cronkhite and Liska have severely weakened this claim, at least in regard to the credibility studies in their "Critique."

The outcomes of experiments provide statistical models of average values. The credibility studies cumulatively suggest that, within a specifiable range, subjects on particular occasions attributed particular characteristics to message sources, and these characteristics exhibit neither perfect covariance nor completely independent variance. It has seemed a fair interpretation of such statistical methods to define dimensions of credibility, i.e., *competence, trustworthiness,* and *dynamism,* which necessarily exhibit different patterns of covariance when measured empirically. That these differences are necessary has to do in part with the particularity of empirical reality discussed above: one would not expect uniform variance among dimensions (or scale items) attributed to different people, say, to Abraham Lincoln (likely to be high on all three) and to Adolf Hitler (high dynamic, low trustworthy). Moreover, in empirical reality, each encounter between receiver B and message-source A will be unique, such that variance in B's attributions toward A is probable, even inevitable.

The strategic value of communication theory's statistical models resides in the fact that some *can* be compared. Concepts in communication theory, the debatable perspectives of laws, rules, systems; the discussions of statistical methods for model-building; argument about scientific motives; all reflect the concern for building, understanding, and comparing statistical models of empirical reality.

CONCLUSION

Structuralism aims ultimately at interdisciplinary methods which can reveal aspects of social structure. The structural study of speech enables comparison of models of different types of speaking, speaking in different cultures, particular "pieces" of speech, and even models of other social phenomena. Both mechanical and statistical models are necessary for a thorough explanation of the phenomena of speech.

Rhetorical studies, by building mechanical models, can both draw from and contribute to social science research in general. History and the historical study of public address collect data and make observations which are empirical; rhetorical theory and criticism present the models for, and mechanical reconstructions of, the same data. Models of rhetorical theory may have predictive value because of the recurrent nature of social phenomena, of which the rhetorical situation is an example. The limits of this predictive facility exist and inhere in empirical reality, and seem to require statistical measurement and modeling.

Communication studies can draw from and add to general social science research through building statistical models. These models can be compared handily with relevant rhetorical-mechanical models and with models of non-speech phenomena. They have predictive value in isolating thresholds of human behavior and perception where particular effects occur or particular laws take over.

Notes

1. This usage differs from the norm somewhat. A fairly full discussion of the distinction between "model" and "theory" may be found in Leonard C. Hawes, *Pragmatics of Analoguing: Theory and Model Construction in Communication* (Reading: Addison-Wesley, 1975), Chapter 9.
2. Gerald R. Miller, "Humanistic and Scientific Approaches to Speech Communication Inquiry: Rivalry, Redundancy, or Rapprochement," *Western Speech Communication,* 49 (1975), 230–39.
3. The suggestion of John Waite Bowers, "The Pre-Scientific Function of Rhetorical Criticism," *in Essays on Rhetorical Criticism,* ed. Thomas Nilsen (New York: Random House, 1968), p. 127. Also see Thomas S. Kuhn, *The Structure of Scientific Revolutions,* 2nd ed. (Chicago: The University of Chicago Press, 1970).
4. A good introduction to structuralism is Terence Hawkes, *Structuralism and Semiotics* (Berkeley: University of California Press, 1977). One worthwhile collection of texts and excerpts from major works of structuralism is Richard and Fernande DeGeorge, eds., *The Structuralists: From Marx to Lévi-Strauss* (New York: Anchor Books, 1972).
5. Hawkes, p. 17.
6. A thorough treatment of this and other foundational assumptions of structuralism can be found in Stanley Deetz, "Structuralism: A Summary of Its Assumptive and Conceptual Bases," *Review of Social Theory,* 1 (1973), 138-63. Also see Hawkes, p. 18; Barbara Warnick, "Structuralism Vs. Phenomenology: Implications for Rhetorical Criticism," *Quarterly Journal of Speech,* 65 (1979), 250–61.
7. Deetz, p. 139.
8. Claude Lévi-Strauss, *Structural Anthropology,* trans. Claire Jacobson and Brooke G. Schoepf (New York: Basic Books, 1963), p. 61. This essay is greatly influenced by Lévi-Strauss's concepts of social science. I have, of course, noted this debt appropriately throughout the discussion in footnotes, but this general acknowledgement also seemed needed.
9. Jean Piaget, *Structuralism,* quoted by Deetz, p. 143.
10. Roland Barthes, "The Structuralist Activity," trans. Richard Howard, *Partisan Review,* 34 (Winter, 1967), 86. Barthes's statement reveals the impossibility of distinguishing structuralism from "semiotics" or, as Europeans call it in deference to Saussure, "semiology," which is the study of signification. Structuralism is present as perspective and method in anthropology, linguistics, psychoanalysis, literary criticism, sociology, and political science. It is, I hope to show, an enterprise in which our discipline should play an active part.
11. Barthes, "Structuralist Activity," pp. 86–87. Emphasis added.
12. Deetz, p. 139. Evidence supporting genetic determinism is overwhelming. I will not cite biologists in its defense, or claim that genetics is more powerful than environment. Indeed, important interaction between the two is the focus of contemporary ecology, which should prove most fruitful. See Garrett Hardin, *The Limits of Altruism: An Ecologist's View of Survival* (Bloomington: Indiana University Press, 1977).

    Structuralism as social science may have its strongest natural science support from genetics and life-sciences. I say this because evidence that language is genetic (see below, n. 30) indeed suggests that *how* language means may be homologous to how we make meaning of (structure) any actions, events or objects. No such case has been established, though Piaget grounds his structuralism in genetics.

13. Hawkes, *Structuralism and Semiotics,* pp. 52–53.
14. Claude Lévi-Strauss, *Totemism,* trans. Rodney Needham (Boston: Beacon Press, 1963).
15. Edmund Leach, *Claude Lévi-Strauss,* rev. ed. (1974; rpt. New York, Penguin Books, 1976), p. 40. Also see Terence Hawkes, *Metaphor* (London: Methuen, 1972), pp. 83–84.
16. Lévi-Strauss, *Structural Anthropology,* p. 279.
17. Barthes, "Structuralist Activity," pp. 83–84. Emphasis in original.
18. Lévi-Strauss, *Structural Anthropology,* pp. 279–80.
19. Lévi-Strauss, *Structural Anthropology,* pp. 283–84. Emphasis added.
20. Peter Berger and Thomas Luckmann, *The Social Construction of Reality* (New York: Anchor Books, 1967), pp. 14–28.
21. Lévi-Strauss, *Structural Anthropology,* pp. 206–11; 286–89; Also see Thomas B. Farrell, "Knowledge, Consensus, and Rhetorical Theory," *Quarterly Journal of Speech,* 62 (1976), 4.
22. See Edward T. Hall, *The Silent Language* (New York: Doubleday, 1959).
23. A different division is well elaborated by the discussion of "territories of self" in Erving Goffman, *Relations in Public* (New York: Harper and Row, 1971), pp. 32–38.
24. Ferdinand de Saussure, *Course in General Linguistics,* trans. Wade Baskin, ed. Charles Bally and Albert Sechehaye (New York: Philosophical Library, 1959); Klaus Brinker, *Modelle und Methoden der strukturalistischen Syntax* (Stuttgart: Kohlhammer/Urban Taschenbucher, 1977), pp. 11–14; Hawkes, pp. 19–21.
25. Saussure, *Linguistics,* rpt. in *The Structuralists,* p. 62*ff.* (See n. 4.)
26. Hawkes, *Structuralism and Semiotics,* p. 21.
27. This is why Kuhn, p. 5, describes "normal science . . . research as a strenuous and devoted attempt to force nature into the conceptual boxes supplied by professional education." Also see parts III, IV and V, *Structure of Scientific Revolutions.*
28. See the discussion of the "appearance" from "reality" distinction in Chaim Perelman and L[ucie] Olbrechts-Tyteca, *The New Rhetoric,* trans. John Wilkinson and Purcell Weaver (Notre Dame: University of Notre Dame Press, 1969), pp. 415–19.
29. Ronald W. Langacker, *Language and its Structure* (New York: Harcourt, Brace and World, 1968). pp. 14–15.
30. Eric H. Lenneberg, *Biological Foundations of Language* (New York: John Wiley and Sons, 1967). There are rare cases in which gene damage eliminates the language acquisition trait. See Langacker, p. 15.

Some readers familiar with the accomplishments of the Yerkes Center's chimps and other simians have questioned this position. One must remember that our acquisition of language is not purely genetic, but also learned, which is, of course, why there are so many different languages spoken. A reasonable person comparing the *uniformity* of human language learning, and the tremendous *speed* with which we learn so complicated a structure, compared to our relative slowness with math or music, might decide that there is strong evidence that our language learning ability is a genetic trait. The weakening of the ability around puberty further supports the position. Finally, it is not a counter argument that animals can learn associations; that my German shepherd, Lilo, comes when called by name does not suggest that she has language. It proves only that to associate certain, specific sounds (or visual symbols) with objects can be learned, indeed must be learned, like a language's phonetic system. Lilo is therefore capable of *communication,* but *not of language.* This very interesting paradox belongs to zoosemiotics, which studies the communication of animals within as well as between species. It never has been at issue whether animals can communicate; but unless one counts all intelligence, communication, or learning as language, there remain some differences between human and other animal communication. See Thomas A. Sebeok and Jean Umiker-Sebeok, eds., *Speaking of Apes: A Critical Anthology of Two-Way Communication with Men* (New York: Plenum Press, 1980).

31. Saussure, *Linguistics,* rpt. in *The Structuralists,* pp. 62–69.
32. Saussure, *Linguistics,* pp. 75–79.
33. Kuhn, pp. 17–18; 174–207; also see n. 20, above. The point is made by Miller, p. 231.
34. This distinction may appear much more simple and less sophisticated or precise than those in recent and current theory within our field. Hawes' *Pragmatics of Analoguing,* for example, treats "scale," "conceptual" and "mathematical" models making distinctions about the substance and structure of analogues (pp. 126-43). However, it is outside the purpose and scope of this paper to compare structuralist metatheory with every other statement on modeling or theory building. And since my purpose is to elaborate a structuralist view of speech research, I propose to elaborate the modeling notions of Lévi-Strauss, which, if they are efficacious, should provide readers adequate evidence of their heuristic value without the burden of claiming that other points of view are worthless or wrong. For clarity and exemplification, the discussion will be grounded in relevant research in speech communication.
35. Charles R. Berger, "The Covering Law Perspective as a Theoretical Basis for the Study of Human Communication," *Communication Quarterly,* 25 (1977), 7–18. Berger's vocabulary and approach are taken from Hempel and Brodbeck; I rely on the nomenclature of Lévi-Strauss for the discussion of models. Berger's description of "Deductive-Nomological Explanation" is equivalent in essence to a "mechanical" model; "statistical" model covers both his "Deductive" and "Inductive-Statistical Explanation." See Lévi-Strauss, *Structural Anthropology,* pp. 277–89.
36. Lévi-Strauss, *Structural Anthropology,* p. 286.
37. Aristotle, *Rhetoric,* I, ii, trans. W. Rhys Roberts (New York: Modern Library, 1954), pp. 31-34.
38. For examples, see *Rhetoric,* I, ii, v, ix, xii, and II, iv–xvii. I do not propose to review here past discussion of the enthymeme to argue whether it is a formal model. However, I think it is apparent that the *topoi* are mechanical models of possible enthymemes. See Donovan J. Ochs, "Aristotle's Concept of Formal Topics," *Speech Monographs,* 36 (1969), 423–24. Ochs's explanation and his diagram of the *topos* of opposites show each topic as a *scale model* of the element shared by all enthymemes which belong under (are modeled by) the topic. Ochs observes (p. 424), "The 'element' shared in common by both examples is . . . the relationship of 'opposition' between the terms of the premises. Each instance of opposition is formally the same." Ochs thus reveals a structural, mechanical model analogous to the opposition "edible-inedible" discussed above, p. 3*ff.*
39. Berger, "Covering Law," p. 10.
40. See J. B. Chassan, "Statistical Inference and the Single Case in Clinical Design," rpt. in *N = 1; Experimental Studies of Single Cases,* ed. P. O. Davidson and C. G. Costello (New York: Van Nostrand Rheinhold, 1969), pp. 26–45.

    As Chassan explains, statistical models based upon data collected from large samples of larger populations (extensive) cannot predict outcomes for individual cases—cannot even discriminate chance effects from deliberate effects in results regardless of significance levels. His recommendation is that intensive statistical models, those based not on one (or two, or three) observations of a sample, but on frequent observations of one subject, be used to overcome the statistical weaknesses which inhere in extensive models. Even these do not solve the problem fully unless one happens into a situation with 1.0 correlations. This simple example may explain. Suppose we study crosswalk behavior "extensively" and find that 52.5 percent of people cross against the light. An "intensive" model might say that John crosses against the light 65 percent of the time. Neither model enables prediction with high reliability of John's behavior on one particular trip to the crosswalk (though all of us know where the smart money will be bet). To say the model of John's behavior is *not on scale* means 65 percent of him won't cross leaving 35 percent behind.

41. Gerald Miller, Frank Boster, Michael Roloff, and David Seibold, "Compliance Gaining Message Strategies: A Typology and Some Findings Concerning Effects of Situational Differences," *Communication Monographs,* 44 (1977), 37–51.

42. Gary Cronkhite and Jo Liska, "A Critique of Factor Analytic Approaches to the Study of Credibility," *Communication Monographs,* 43 (1976), 91–107.

43. Douglas Ehninger, "On Systems of Rhetoric," in *Contemporary Rhetoric,* ed. Douglas Ehninger (Glenview: Scott, Foresman, 1972), p. 56.

44. Lloyd F. Bitzer, "The Rhetorical Situation," *Philosophy and Rhetoric,* 1 (1968), rpt. in *Contemporary Rhetoric,* pp. 39–48.

45. Bitzer, "The Rhetorical Situation," p. 39.

46. Bitzer, "The Rhetorical Situation," p. 47. See Bitzer, "Rhetoric and Public Knowledge," in *Rhetoric, Philosophy, and Literature,* ed. Don M. Burks (West Lafayette, Indiana: Purdue University Press, 1978), pp. 67–94.

47. Lévi-Strauss, *Structural Anthropology,* pp. 206–11; 286–89. Lévi-Strauss equated diachronic or non-reversible time with both historical and "statistical" time. In this sense, statistical models are interested in *evolution through time.* Mechanical models use mechanical time, which is reversible; mechanical models do not show the evolution of a phenomenon but display it as it is at a frozen moment. When Lévi-Strauss builds a model of a kinship system, for instance, the model does not show whether the system always has been in its modeled form or has evolved to that form from another. To historians the evolution is the paramount question.

   In communication studies those identified as *empiricists* may claim a disinterest in "the Historical." But on a micro-historical time scale, most statistical designs, observational or experimental, cannot be used without measurements collected at t1 and t2, or stimulus-post-test measures, and these concepts are of historical, non-reversible time. On the other hand, when Bitzer elaborates the rhetorical situation, it appears in a timeless model: the question, "was it also that way at t1?" is irrelevant to the model. If the word *"process"* (and other process words like *"transaction"*) has dominated communication theory, the word reveals an orientation toward historical, statistical time. On the other hand, rhetorical theorists and critics have used words like *"Function and Scope," "Identification," "Structure," "Persona,"* and *"Stance,"* none of which involve diachronic time, but which are suited to the building of structural, mechanical models.

48. Kenneth Burke, *A Grammar of Motives and A Rhetoric of Motives* (Cleveland: The World Publishing Co., 1962).

49. Burke, "The Philosophy of Literary Form," in *The Philosophy of Literary Form* (Baton Rouge: Louisiana State University Press, 1941), p. 20.

50. Burke, "Literary Form," p. 25.

51. For example, "rules" research such as John Waite Bowers, Norman D. Elliott and Roger Desmond, "Exploiting Pragmatic Rules: Devious Messages," *Human Communication Research,* 3 (1977), 235–42; and Robert E. Nofsinger, Jr., "The Demand Ticket: A Conversational Device for Getting the Floor," *Speech Monographs,* 42 (1975), 1–9, is essentially not statistical.

52. Lévi-Strauss, *Structural Anthropology,* p. 280.

53. Charles Osgood, William May, and Murry Miron, *Cross-Cultural Universals of Affective Meaning* (Urbana: University of Illinois Press, 1975).

54. C. E. Osgood, G. J. Suci, and P. H. Tannenbaum, *The Measurement of Meaning* (Urbana: University of Illinois Press, 1957), p. 25.

55. Osgood, et al., *Measurement of Meaning*, p. 26.

56. David K. Berlo, James B. Lemert and Robert J. Mertz, "Dimensions for Evaluating the Acceptability of Message Sources," *Public Opinion Quarterly*, 33 (1969), 563-76.

57. James C. McCroskey, "Scales for the Measurement of Ethos," *Speech Monographs*, 33 (1969), 65–72.

58. See Cronkhite and Liska for a systematic review.

A Materialist's Conception of Rhetoric

Michael Calvin McGee

T**he contemporary history of rhet-**
oric is the opposite of the typical history of other social sciences. In
sociology, for example, early thinkers were overwhelmed by phenomena, so awed by the gargantuan presence of "society" that they forgot the
first task of theory, to name and describe phenomena. There were so
few *concepts* of "society" that, as late as 1940, Ortega could bemoan his
reading of all sociological theory to that date, claiming not to have
found a single definition even of "society," let alone the more telling
phenomena which comprise "society."[1] Rhetoricians battle an opposite
problem: we are overwhelmed with a history which goes back through
two millennia of conceptualizing to pre-Socratic Greece. Supposedly,
each writer who creates or modifies a concept does so on the warrant of
experience with real phenomena, actual cases of "rhetoric." Over time,
however, the connection between theory and practice is muddied. A
proliferation of concepts forces us to pay more attention to what has
been said about rhetorical practice than to actual public address.[2]

Today, the typical course in rhetorical theory is a *history of* rhetoric,

MICHAEL CALVIN McGEE *is Associate Professor of Rhetorical Studies at the University of Iowa.*

and the "cutting edge" of scholarship in rhetorical theory seems to be the *philosophy of* (if not more specifically the epistemology of) rhetoric. The terms "history of" and "philosophy of" presume common knowledge of "rhetoric." The knowledge which is presumed, I believe, is of a "rhetoric" which is on its face uninformed by historical or immediate contact with actual practice.[3] The problem is not a new one, though in the past it has been regarded as primarily or essentially terministic. So when Donald Bryant listed the several meanings "rhetoric" has had through the centuries, he proposed that we distinguish between the theory and the practice of "rhetoric" by coining the term "rhetory" to refer to actual discourse.[4] It is not enough, however, merely to *distinguish* theory and practice at a definitional level. One must also decide what *relationship* exists between theory and practice—which "comes first" in a common desire to understand human communicative behavior. When the content of a *history of* rhetoric includes a treatise by Juan de Vives on figures and tropes, and when the content of a *philosophy of* rhetoric purports speculatively to account for the psychology of knowing, the implicit claim is that the theory and technique of rhetoric come less from human experience than from the metaphysical creativity and inspiration of particular writers. So, as Natanson observed, what has been called "rhetorical theory" through much of our tradition is not theory at all, but a set of technical, prescriptive principles which inform the practitioner while, paradoxically, remaining largely innocent of practice.[5]

The obvious alternative is to believe that practice "comes first," that the essential mission of rhetorical theory is not to *prescribe* technique but formally to account for what seems to be an essential part of the human social condition. The problem posed by such an alternative is the classic confrontation between idealism and materialism. Karl Marx's initial response to Feuerbach's *Das Wesen des Christentums* puts the question vividly:

> *The production of ideas, of conceptions, of consciousness, is at first directly interwoven with the material activity of men—the language of real life. Conceiving, thinking, the mental intercourse of men at this stage still appear as the direct efflux of their material behavior. . . . Men are the producers of their conceptions, ideas, etc., that is, real, active men. . . . In direct contrast to German philosophy [idealism] which descends from heaven to earth, here it is a matter of ascending from earth to heaven. That is to say, not of setting out from what men say, imagine, conceive, nor from men as narrated, thought of, imagined, conceived, in order to arrive at men in the flesh; but setting out from real, active men, and on the basis of their real-life-process demonstrating the development of the ideological reflexes*

and echoes of this life-process. . . . It is not consciousness that determines life, but life that determines consciousness. For the first manner of approach [idealism] the starting-point is consciousness taken as the living individual; for the second manner of approach [materialism], which conforms to real life, it is the real living individuals themselves, and consciousness is considered solely as their consciousness.[6]

If we begin the construction of rhetorical theories as we would begin a textbook on public speaking, with an imagined picture of a human being assigned to compose a piece of persuasive discourse, and if we then make rules to help this fictional person succeed in the imagined task, we lose contact with the brute reality of persuasion as a daily social phenomenon—and even our rules for good speaking thereby lose force. A material theory of rhetoric, in contrast, begins with real speeches which are demonstrably useful to an end or are failures. Such an approach to theory would not aim at making rules of composition, but rather at the description, explanation, perhaps even prediction of the formation of consciousness itself.

With the possible exception of Kenneth Burke, no one I know of has attempted formally to advance a material theory of rhetoric. The task is imposing, for in many ways the world of traditional rhetorical theory would have to be turned upside-down to resolve a host of complicated philosophical issues. The "epistemic function" of rhetoric will become a cornerstone of theory-building rather than an interesting alternative approach to criticism.[7] Discourse, even language itself, will have to be characterized as material rather than merely representational of mental and empirical phenomena.[8] Such difficult and controversial concepts as "consciousness" and "ideology," "myth" and "phenomenon" will have to be explored.[9] Various methods of data-based historical research and theory building will have to be examined, and the mystifications of "semiotics" and "hermeneutics" resolved and eliminated.[10] Since none of this could occur in a vacuum, it also will be necessary at every point to justify distinctions between a material rhetorical theory and both rhetorical criticism and empirical communication research. Finally, since no materialists have been essentially concerned with rhetoric, apparently heretical rhetorical adaptations of such concepts as "phenomenology" and "dialectics" will have to be justified against methodological purists on both sides of the Atlantic.

Because it is the most direct strategy, I do not blush to advertise this essay as an exercise in fundamental conceptualization: I want to define the term "rhetoric" from a material perspective. My concern is with the creation and application of rhetorical theories. I do not ask the question *What is rhetoric?* so much as the question *What legitimizes the theory of rhetoric?* The alternative to *idealism,* I will suggest, is to think of rhetoric as an *object,* as material and as omnipresent as air and water. Just as oceanographic theory is controlled by the existence of water in nature, just as meteorological theory is warranted by the behavior of air, so a theory of rhetoric can be legitimate only when measured, directly and explicitly, against the objects it purportedly describes and explains.

IDEALISM IN RHETORIC DEFINED

By the late eighteenth-century, the Renaissance-inspired "scientific revolution" had produced so many discoveries in physics, chemistry, and mathematics that such lights of the *Academie Francaise* as De Stutt de Tracy sought to apply the same naive empiricism to the study of philosophies of the past. There was to be a "science of ideas," *ideology,* invented in the belief that the future was determined by the ideas of the past and that we can therefore predict the future by counting ideas. The difficulty, of course, is that a philosopher's idea of the world is neither empirical nor very influential. As Marx suggested in the passage quoted earlier, effective ideas are thoughts of *actors,* not of cloistered academics, and they are produced in the context of material necessity, not abstractly, naked of human passion. Marx did agree that the future could be predicted, but by the twentieth century, the pace of technological, economic, and political change was too rapid for even philosophers to understand and synthesize the principles involved. Materialists and idealists alike gave up any but the mythical vision of predicting broad swaths of the future. Such social scientists as Neil Smelser continue to treat human attitudes and opinions as defined and determined by situation, and the old "science of ideas" notion has been translated into a "history of ideas" dreamed by academics and only purportedly influential.[11]

Departments of "speech," concerned primarily with rhetoric, were birthed and brought to maturity in the climate of controversy I have just described. Early rhetoricians seemed to share Marx's anti-idealist impulses, for they were dissatisfied by the failure of literary scholars to account for *practical* discourse, communication designed to act upon and to be useful in the work-a-day world. In the end, however, two interests in practical discourse resulted more in the appreciation of bad literature than in the study of material functions of discourse. First, there was concern for ordinary discourse as a genre of literature, "public address," unique because it was meant more to be effective than to be timeless or beautiful. A valiant effort was made to use ancient pedagogical principles to deal with this literature on its own terms; but since most early rhetoricians were accustomed to think of all writing as literature, and since ancient treatises were meant to be textbooks, public address was treated as a specialized "art" form. Early writers were distinct from critics of poetry or the novel only in their appreciation of a particular author's intention to persuade or inform an audience more than entertain them.

This interest in the aesthetics of oratory carried over into a second concern, the teaching of composition skills. Because a public speaker can choose better or worse strategies of communication, and because there is an ancient literature consisting of specific advice on the making of such choices, rhetoric was thought of as a "body of principles" useful in practical classroom instruction. Ancient treatises on rhetoric were studied almost bibliographically at first, and then as themselves a kind of literature. Early writers were historians, distinct from literary and cultural historians only in the titles of books they read. Through the 1950's there was a heated debate among those who sought to test ancient advice experimentally and those who tried historically to understand the ancient advice and discover whatever was missed in our original search for books about rhetoric. With few exceptions, however, everyone seemed agreed that persuasive oratory was a peculiar "art" form, and that rhetoric was a "body of principles" giving advice on how to become proficient in that art.

It is possible to think of a public speech as "art." To do so, however, is to distort both material and ideal conceptions of theory and practice: from a materialist's perspective, ordinary discourse is a social function which permits interactivity among people. It is a medium, a bridge among human beings, the social equivalent of a verb in a sentence. To treat such a thing as if it were "art" is to see it as a product instead of a function, as goal, the equivalent of a noun in a sentence. If one tricks the mind to make process into product, the end result can be unhealthy preoccupation with the performance itself, a "sophistic consciousness" wherein the saying is more important than the doing. From an idealist's point of view, the "art/body of principles" notion of public address and rhetoric establishes a contradictory relationship between theory and practice. Theory in such a conception is said to be related to practice as instruction is related to performance. So Plato admits that there may be an "art" in rhetoric as there is an "art" in cooking. But it is a strange conception of both theory and art to believe that a football game is "art" because the coach teaches technique, or to believe that recipes are "theories" because chefs serve better and worse meals.

Perhaps because we have been teachers of composition and public speaking, we have been incredibly sensitive to idealists' reservations about the "artistic" status of oratory and about the ethics of teaching students the techniques of persuasion. When we first hear that rhetoric is a knack and not an art, we set out intently either to prove that Plato is wrong or to find a perspective on rhetoric which meets Plato's moral criteria. When we hear a journalist using Webster's definition of rhetoric as bombast and eristic, we cringe either in formulary apology or angry indignation.

Each such apology, retreat, or equivocation perpetuates a systemic contradiction in rhetorical theory: ours is a practical art, presumably in contact with the work-a-day world; but at the same time, we are much more involved in condemning unethical or ineffective speeches (with the warrant of *a priori* prescriptions) than with creating precise descriptions and explanations of prevailing persuasive practices. The typical rhetorician, theorist or critic, seems to emulate Plato: we judge a piece of discourse to be deformed, imperfect, or perverted. We then imagine it possible to reform, perfect, or recreate it. Using our prescriptive rhetorical "theories," we dream a more effective or more moral speech than the one we have heard. Finally, we turn the world upside-down by thinking that our imaginings are "real." From the idealist's perspective, rhetoric is concerned with practical discourse not as a process requiring description and explanation, but as the product of an imperfect world which has dictated the production of bad literature, prose too clear and intentional to be beautiful. Instruction begins with general knowledge of the subject matter of a discourse and ends with a finished speech or essay. The steps in between constitute a naive psychological model of the creative process: an advocate first "invents" instrumental arguments, "disposes" the arguments like soldiers on the battlefield, "styles" them in attractive language as one arms a warrior, "memorizes" specific passages to conceal the labor of artifice, and finally "delivers" the whole discourse. In the typical book on rhetoric, "principles" are taught in their proper order under the individual headings of a product-conception and product-model of rhetoric: rhetoric is the "invention/disposition/style/memory/delivery" of discourse.

THE MATERIAL MODEL OF RHETORIC

If we pay more attention to *how* rhetoricians arrived at their advice than to *what* that advice was, however, there is a process-model inherent in all textbooks on rhetorical technique. Aristotle, for example, did not pretend to have the experience of an effective orator, nor did he psychoanalyze the outstanding advocates of his day. Rather, he arrived at descriptions of internal motivations and mental processes by inference from observing the function of communication in Greek societies. He observed individual advocates ("speaker") delivering a finished discourse ("speech") to a group of human beings ("audience") in a particular social context ("occasion") with the intention of using the collective power of the group to control some problematic element of the shared environment ("change"). The conventional rules designed to improve students' language skills all consisted of his interpretation and description of particular communication events. The product-conception and product-model of rhetoric superseded the original material conception and model because of Aristotle's primitive attitude toward elements of the phenomenon he witnessed. "Audience," for example, was nothing but a lump of clay to be molded, important only in having properties resistant to the creative touch of "speaker." Like Carlyle's heroic shapers-of-destiny, Aristotle's "speaker" stood above and apart from the society of which she/he was a part, an autonomous individual who acted in an egocentric world of trickery and manipulation. "Occasion" was merely an excuse for "speaker" to work magic, and "change" was the glory of the advocate, the working of his/her will on a faceless, soul-less (if not mindless) mass of human flesh. Aristotle's primeval elitism is reminiscent of his teacher's *Republic* and consistent with his office as adviser to the despot Philip of Macedon. But if we ignore the *product* of his attitudes, there is in Aristotle's *method* a process-conception and process-model of rhetoric: Rhetoric is "speaker/speech/audience/occasion/change" operating in society through time.

Everyone who observes persuasion functioning in a society, and is impressed enough to write a treatise on technique, consciously uses a material conception of rhetoric, if only in formulary recognition of situational constraints on a would-be advocate's choice of strategy and technique. Not only idealism confuses the conception, however, for it is easy to let equivocations of the terms "object" and "material" cloud thinking. Though it is the only residue of rhetoric one can hold like a rock, it is wrong to think that this sheaf of papers, this recording of "speech," *is* rhetoric in and of itself. It is surely "object," and the paper and ink scratches are "material." But the whole of rhetoric is "material" by measure of human *experiencing* of it, not by virtue of our ability to continue touching it after it is gone. Rhetoric is "object" because of its pragmatic *presence,* our inability safely to ignore it at the moment of its impact. "Speech" bears exactly the same categorical relationship to rhetoric whether one conceives "rhetoric" as a body of prescriptive principles or as an objective social interaction. From the idealist's viewpoint, "speech" is the surviving evidence of an "invention/disposition/style/memory/delivery" mental process. From the material perspective, "speech" is an integral part of a "speaker/speech/audience/occasion/change" phenomenon, peculiar as an element of rhetoric because it survives and records the moment of experience.

The distinction between objective experience and objective sensation is important in dealing with all elements of rhetoric. Though one can hardly sense something without experiencing it, and though it seems impossible to experience what has not at one time or another been sensed, there is both a conceptual and procedural difference between specific cognitions and the overall impression one comes away with upon experiencing a set of particular cognitions. So, for example, I can study rattlesnakes by watching a peculiar caged beast perform in my laboratory—I can sense its every move, even kill and dissect it until I have perfect empirical knowledge of the creature. But this set of facts pales before my accidental confrontation with a rattlesnake coiled in my path, ready to strike. I pay attention to different facts in the forest, and it is the *relationship* which those facts bear to each other and to me which I regard as salient, not the facts in and of themselves. In like fashion, I can study the empirical characteristics of "audience," the biography of "speaker," the content of "speech" in my laboratory—I can collect a set of facts, in other words, a set of sensations. But in the social world, such knowledge matters less than the specific *relationships* which "speaker/speech/audience/occasion/change" bear to one another in actual human experience.

Conceptually, only two of rhetoric's elements *could* be studied as a kind of sensation rather than as part of an experience. I can conceive a potentially rhetorical "occasion" which appears to invite "speaker/speech/audience/change" where none materialized, and the element "change" can be conceived and studied as the product of another process or even as a naked product, conceptually stripped of its rationale. But it is impossible to think of "speaker/speech/audience" existing in a vacuum, discrete and apart from one another. These elements each suppose one another. The terms themselves have meaning only in relation to one another—"speaker" puts one human being in a role vis-à-vis other human beings cast as "audience" in a social drama mediated by "speech."

Rhetoric is thus an almost mathematical paradigm of terms, for the "speaker" (2) can be linked through "speech" (+) to an "audience" (2), and because of the configuration of restraints and potentials present in an "occasion" (=), predictable "changes" (4) can occur. Of course rhetoric is like mathematics only in its structuring, in the fact that it is a form of relationships and not a set of facts. The necessity which characterizes a mathematical sequence does not adhere to predictions of "change" from observing a rhetoric because the human beings who play the roles of "speaker" and "audience" are not so obedient as arabic numerals. Procedurally, the distinction between experience and sensation establishes a relationship between rhetoric and communication research: the study of rhetoric is to the study of communicative behaviors as mathematics is to mechanics, as form is to content, as phenomenon is to cognition.

A principle begins to emerge in consequence of relocating rhetoric in the material world of objects: because rhetorics are forms, I can perceive them in any arena of experience where I am able to see the paradigm of relationships. "Speakers" do not have to be single individuals; "speeches" do not have to be words uttered in one place and at one time; "audiences" need not be present immediately; "occasion" is not restricted by time or space; and "change" may occur gradually over centuries as well as immediately in the presence of a single "speaker." Rhetoric, in other words, exists on a continuum from the absolutely specific experience of being persuaded to the absolutely general experience of having been conditioned to a pattern of social and political opinions. There are as many nuances of rhetorical experience as there are points on a line; but to make the argument clear, I will briefly describe the ends and middle of the continuum.

Microrhetorical Experience

An absolutely specific rhetoric could occur only when a single speaker sought to influence a single auditor—as the number of auditors increases to make the term "audience" appropriate, the experience is inherently abstracted by the listener's sense of being part of an entity larger than self, "audience." As a category of experience, however, it seems useful to conceive the most specific rhetoric occurring when a single "speaker" confronts a specific "audience" in one place, at one time, with a recommended belief or behavior which may not have been contemplated by "audience" without the agency of "speech." Thus "speaker" is absolutely specific when we refer to a human being making symbolic claims through any medium of communication. "Speech" is specific if we refer to the words of a single individual. "Audience" is specific *in relation to* a particular "speaker/speech"; that is, we may not always be able to pinpoint each individual auditor, but we can nonetheless give a name to an otherwise faceless "audience" by referring to "speaker" and/or "speech," as in the sentence "Oral Roberts' sermon of November 5, 1974 convinced his television audience to contribute five million dollars."

Like "audience," the "occasion" is made specific with reference to "speaker/speech." In theory, "occasion" is "speaker's" reason for being in a particular material setting (replete with altars, books, lamps, chairs, whatever) coupled with "audience's" reason for sharing the same time and space. My reason for addressing the Rotary Club may be as immediate as last week's invitation or as remote as my grandfather's charter-membership in the organization. The only thing preventing my "speech" from being the focal point for a history of civilization is Occam's Razor, for a skillful analyst could broaden the concept of "occasion" so much as to include the ontology of every person and thing present. But "occasion" is usually *made* specific by "speaker/audience" themselves—the various reasons-for-being-there are truncated by "speaker's" stated intentions ("I want to discuss Soviet policy in Afghanistan") and "audience" expectation ("We'd like you to speak on the subject of a free press"). Finally, "change," when specified, means *effect,* the sort of attitude and behavior modification rhetorical critics and communication researchers look for among auditors as a consequence of hearing "speech." I call this category of "speaker/speech/audience/occasion/change" experience *microrhetorical* because it is quantitatively concrete: specific human beings play the important roles—people with names which could in theory be called out, people with opinions to be counted engaging in behaviors empirically evident.

Sociorhetorical Experience

Human beings constantly fantasize roles larger than themselves, "playing like" they are "grocers," "unionists," "judges," "Christians," "Democrats," etc. Of course the term "fantasy" may be too strong, for our conditions of life force us to play social and economic roles simply to earn a living. But there is a clear distinction between the behaviors and beliefs of a grocer in his store, a judge in her chambers, and the behaviors and beliefs of the same persons at home, at a football game, or at the beach. It is a chicken-and-egg problem, often too difficult for even an experienced psychotherapist, to decide which is the "real" person, the private, flesh-and-blood human being, or the economic and political *persona* that human being portrays. Indeed, sorting out the various *personae* of the people around us is a chronic interpersonal and social problem: is Sue "playing like" my neighbor when she tells glowing stories of her trip to Florida, or is she a "real estate agent" bent upon selling me a plot of land in Aqua Acres?

The human role-playing capacity creates for everyone a more abstract and more sophisticated "speaker/speech/audience/occasion/change" experience. "Speaker" is identified by his/her membership in a social group, and it is the *public persona* which we pay attention to. We are not conscious of "speaker's" individuality—he/she takes little personal risk in the interaction, knowing that it is a *role* speaking, not a private person. So even though a used car salesman identifies himself in a television commercial, it is "salesman" who speaks and "salesman" we hear, not "John Honicutt." "Speech," too, is role-defined, for having learned to survive in a particular political economy, we are accustomed to hearing set arguments in set order. "Audience" is also impersonal and abstract, for their interest is defined by the drama being enacted. Individuals in the audience matter only because they have a few dollars to spend, a vote to cast, a soul to save, a law to abide by, etc. Hence, "audience" is identified as "consumers," "constituency," "congregation," "citizenry," etc., to denote that they are playing one particular role in a social ritual, one of the many roles they assume willingly and unconsciously in day-to-day business. "Occasions" are as formulary as the roles being played—we resent being sold used cars in church, being converted to Christianity in the local supermarket, etc. There are thus fewer difficulties in limiting "occasion" conceptually here than in more specific rhetorics, for we learn to recognize particular "occasions" as we learn to manoeuvre in society. Finally, "change" in sociorhetorical experience means *success*. Groups are formed in societies, political and economic rituals are followed, to increase the individual's comfort, to parcel out the wealth and power of the society, to provide for some measure of collective security and stability. "Change" is an alteration of circumstance, moving from having less money to having more money, from having less influence to having more influence, from being lonely or forgotten to being part of a group and accounted for.

Macrorhetorical Experience

In addition to playing group-defined roles ourselves, human beings also create institutions, artificial entities animated and endowed with human characteristics. "Labor," "Government," "the Law" all are spoken of as having human abilities, including the ability to persuade. Individual "speakers" in a public *persona* literally announce a policy or make legal decisions; but there is a distinction between officers or agents speaking in an official capacity and those same people *speaking for* the institutional entity they represent. So, for example, there is a difference between union leader Lane Kirkland saying, "I demand higher wages for American workers" on one occasion, and saying on another, "The voice of Labor cries out for higher wages." In the first instance, Kirkland's demand is warranted by the power inherent in his office; but in the second sentence, he exercises collective power remanded to him by a mute giant, "Labor," for whom Kirkland must speak. In radically positivistic moods, we recognize that the personification of "Labor" is only a figure of speech. But we *make* such animations as "Constitution," "People," and "Destiny" real by emphasizing the coercive power of large groups of human beings:

"Congress" never literally "speaks," but if we treat a new law as if it were conversation from an ordinary citizen, or even as if it were a policy statement issued in an election campaign by our local representative, we run the risk of being punished for defying "the will of Congress."

In our most general "speaker/speech/audience/occasion/change" experiences, institutions are cast in all the human roles, "occasion" is the totality of human experience, and "change" is the Utopian fantasy of "Society's" direction and goal. Unlike more specific rhetorics, however, *the same institution can be cast in nearly every role*. So from time to time "the People" are said to "speak." Nearly every officer of state has at one time or another characterized a particular "speech" as being "the will of the People." In all Anglo-American political systems, "the People" choose leaders and thus constitute the "audience" for all political discourse. "Occasion" is defined by the historical and circumstantial development of "the People's" interests and identity. Finally, "changes" of any sort are defined by "the People's" ideal vision of themselves living in a more perfect world. In macrorhetorical experiences, even the most concrete elements are normative and attitudinal, the creation of human dreaming, so that in this arena "peoples" can speak to "peoples" when China and the United States send representatives to negotiations in Geneva. Even the dead can participate, as in the sentence "Our founding fathers did not intend to allow the Nazis freedom of speech in Skokie."

In describing three categories of rhetorical experience, I have discussed "speaker/speech/audience/occasion/change" element by element, perhaps giving the impression that rhetoric is discretely analyzable by parts. That is, my procedure in treating rhetorical elements could imply that because "speaker" is listed first and "change" last, "speaker" naturally "comes first" when one describes rhetoric, just as "invention" naturally "comes first" when one creates a public speech. If this were so, we might create an *orthogonal* model of rhetoric: on the horizontal axis, we could represent the five discrete categories, picturing "speaker" confronting "occasion" by producing a "speech" which moves an "audience" to "change" belief and/or behavior. On the vertical axis, we might account for abstractions of rhetorical experience by labelling each element as it generalizes from individual to group to whole collectivity. Such a model would miss the point that rhetoric is a *gestalt* of relationships, because one could believe in error, for example, that the sociorhetorical experience of "audience" can become the subject of specialized research, that theorists can consider human membership in groups in isolation from "speaker/speech/occasion/change" elements. More importantly, the orthogonal model would be in one way too simple a description of rhetoric, and in another way much too complex.

Orthogonal conceptions of rhetorical experience are too simple because they encourage the mind to think in terms of categories. If we think that "speaker" actually "comes first," for example, we might be inclined to underestimate the coercive power of other elements on the "speaker." "Audience," we know, can so thoroughly intimidate "speaker" with its expectations that "speaker" is literally forced to say what the "audience" wants to hear, nothing more and nothing less. We have no trouble finding a situation in which "occasion" coerces "speaker" as well as "audience" into "speech," nor are we pressed to see "speech" trapping both "speaker" and "audience" in a web of argument which nobody likes, but from which no one can escape. Further, the elements do not constantly maintain the dominance-configuration they first assume: "speaker" could begin as the dominating element, coercing all others; but with the passage of time, "audience" can assert itself, coercing "speaker" into unpredicted and unwanted lines of argument. In time, "speaker" can regain dominance, or "occasion" could come back to dominate both "speaker" and "audience" with the press of events. Rhetoric, in other words, seems too dynamic a process to be represented by relatively static orthogonal models.

In another sense, orthogonal models of rhetoric are overly complex, for we could read each horizontal line of the grid as an independent model, judging that there are structured differences among rhetorical, sociorhetorical, and macrorhetorical experiences. One even could come to believe that it is necessary to look for macrorhetorical experience in every document if complete theoretical explanation is to be provided. In this mood, for example, we might see Lane Kirkland give a speech of encouragement to his grandson's football team. Is Kirkland simply encouraging athletes to perform well in an important game? Is he using his official power to endorse high school athletics? Must we search and strain for the sense in which Kirkland is acting as "the voice of Labor," showing how support for adolescent games is part of the American social and economic order? These mistakes, seeing three independent models and forcing abstractions unnaturally on wholly specific rhetorical experiences, derive from failing to recall that rhetoric exhibits a common structure of relationships. The differences among microrhetorical, sociorhetorical, and macrorhetorical experiences are differences in degree of abstraction. The "speaker/speech/audience/occasion/change" paradigm exists in a wide range of human experience, from the barely-social to the wholly-social. The relationships are a constant; hence, when a rhetoric exists at one level of abstraction, we are not obliged to make it seem larger or smaller than it appears to be, nor are we making our description more elegant and sophisticated by hypostatizing evidence.

A model of rhetoric, I suggest, should be *molecular* (see Figure 1). Nothing here necessarily "comes first" to the eye or to the mind. We can focus on one element, but we see as we attempt to make it discrete that separating it from other elements is a complex manoeuvre involving the conceptual severance of four sets of relationships. It is not difficult to imagine the effect of such surgery on the integrity of the whole structure. Further, we can see that no element is necessarily dominant. It is perspective or orientation which creates the impression of "occasion/speaker/speech" elements existing in the foreground, the same perspective which made "speaker" John F. Kennedy seem to dominate the politics of the early sixties and made the "occasion" of the Vietnam War seem to dominate the politics of the late sixties. Because the model is three dimensional it can be rotated to make any element appear larger or smaller (see Figure 2). This forces us to check theoretical claims that one element dominates a particular rhetoric by

Figure 1
A Molecular Model of Rhetoric

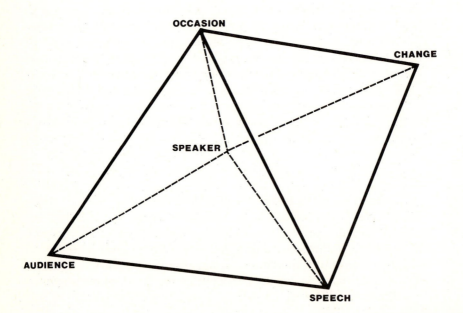

Figure 2
Different Orientations to the Molecular Model

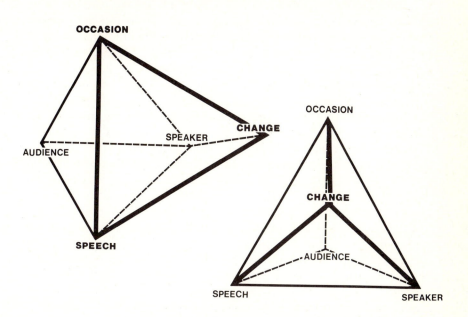

conceptually putting all the other elements momentarily in the foreground of contemplation. Finally, the molecular model does not refer to the levels of abstraction at which one might experience rhetoric. This encourages the mind to think of the common structure exhibited by all rhetorics rather than to sense differences in kind resulting from nothing more than degree of abstraction. It also inclines us to see that when abstract rhetorics *are* experienced, there seems to be a *unity of abstraction;* that is, with this model before us, it would be hard to conceive an abstraction of "speaker/speech" which was not accompanied by a corresponding, almost a mathematically proportional, abstraction of "audience/occasion/change."

A MATERIALIST'S DEFINITION OF RHETORIC

Idealists could hope to isolate the ultimate formal definition of rhetoric, for though the strains of usage are often inconsistent and always complex, the question *What is rhetoric?* is conceivably answerable if we translate it to mean *How has the word "rhetoric" been used by persons claiming to instruct would-be advocates?* Conceiving rhetoric materially, however, makes it necessary to define it with regard to the solution of problems posed by the persistent recurrence of "speaker/speech/audience/occasion/change" at every level of social experience. Formal definitions must thus be truly theoretical, grounded in objective data rather than in the practice and opinions of cloistered academics using the word "rhetoric" in treatises on composition.

Since material theory in rhetorical studies is rare, any definition offered must be regarded as purely operational, designed to guide the mind toward solution of a special question which must be answered in the process of creating descriptions, explanations, and predictions. This essay is focused on the fundamental problem of linking theory with practice, hence the question *What warrants and legitimizes the theory of rhetoric?* My definition of "rhetoric," therefore, is intended to expose the questions which arise from an attempt to determine the material criteria of theory. I am not positing essence so much as continuing to define the issues which occur in the clash between idealism and materialism in rhetorical studies.

I will hazard one of the those infamous italicized sentences which begin "rhetoric is . . ." and then call specific attention to the issues I want to raise with the chosen wording. *Rhetoric is a natural social phenomenon in the context of which symbolic claims are made on the behavior and/or belief of one or more persons, allegedly in the interest of such individuals, and with the strong presumption that such claims will cause meaningful change.*

The phrase "natural social phenomenon" is meant to suggest that rhetoric is a paradigm of relationships as described in the previous section. The material model of rhetoric is a portrayal of social process, a naturally recurring phenomenon with which we must cope, and in which we must participate. It is the *naturalness* of the phenomenon that creates the necessity to account for it. Bitzer speaks of "exigencies" created by material factors "inviting" a particular "discourse."[12] But his conception of "exigence" is serendipitous, for he holds between the lines a possibility that we might ignore or transcend the phenomenon which invites persuasion. We cannot. The "exigence" of rhetoric is that the phenomenon itself seems inescapable; indeed, as Augustine suggested, the phenomenon persists so much that skill in participating in it seems to come with raw and untutored socialization as well as with particular education.[13] The first requirement of a material theory of rhetoric which purports to account for practice would seem to be actual *description* of "exigence," not the supposition of it. Without resort to paradox, traditional vocabularies simply do not give us the resources to describe the experience of rhetoric as it impinges on us, as it exists "naturally."

The phrase "in the context of which" is intended to suggest the relationship between "discourse" and "rhetoric" which makes usage of the two terms theoretically problematic. In Foucault's terms, human discourse is an "archaeological" remnant of a larger phenomenon. It stands out from other elements of the phenomenon because it persists as the track, the spoor, the evidence of a social process.[14] As I suggested earlier, to say that we study rhetoric in a material way is not to claim that rhetoric is material because it is a sensible discourse I may handle and manipulate like rock. Rather, discourse is *part* of a material phenomenon particularly useful because it is residual and persistent. We can reconstruct the nature, scope and consequence of a nuclear explosion by analyzing its residue when the raw matter and even the energy inherent in its occurrence have dissipated. Thus it is possible to reconstruct the nature, scope, and consequence of rhetoric by analyzing "speech" even when "speaker," "audience," "occasion," and "change" dissipate into half-remembered history. Reconstruction *of the whole phenomenon*, it seems to me, is a *prius* to an accounting of the rhetorical, for it is the *whole* of "speaker/speech/audience/occasion/change" which impinges on us: to confuse rhetoric with a discourse is the same error as confounding fallout with nuclear explosion. Traditional ideal conceptions of rhetoric not only make it possible to equate the terms "rhetoric" and "discourse," they can encourage such confusion by falsely suggesting an inverse relationship between the two terms. Thus, for example, it is often said that rhetoric is a type or genre of discourse distinct from philosophy, poetry or scientific discourse. As we busy ourselves trying to locate an exclusionary principle with which generically to mark out rhetorical discourses, we too often forget that *there is no type of discourse which cannot function as "speech" in a material rhetoric*. If we can say that all distinguishable forms of discourse *may* function rhetorically, we are thereby suggesting that rhetoric is greater than a discourse; "rhetorical" is a quality of discourse derived from the discourse's presence and function within the larger phenomenon "rhetoric."

The phrase "symbolic claims" is meant to be more than a synonym for "discourse" and/or "persuasion." *Every* interactivity of society contains or comprises a claim on some human being's belief and/or behavior. Nothing in the environment bespeaks our free-agency; indeed, we most often mark out our own free-will as Nietzsche described in *The Will to Power*, by listing the ways in which we may in fact constrict the free-will of others.[15] In the paradox that the proof of freedom for one is simultaneously the proof of the necessity which restrains another, there is the truth that society itself is nothing but formal interaction, a process of mutual claims upon and controls of each individual's belief and/or behavior. Rhetoric is one of the phenomena in the context of which claim and control are possible:

whenever an "audience" exists, it puts claims upon and to some extent determines the belief/behavior of "speaker," and nearly simultaneously "speaker" puts claims upon and to an extent controls the belief/behavior of an "audience." "War," "police power," and "economy" are other phenomena (perhaps not entirely distinct from "rhetoric") in the context of which claim and control are possible. Rhetoric would appear to be the most common context of claim and control because it is the most comfortable context: the claims and controls are *symbolic,* the representation and consequent sublimation of painful physical claims and controls. There is in rhetoric a sense of seduction, of control which, if it is not voluntary, is at least an acquiescence wherein a human being feels accounted for in some more personal way than a gun shoved into the rib. Rhetoric, I mean to say, Parke Burgess notwithstanding, is a species of coercion.[16] And it seems important in any material theory of rhetoric to describe the phenomenon *as* a coercive agency: traditionally, we pay more attention to the *degree* of force in claiming and controlling than to the *fact* of coercion. So we see a so-called "ethical argument" differing in kind from purely physical threats associated with fascist stormtroopers. Certainly it is more comfortable and preferable; but neither the motive of the advocate, nor the means of seducing agreement, nor the resulting degree of pain change the form of using symbols, whether called "argument" or "threat," to restrict the freedom of a human being to do and to believe as he/she alone thinks fit. That which is preferable in "rhetoric" as opposed to "war" is precisely the symbolic sublimation of pain, not the lack or absence of coercion in the act of controlling behavior/belief.[17]

The wording "behavior and/or belief" is meant to recognize that there is usually a congruity of thought and action when human beings interact socially, but at the same time to suggest that symbolic control is sometimes accomplished with great indirection through manipulation of belief structures alone. Traditional conceptions of ideal "rhetoric" have been able to cope well with the connection between a specific rhetorical phenomenon and the subsequent behavior of people who played the role of "audience." Thus, for example, those critics Black calls "neo-Aristotelian" have been able to build the arguments which plausibly suggest a link between a behavior recommended in the "speech" and subsequent actualization of that behavior in reality by "audience," as when a politician asking for the votes of certain constituencies receives them. Of course, as Black suggests, one cannot be certain that there is a cause-effect relationship between requesting and getting votes: dozens of variables intervene to make such a conclusion logically dubious. Still, when "audience" ratifies their "speaker's" claim upon them by acting out recommendations in reality,

"People") has the capacity to *create* "change" by fiat of collective belief and behavior.[25]

The "speech" as theory, in other words, is distinct from ordinary theory in that those who react to it have the power to *make* it "true" if it happens to be technically (that is, logically or empirically) "wrong." We see, for example, the long line of political theorists who argued the impossibility of "democracy," on sound and reasonable principles, literally made "wrong" in their predictions by the collective belief and behavior of Anglo-Americans. Reading "speech" as if it were the favored theory of "change" at the moment of its utterance, I believe, could yield powerful descriptions and explanations of social process. Even predictions are possible in either or both of two circumstances: (1) if analysis of several rhetorics over long periods of time seems to reveal a high degree of redundancy in the models of "change" they contain, and if it seems that events did alter the world in the same direction recommended by "speech," we would have some reason to characterize the redundant model as potentially predictive of "change" in the future; (2) further, if we can find evidence to prove claims of a contemporary "speech's" effectiveness, it is not improbable that a gambler's prediction of the shape of "change" might be verified. Of course such predictions could be reliable only by the standards of critical social science, not by the more rigid criteria of academic positivism.[26]

The definition just elaborated cuts across so many issues, real and imagined, and there are therefore so many lines of refutation to be adduced against it, that I am obliged to leave it as a caveat for those who might see less heresy than I intend: conceiving "rhetoric" as a material phenomenon alters the meaning of all rhetorical theory, for it puts upon a theorist the requirement that he/she begin with a body of data and not with a corpus of philosophical speculations and prescriptions.

CONCLUSION

Today, the typical course in rhetorical theory consists of the analysis, not of public address texts, but of philosophical manuals of instruction. Most of those manuals at least purport to be constructed from observations of "speaker/speech/audience/occasion/change" interactions—so if one wished to recover theoretical descriptions, explanations, and postdictions of the function of communication in historical societies, ancient treatises about rhetoric would be useful documents. The problem is not in traditional books about rhetoric, therefore, but in our reading and use of the classics. Instead of

there is such a strong presumption of causal effect that challenging the link on logical grounds alone seems nitpicking.[18] Black's point is more profound, however, for in his stunning critique of Chapman's "Coatesville Address" the question turns not on the behavioral power of "speech" so much as on the attitudinal power of material rhetoric exhibited over long periods of time. As I already have argued, rhetoric need not always be particular. When "speaker/audience/occasion/change" elements are abstract, particularly in the realm of morality, the "effect" is not on any human agent particularly, but on everyone indirectly, as each of us participates in a public, shared agreement as to the normative conditions of belonging to society. Behavior is often recalcitrant, "variable in every direction" as Ortega suggests, but it is always tugged by belief, coerced into new patterns by pure doubt as to its justifiability.[19] Since behavior and belief must be perceived as congruent, the attitudinal power of rhetoric must be described—and as Black argued, traditional ideal conceptions simply cannot cope with describing fabrications of normative structures, of "public morality" and "ideology."[20]

By the phrase "allegedly in the interest of such individuals" I mean to say that every "speaker" claims to be motivated by "audience's" interest. This calls to attention the relationship between "speaker" and "audience" as "leader" to "follower." Though idealists pay lip-service to the need to adapt to audiences, and though a great deal of technical effort has been directed at formulating check-lists to use in analyzing audiences, almost no attention has been given in traditional rhetorical studies to the leader/follower relationship obvious in nearly every material rhetoric.

Idealists merely *suppose* that "speaker" is active and a leader while "audience" is reactive and the constituency of followers. Even a tiny survey of material rhetorics quickly shows that the relationship between "speakers" and "audiences" is not so clear: like a spider crawling on the polished surface of a mirror, the interpenetration of "speaker" and "audience" is so complete that only rarely can one distinguish the reality from the image. Every "audience" comes together with an interest and the expectation that "speaker" will aid in procuring that interest. And every "speaker" comes to "audience" with the desire to accomplish an otherwise impossible task by mobilizing a collective force. What we see is almost a negotiation wherein "speaker" articulates the wishes and needs of "audience," and "audience" agrees to "speaker's" leadership as a means of securing their interest. Do "speakers" lead when they, in Plato's words, "do only what they think best," not "what they will"?[21] Will "speaker" be accorded the right of leadership if "audience" does not hear an articulation of their interest? Is "speaker" merely the "voice" of "audience"? Or is "audience" like clay and so pliable that they will sacrifice even their most heart-felt interest for the sake of "speaker," their leader?

When practice is the guide, the answer to each of these questions is at one time or another "yes." And at one time or another each leader/follower relationship appears to have been productive and disastrous, whether measured by an ideal Platonic "good" or by more pragmatic "general welfare" criteria. The nature of "leadership," in other words, is so equivocal that one must think in terms of "styles of leadership" fit for "audiences" in particular circumstances. The task of a material theory of rhetoric, it seems to me, is to account for leader/follower relationships. To achieve this goal, it would seem advisable to catalogue and to study what "speakers" allege to be the interest of "audiences" in "speeches," the documentary residue or rhetoric.

The "alleged interest" of "audience" also focuses attention on one of the central concerns of ideal rhetoric, the problem of discovering and describing "motive." One need not dwell long on the topic, for Kenneth Burke has described a material alternative to both the normative and behavioral conceptions of "motive."[22] The molecular model presented in the previous section, however, invites more general attention to "motive" than Burke or his predecessors intended: with the exception of a few arguments taken up tangentially by Burke, "motive" has been characterized less as a discrete category of experience than as a property of "speakers." Thus, for example, the interest and intention which "speaker" brings to "audience" is conceived as a motive which is more or less reprehensible as it approaches or ignores the general welfare allegedly present in the "speaker/audience" relationship. In arguing that the concept "motive" is in fact a short-hand term for "situation," Burke called attention to the error of confusing an agent's "purpose" with his/her "motive," the latter being a product not just of intent, but also of interactivity with other agents. Burke seems correct that a complete description of "motive" would be an elaboration of "occasion." But as "motive" is an abbreviation for "occasion," so one might claim that "speech" is an abbreviation of "motive" ("speech," of course, understood as part of material rhetoric and not as a synonym for "discourse"): as Wallace suggested, the interest of both "speaker/audience" exists in "speech" as the "good reasons" which warrant accepting "speaker's" recommendations.[23] Such "good reasons" are not identical to "speaker's" intentions and purposes because they must be persuasive, adapted to "audience" and made to appear interested only in the general welfare. Insofar as "speaker" frames "good reasons" to *move* "audience" toward a position consistent with but not wholly the same as their interest, such "good reasons" are also apart from "audience."

The interest of "audience" as portrayed in "speech," therefore, is a

record of *interactive motive,* of "speaker/audience" interests skewed for the purpose of accommodating each other. In motives are a property of neither "speaker/audience" but discrete category of experience. Significantly, as Wallace su such motives are empirically accessible in the "speech" which rhetoric as residue of the phenomenon. Though the *intent* of "s remains hidden in his/her psyche, to be guessed at with the h *priori* paradigms, *interactive motives* are available and warrantabl evidence of "speech." Further, because *public* behaviors and bel be guided *only* by interactive motives, the private interest "speaker" seems all but irrelevant to rhetoric—interactive govern *collective* beliefs whether "speaker" be Pope John Paul Ayatollah Khomeini.

The potential of a material theory of rhetoric is exposed suggestion that rhetoric implies "the strong presumption tha claims will result in meaningful change." As foreshadowed previous discussion of levels of rhetorical experience, this phrase intended to say that "speech" has "effects." The whole probl "effect" seems picayune when one realizes that what actually ha as a result of "speech" is less important than the fact that every "sp is a miniature predictive model of the "changes" which it recomm Every "speaker," in other words, creates a picture of the world suggestion that "audience" perceives reality through the term with the resources of "speech." That world is a distorted structu facts and inferences selected not for their reliable representation objective world, but rather for their salience to the satisfactio intersubjective desires.

Insofar as "speaker/audience" have the power collectively to a their world, "speech," regardless of its ultimate effects, is alwa contingent model of (1) the existing environment essentialized into of salient facts; (2) estimates of activity sufficient to change esse facts; and (3) a predicted environment altered by intersubjec activity. Any who have worked with models of social cha understand the difficulty of finding even an explanatory instrum never mind the dream of prediction.[24] Yet in the work-a-day world conduct a continual deliberation based on our ability to model environment and to predict the consequences of changing it. How such models constructed? What does "change" mean in the contex these models? How in actual material rhetorics do "speaker/au ence/occasion" seem related to "change"? These questions ar regardless of the actual effects of "speech." But the possibility th "speech" is indeed an effective agency of "change" makes the model "change" sketched in "speech" *theoretically* powerful, for, as I ha argued elsewhere, an "audience" (or in its most reified sense

communicative interactions, most rhetoricians have seen a creative process, "invention/disposition/style/memory/delivery." Rather than ask what Aristotle *saw* in ancient Greece, we have concerned ourselves with what Aristotle *said* in Greek. It is good to use Aristotle in the same spirit and for the same reasons one would use Copernicus' *Heavenly Spheres* or Redi's theory of spontaneous generation. To say upon reading Aristotle's *Rhetoric* that one is "studying rhetoric," however, is to commit the most egregious of errors, for one is studying an honorable and ancient treatise *about* rhetoric, not *the thing itself*. A study of rhetoric, I have suggested, is predominantly a study of practice, and a "rhetorical theory" should be related to practice as generalization to data, not as prescription to performance. In this view, rhetoric is not an "art," nor it is a "body of principles"—it is a thing, a material artifact of human interaction.

I have approached my thesis conceptually, first constructing a molecular model of material rhetorics, then offering a formal definition of rhetoric-as-object, because I believe that a fundamental alteration of perspective is necessary to counterbalance the overwhelming influence of idealism in rhetorical theory. The problem Black exposed in his critique of the methods popular among rhetorical critics still bothers rhetorical theorists, biasing and inhibiting the development of grounded theories of rhetoric. To survey practice while counting enthymemes, acknowledging that people arrive at conclusions through thought, feeling, and intimidation, all in the context of writing formulary biographical prose—this is an exercise in futility which glorifies the obvious. Exactly the same mind-set is involved in studying Juan de Vives or Hugh Blair with the intention of understanding "rhetoric" when we know of material rhetorics in the context of which a set of "speakers" such as Burke, Franklin, Jefferson, Chatham, Adams, Fox, Madison, and Erskine acted in and on the real world.

If history matters at all to rhetorical theory, and I am convinced that it does, it is material history, not the history of ideas. For centuries those enamored of links in the great chain of being have read each other: bureaucratic thinkers from Aristotle to Bacon to Howell have thought it reasonable, usually on purely normative grounds, to restrict the "office" of rhetoric. If we were dealing with an Idea, reassignment of topics and thoughts might make as much sense as the shuffling of secretaries and clerks in business offices. But we are not. Human thought cannot be bureaucratized unless there are "offices" corresponding to material realities. The sun does not go away by assigning or reassigning thought about it to the "office" of chemistry rather than physics—and wherever topics relating to "sun" are pursued, thought must be controlled *by the sun* rather than by administrative procedures in the "office" of thinking. Similarly, if we think to purify argument of non-rational passions by reassigning it from the "office" of rhetoric to that of ethics or logic, the real rhetorics which inspired us to investigate argumentation in the first place do not go away. Should we define rhetoric as an art or as a genre of literature or as a body of principles, we distort our own sociality, for we divert attention from the coercive power of the symbols which unite society and focus instead on the tricks of pretty language or on the gamesmanship of forensic and deliberative competition. These narrow notions of "rhetoric" permit no more than a debunking of practice—saying what it is *not*; and they almost preclude real understanding of practice—saying and appreciating what it *is*.

Notes

This essay, still imperfect after ten years' revision, began in Douglas Ehninger's passing curiosity as to what a "material" pre-Socratic or neo-Marxian theory of rhetoric might look like. Perhaps this adumbration gives some notion short of caricature.

1. José Ortega y Gasset, *Man and People*, trans. Willard R. Trask (New York: W. W. Norton, 1957), pp. 11–16.
2. See, e.g., Lloyd F. Bitzer, "The Rhetorical Situation," *Philosophy & Rhetoric*, 1 (1968), 1–14.
3. Howell's "history of" eighteenth-century British logic and rhetoric, for example, is so committed to the primacy of textbooks on composition that he takes Boulton to task for failing to consider that the fashionable recipes for speech-making actually established criteria for public debate over the French Revolution: "James T. Boulton discusses Priestley's contribution to the debate in Britain between 1790 and 1793 over the French Revolution. . . . But Mr. Boulton does not recognize that the rhetorical theories of that era, and particularly Priestley's *Lectures on Oratory,* are important to the modern critic in defining the standards which the participants in that debate themselves observed." In my reading, there is not a single British politician or orator between 1761 and 1845 who appears to have adhered to or explicitly recognized a "standard for participation in debate" even remotely resembling the "rhetorical theories of that era." If one wished to correlate Priestley's theory and practice of rhetoric, the useful theoretical treatise is his *Lectures on History and General Policy* (1764), not his *Lectures on Oratory.* See Wilbur Samuel Howell, *Eighteenth-Century British Logic and Rhetoric* (Princeton: Princeton University Press, 1971), p. 647, fn. 536; and Joseph Priestley, *Lectures on History and General Policy,* 3rd. ed. (1764; Dublin: Luke White and P. Byrne, 1791), esp. pp. 23–87, 228–80; Priestley, *A Course of Lectures on Oratory and Criticism,* ed. Vincent M. Bevilacqua and Richard Murphy (1777; rpt. Carbondale: Southern Illinois University Press, 1965).
   Among those committed to a *philosophy of* rhetoric, Perelman is perhaps the most sensitive to actual practice—he consistently, impressively illustrates principles of "the new rhetoric" by citing examples from the literature of public address. But they appear to be *nothing more* than examples, bits and pieces carefully ornamenting metaethical speculation, snippets from "great speeches"—emphatically *not* from ordinary persuasive discourse—which illustrate the mechanics of practical reason.

So, for example, Perelman examines a relationship between social inertia and social change, noting that an advocate of change has the more imposing task. He makes the point by an analogy between physics and human consciousness, by referring to a quip by Jean Paulhan, by persuasively defining "change," by asserting the commonality of appeals to inertia, and finally, at long last, by quoting two sentences from a speech by William Pitt. Perelman's new rhetoric has no closer contact with actual rhetoric than metaphysics with social science, for he has not so much rediscovered rhetoric as he has redefined philosophy along more reasonable lines. As Eco suggests, "the so-called 'new rhetoric' (Perelman, 1958) has definitely reduced apodictic discourses to axiomatical systems alone, and has listed all other types of discourse (from philosophy to politics or theology) under the rhetorical heading." See Chaim Perelman and L. Olbrechts-Tyteca, *The New Rhetoric*, trans. John Wilkinson and Purcell Weaver (South Bend: University of Notre Dame Press, 1969), esp. pp. 104–6; and Umberto Eco, *A Theory of Semiotics* (Bloomington: Indiana University Press, 1976), p. 277.

4. Donald C. Bryant, *Rhetorical Dimensions in Criticism* (Baton Rouge: Louisiana State University Press, 1973), pp. 3–4.
5. Maurice Natanson, "The Limits of Rhetoric," *Quarterly Journal of Speech,* 41 (1955), 133–39.
6. Karl Marx and Frederick Engels, *The German Ideology* (1845–46) in Karl Marx and Frederick Engels, *Collected Works,* 9+ vols. (Moscow: Progress Publishers, 1976), V, 36–37.
7. See, e.g., Walter M. Carleton, "What Is Rhetorical Knowledge? A Response to Farrell—and More," *Quarterly Journal of Speech,* 64 (1978), 313–28.
8. Though it is a feeble effort at difficult synthesis, see, e.g., Rosalind Coward and John Ellis, *Language and Materialism* (London: Routledge & Kegan Paul, 1977).
9. For an excellent synthesis of the current state of thinking on such subjects and others, see Anthony Giddens, *Central Problems in Social Theory: Action, Structure and Contradiction in Social Analysis* (Berkeley: University of California Press, 1979).
10. See Fredric Jameson, *The Prison-House of Language* (Princeton: Princeton University Press, 1972); John R. Lyne, "C.S. Peirce on Rhetoric and Communication," Diss. University of Wisconsin-Madison 1978; and Michael J. Hyde and Craig R. Smith, "Hermeneutics and Rhetoric: A Seen but Unobserved Relationship," *Quarterly Journal of Speech,* 65 (1979), 347–63.
11. Cf. Neil J. Smelser, *Theory of Collective Behavior* (New York: Free Press, 1962), esp. pp. 2–21; and Michael Calvin McGee, "Social Movement: Phenomenon or Meaning?" *Central States Speech Journal,* 31 (1980), 233–44. Also, c.f. A. O. Lovejoy, *The Great Chain of Being* (Cambridge: Harvard University Press, 1936); A. O. Lovejoy, "Reflections on the History of Ideas," *Journal of the History of Ideas,* 1 (1940), 3–23; and Michel Foucault, *The Archaeology of Knowledge,* trans. Alan M. Sheridan-Smith (1969; Eng. trans. New York: Harper Colophon, 1972).
12. Bitzer, "Rhetorical Situation," pp. 7–8.
13. Augustine, *On Christian Doctrine,* trans. J. F. Shaw, in *Great Books of the Western World,* ed. Robert M. Hutchins (Chicago: Encyclopedia Britannica, 1952), XVIII: 4. 7. 5–9; 4. 7. 14; and 4. 7. 21.
14. Foucault, *Archaeology of Knowledge,* pp. 215–37.
15. Friedrich Nietzsche, *The Will to Power,* trans. Walter Kaufmann and R. J. Hollingdale (New York: Vintage Books, 1968), pp. 382–418.
16. Parke G. Burgess, "Crisis Rhetoric: Coercion vs. Force," *Quarterly Journal of Speech,* 59 (1973), 61–73.
17. I recognize that I use the terms "freedom" and "constraint" eccentrically. Most Anglo-Americans who take up the topic of coercion see it as a direct opposite of

freedom, much as Arendt acts an an ideologue in arguing for a communications concept of "power" antithetical to totalitarian employment of force and sheer terror. I have little quarrel with the conclusions of such arguments, though for me it is impossible to know reflexively whether or not my assent is ideologically conditioned by participation in Anglo-American culture. It seems to me that ideological conceptions of freedom as the opposite of force are clearly derivative from a dialectical opposition between unconstrained action and constrained action. Freedom, for most of us, is usually and erroneously associated with lack of constraint. In fact, I believe, to live in society is to experience a complex of constraints. "Pure freedom" as unconstrained action is a phantom, a vision made real only by intersubjective agreement or by ideological conditioning. The huge majority of us, from the time we are toilet trained if not before, develop a habit of acquiescence inconsistent with the idea of rational assent. We are pulled fighting and screaming into the world of civilized social animals, resenting and resisting laws and rules of all sorts. More and less preferable methods are used to overcome our resistance and resentment: we are paddled, bullied, caged, tied, persuaded, and threatened until we agree to behave "like a grown-up." Historically and presently, governments treat the general citizenry as adolescents, using all the tools of manipulation and indoctrination. If television commercials are an indication, even business corporations increasingly treat the people as willful children. Adults, however, are strong enough, particularly in groups, to offer more effective resistance than can toddlers to parents. So those with economic, political, or military power paddle with reluctance, preferring instead to persuade. Rhetoric in their hands is an instrument of coercion or constraint, a symbolic placebo replacing bayonets and the company store as a matter of pragmatic efficiency. Rhetoric, I conclude, is clearly *preferable* to more violent and ruthless means of social control; but it is, in its function, *distinct* from that which it sublimates only by measure of the degree of its force. See Hannah Arendt, "Lying in Politics," in *Crises of the Republic* (New York: Viking, 1972), pp. 1–47; and Jurgen Habermas, "Hannah Arendt's Communications Concept of Power," *Social Research,* 44 (1977), 3–24.

18. Edwin Black, *Rhetorical Criticism: A Study in Method* (1965; rpt. Madison: Univ. of Wisconsin Press, 1978), pp. 27–90.
19. José Ortega y Gasset, *History as a System,* trans. Helene Weyl (New York: W. W. Norton, 1961), pp. 199–216.
20. Black, *"Rhetorical Criticism,"* pp. 132–47.
21. Plato, *Gorgias,* in *The Dialogues of Plato,* ed. and trans. Benjamin Jowett (New York: Random House, 1937), I: 466B.
22. Kenneth Burke, *Permanence and Change: An Anatomy of Purpose,* 2nd ed. rev. (1954; rpt. Indianapolis: Bobbs-Merrill, 1965); Kenneth Burke, *A Grammar of Motives* (New York: Prentice-Hall, 1945); Kenneth Burke, *A Rhetoric of Motives* (New York: Prentice-Hall, 1950).
23. Karl R. Wallace, "The Substance of Rhetoric: Good Reasons," *Quarterly Journal of Speech,* 49 (1963), 239–49.
24. See Herbert W. Simons, Elizabeth Mechling and Howard N. Schreier, "Mobilizing for Collective Action From the Bottom Up: The Rhetoric of Social Movements," unpub. MS, Temple Univ., pp. 48–106, forthcoming in Carroll C. Arnold and John Waite Bowers, eds., *Handbook of Rhetorical and Communication Theory.*
25. Michael Calvin McGee, "In Search of 'The People': A Rhetorical Alternative," *Quarterly Journal of Speech,* 61 (1975), 235–49.
26. See Giddens, *Central Problems,* pp. 234–59.

Polanyi's Epistemology of Good Reasons

Samuel D. Watson, Jr.

In extending Robert L. Scott's analysis of the systems of western rhetorics, Douglas Ehninger observed that "perhaps to do so is to fall prey to a rashness that Professor Scott wisely resisted."[1] Nonetheless, his response yielded a reasoned account of the developments marking a "new" social rhetoric and confirmed my belief that rashness is a reasonable, even necessary, risk to run in an effort of inquiry. It is both an assumption and a conclusion of this essay that such an effort also can be an exercise of reason. What concerns me is both epistemology and reason, particularly as these concepts are construed by Michael Polanyi.

James Wiser accurately notes that Polanyi, "proceeding in a manner reminiscent of the Classical Greek tradition, . . . constructs a philosophical anthropology by examining the structures of man's highest faculty, reason."[2] Yet the "structures of man's highest faculty" did not provide a self-evidentially clear starting point for Polanyi, any more than they do for us. Unfortunately, Polanyi never drew together,

Samuel D. Watson, Jr. is Associate Professor of English and Co-Director of the UNCC Writing Project at the University of North Carolina at Charlotte.

in some one place, his distinctive view of human reason. To do so, in a way which is openly exploratory rather than definitive, is this essay's purpose.

To place Polanyi in a broader context, specifically a rhetorical one, is to discover a warrant for this task. Polanyi's name has become familiar to rhetoricians. A recent article claims in passing that he "explains more about the nature of modern rhetoric" than virtually any other thinker.[3] Still, much of his work remains untapped by rhetorical theorists; significantly, they have quietly ignored the most distinctive dimension of his thought, his epistemology. Theorists of the "good reasons" school, probably the most important movement in contemporary rhetorical theory and certainly the movement whose members most consistently take him seriously, have hardly begun to attend to Polanyi's epistemology. A brief review of their concerns and of their approving, though strikingly incomplete, application of his thought suggests their reluctance directly to address epistemological issues. With this as a basis, I shall explore Polanyi's contribution to rhetorical thought, with specific emphasis on his epistemology and the conception of human reason it engenders. It is this conception of reason which offers us an important view of the relationships between acts of inquiry and statements which are rhetorical.

GOOD REASONS AND BAD EPISTEMOLOGY

When Karl Wallace entitled his seminal article "The Substance of Rhetoric: Good Reasons,"[4] he established a term, *good reasons,* which has come to characterize an important if loosely affiliated "school" of contemporary rhetorical theorists,[5] including such persons as Chaim Perelman, Henry Johnstone, Robert Scott, Wayne Booth, Lloyd Bitzer, and Carroll Arnold. He also indicated two concerns which continue to be central for this school: one is a search for some conception(s) of reason which, not restricted to formal inference, functions in the human realm of individual and communal decision; the other is a renewed interest in the content, substance, and significance of rhetorical discourse (i.e., in "invention" as a revitalized canon of rhetoric). Both of these concerns raise questions of epistemology. Indeed, as Perelman and others have shown, it was a distinctive epistemological orientation which, as much as anything, encouraged the demise of rhetoric, including invention, as a serious branch of study through the last few centuries of Western thought.[6]

Theorists of "good reasons" have been slow to embrace directly the epistemological challenge. By default they have tended to assume a still prevalent epistemology—which, following Polanyi, I will call "objecti-vist"—and have delineated their rhetoric by contrast to it.[7] Ironically, such an attitude, were it embraced, would consign rhetoric to irrationality. As Walter B. Weimer's searching critique shows, "rhetoric is endorsed in a retreat from higher, but unfortunately unobtainable, critical and epistemic standards. . . . Even though rhetoric is given 'primacy' in these accounts it still has second-rate status."[8] Indeed it must have, as long as it is measured by the standards of an epistemology that, rooted in formal demonstration, denies legitimacy to the informal methods and even to the uncertainties which, characterizing the human world, are rhetoric's reason for being.

Michael Polanyi was not a rhetorician, but it was these uncertainties of our world that called him from his productive career as a research scientist to attend to philosophical concerns. Polanyi sought a philosophic position from which to defend freedom of thought, in the sciences and elsewhere, and to understand the philosophic bases of contemporary threats to that freedom. The most significant threats were ideologies, especially Marxism, which deny autonomy to individual thought and to the informal and irreducibly rhetorical operations of communities, within which thought is exercised.

Polanyi traces the persuasive force of contemporary ideologies to an unstable union of man's moral passions and objectivist epistemol-ogy. Their current fusions threaten the unspoken trusts and beliefs on which any human culture rests. As Polanyi states in *Personal Knowledge*, he "faced the task of justifying the holding of unproven traditional beliefs."[9] *Personal Knowledge* gives the first clear view of the epistemology of tacit knowing, which Marjorie Grene claims to be "Polanyi's unique contribution to philosophy. . . , the thesis that all knowledge necessarily includes a tacit component on which it relies in order to focus on its goal."[10] The theory of tacit knowing seeks to account for acts of inquiry, first in the hard sciences but later also in such comprehensively human areas as ethical action, aesthetic experiences, and religious faith. Extending the epistemology of the tacit in these directions, while continuing to show that tacit actions inform all human efforts to achieve meaning, was Polanyi's continuing endeavor until his death in 1976.

A survey of the direct uses "good reason" theorists have made of Polanyi's work illustrates the epistemological reticence I have noted already. It also provides some orientation to his thought. Wayne Booth credits Polanyi with giving us "the most important critique of systematic doubt in the name of what I have called systematic assent."[11] In Booth's book-length search for good reasons for assent, he, like Polanyi, gives belief primacy over doubt, embraces our common and communal sense, sees that qualified communities play a necessary role in inquiry, and would restore to rationality forms of assent which under the "modern dogma" of doubt often are considered irrational. Throughout Booth's book, however, Polanyi's epistemology remains unmentioned.

Lloyd Bitzer reveals a similar ambivalence.[12] Bitzer relies extensively on Polanyi in studying the repository of some truths and thus the authoritative ground of a class of decisions and actions which Bitzer calls "public knowledge"—a confluence of "personal facts" which "very nearly coincides with" Polanyi's "superior knowledge." A public's knowledge comprises the entire heritage of man's achievements within a culture, though most of those achievements are known only tacitly by any single member of the culture. But Bitzer is at pains to limit his essay's scope by distinguishing "public knowledge" from scientific findings, assuming some absolute distinction between knowledge and opinion. In effect, he uses Polanyi's understanding of communities, while ignoring the epistemology which extends and undergirds that conception.

Chaim Perelman[13] states directly the same ambivalence concerning Polanyi which Booth and Bitzer exhibit. In Polanyi's critique of objectivism and his concern with invention, Perelman finds important kinship with his own position. However, Perelman objects that scientific knowledge enjoys a privileged status in our culture, existing without appeal to authority and presenting a body of truths which win universal acceptance in ways not accessible in other fields. Like Bitzer, Perelman would exempt scientific discourse from the realm of rhetorical interactions.

Walter B. Weimer would not. In an article deeply coherent with Polanyi's views (though it only mentions him in passing), Weimer finds knowledge to be "a matter of warranted assertion," and he argues against exempting science from the realm of rhetoric.[14] Such an exemption appeals to a conception of reason which is mistaken; it consigns even science to irrationality and can offer no account of scientific change. Following Weimer's lead, Michael A. Overington constructs a model for the rhetorical study of scientific discourse, placing such discourse firmly in the context of scientific communities as Polanyi understands them.[15] Robert Scott has urged that rhetoricians study Polanyi's epistemology.[16] He has offered a partial response to his own challenge, arguing that auditors are agents in the creation of meaning and that the commitments which persons claim can appropriately be tested by their willingness to engage in authentic argumentation within their communities.[17]

Thus various theorists of the "good reasons" movement have found important but, to this point, limited kinships with Polanyi. They see themselves opposed to the same philosophic positions he is combating, and they have drawn on his understanding of communities. But their relatively scant references to Polanyi's theory of tacit knowing underscores an epistemological reticence which encourages us to overlook the relationships between changes we call epistemic and those called rhetorical. A view of human reason which could undergird both is thus obscured from us.

POLANYI'S EPISTEMOLOGY OF INQUIRY

The starting point of Polanyi's thought is not a quibble about philosophy; it is instead this century's wars, enslavements, and other threats to human culture.[18] He traces these threats to philosophic causes; in essence, the major cause is the absence of a view of human reason which can function persuasively while also claiming epistemic (and ontological) status for itself. In its absence we have ideological forces whose great persuasive powers are destabilizing and destructive. What happens when persons seek to restrict reason to formal operations, and knowledge to what can be seen through the objectivist lenses of doubt, explicitness, impersonal observation, and formal demonstration? Such restrictions, Polanyi consistently implies, are never actually possible. Yet the power of Marxism and other contemporary ideologies, he believes, graphically illustrates the consequences of seriously attempting them. One effect is that knowledge becomes seen as much more reliable than it actually ever is. Far from guaranteeing critical judgment, in contemporary ideologies objectivist epistemology ends by giving knowledge—and those who claim to hold it—an authoritative cast which renders judgment unnecessary and even unthinkable.

In Polanyi's interpretation, this objectivist fervor is furthered by human passion for the perfection of knowledge and of social institutions. Of all creation, humanity alone seeks justice, beauty, and truth. Moral passions, which distinguish humans from other beings, are the primary motive.[19] That is not a benign view. Humans, who alone seek to act morally, are alone capable of the kinds of failure we call evil. In accounting for the unprecedented evils which ideologies have caused in our century, Polanyi traces them largely to our perfectionist moral aspirations, intent to remove injustice completely from social institutions, confident of success because of an ideology's presumed scientific foundation. Thus what Marxism did "was to dress up a utopia as a science and thus render it unquestionable by an age to which science was the ultimate truth."[20]

These same human passions lead us also to insist on perfection in knowledge. But only certain matters can even seem to meet the objectivist standards of impersonality and explicitness; the distinctively human commitments to justice and to the power to seek truth actively are not among them. Thus objectivist epistemology, seriously embraced, is reductive; man comes to be seen as a lower animal at best, to whom it is senseless to attribute any motives higher than selfish drives and appetites. As Polanyi suggests, "all rational action becomes a lifeless banality,"[21] because appeals to reason, which can never match objectivist standards, are unmasked as the self-serving causes they are presumed only to be. All invocations of higher value are embraced superstitiously by persons who do not think clearly or hypocritically by those who do. Thus moral passions, in Polanyi's view, impel us to an ever more strident grasp of a view of knowledge which insists ever more firmly that those moral passions do not exist.

Man's moral passions and his objectivist epistemology, though contradictory to each other, do not cancel each other out. Instead they fuse into a "dynamo-objective coupling," which in contemporary ideologies provides "the joint satisfaction of a belief in moral perfection with a complete denial of moral motives."[22] The very internal inconsistency of this coupling lends it tremendous persuasive force:

> Alleged scientific assertions, which are accepted as such because they satisfy moral passions, will excite these passions further, and thus lend increased convincing power to the scientific affirmations in question—and so on, indefinitely. Moreover, such a dynamo-objective coupling is also potent in its own defense. Any criticism of its scientific part is rebutted by the moral passions behind it, while any moral objections are coldly brushed aside by invoking the inexorable verdict of its scientific findings.[23]

Polanyi traces to a dynamo-objective coupling contemporary self-doubt, alienation, and nihilism, as well as the spectacle, offered by behavioristic psychology and other reductionist social sciences, of human consciousness seeking to persuade itself that it does not exist. However, it is twentieth-century ideologies which most fully benefit from man's homeless condition and exhibit the disastrous consequences which that condition can hold for human culture, including the cultures of science. Those consequences are graphically illustrated by Stalinist attempts to control scientific thought, attempts which led to purges of scientific communities. "I was struck," Polanyi writes of his encounters with Soviet ideology, "by the fact that this denial of the very existence of independent scientific thought came from a socialist theory which derived its tremendous persuasive power from its claim to scientific certainty."[24]

The causes of this threat to free scientific thought should not be difficult to see. If human motives are what an objectivist epistemology claims them to be, then pure science, the pursuit of truth for its own sake, is unmasked as self-serving technology. If science is really technology, the directions of scientific work should be set not by scientists but by political rulers, who can best see what technological advances would bring practical, social benefit. Also, because discourse of reasons is unmasked, it becomes inconceivable that persons can constitute autonomous communities, partly through discourses.[25] And if science itself consists only of impersonal, formal operations in the ways that objectivist epistemology claims, then there can be no need for the inherently *informal* operations of communities of scientists, in which aspirants are trained, scientists' findings are accredited or discredited, and promising problems for future inquiry are identified. The logic is understandable, but the consequences are disastrous, Polanyi believes, for the exercise of responsible choice and free thought in the sciences and in other dimensions of human culture.

Harry Prosch accurately suggests that ethical concerns led Polanyi to consider epistemology.[26] Certainly, by tracing contemporary threats to human achievements, including those of science, in part to their origins in epistemological assumptions, Polanyi provides ample reason to become uncomfortable with an epistemology which is thoroughly objectivist.

Yet objectivism's specifically epistemological failing provides the opening for Polanyi's theory of tacit, personal knowing, a kind of knowing which both complements and undergirds the formal operations which objectivists embrace. Objectivism offers a plausible though misleading view of knowledge which already exists, beyond current dispute, in a discipline, most especially in the hard sciences. That is the knowledge which likely is visible to outsiders, for example to rhetoricians viewing science. From this perspective, which objectivists share, knowledge seems comprised of unproblematical, self-evidential facts. Theories are merely convenient summaries of such facts. If knowledge is strictly formal and explicit, there can be no middle ground between ignorance and knowledge, and we must move from the one to the other through blind "trial and error." Thus objectivism can offer no account of acts of inquiry and achievements of discovery.

In contrast, that persons seek to understand reality is Polanyi's most fundamental assumption, an assumption which can have no place in a strict objectivist framework. He is asking how persons strive to know what they did not previously know, whether the knowledge being striven for is new to all persons, as in the case of discovery (and *all* knowledge *was* discovered at one time or another) or whether the knowledge is new only to the person striving to grasp it, as in the case of learning in general. Polanyi's focal concern is with knowledge coming into being; his is, in short, a thoroughly heuristic epistemology, grounded most firmly in persons' abilities to address problems and to achieve discoveries of reality. And his view of reality, his ontology, comprehends not only tangible objects but the reality of human constructs and of human consciousness itself. In epistemology and ontology, Polanyi's thought seeks to comprehend the dynamics of epistemic change.

A problem is something which I know in some senses but not in others. If I had no knowledge, I would not yet perceive a problem; if my knowledge were complete, I would have not a problem but a solution. We know, Polanyi says, in two quite different ways: we can know an entity which we focally grasp and often can *explicitly* delineate; and we know myriads of clues *from* which we take our bearings on that entity, items which we literally or metaphorically embody and therefore can never fully specify. As clues, these items function *tacitly*. All our explicit knowledge is grounded in our tacit knowledge. As Polanyi frequently puts it, "All knowledge . . . is either tacit or rooted in tacit knowledge."[27] To know a problem is to know by attending from a cluster of clues, without yet having grasped the joint significance toward which they point. The following discussion gives some attention to Polanyi's ontology, while attending to the epistemology of tacit inference as illustrated in the act of visual perception, in the use of tools, in the act of discovery, and in the consideration of a discovery by an accredited community. These dimensions provide us with a rich cluster of clues pointing toward Polanyi's conception of distinctly human reason.

Polanyi states:

> The triad of tacit knowing consists in subsidiary things . . . bearing on a focus . . . , by virtue of an integration performed by a person; . . . in tacit knowing we attend from one or more subsidiaries to a focus on which the subsidiaries are brought to bear.[28]

The dynamics are illustrated in perception. In perceiving something, I attend from innumerable clues, in the object, in its context, and—for example, eye contractions and simultaneous but different retinal images—within my body itself. I am committed to my own body as a generally reliable instrument; I accredit myself as a knower. Though a particular perception may be mistaken, its validity can in no way be formally "proven." I cannot exhaustively specify the clues which inform my perception. Furthermore some clues "contradict" others; it is precisely such "contradictions" which make possible stereoscopic perception. Finally, to attempt to specify and test a clue is to destroy, at least for that time, its function *as* clue. It is rendered meaningless as a clue when I attend *to* it, rather than *from* it as a clue to the coherence toward which it points. Something serving as a clue "ceases to do so when focal attention is directed on it."[29] To insist on the specification of the clues informing a perception would be to destroy the perception, leaving only a "boundless variety of raw experience . . . devoid of all meaning."[30]

Furthermore, a coherent perception is never merely the equivalent of the clues which point toward it. Interpretive effort makes the difference; it is by interpretive effort that I bridge the gap which separates clues from coherent perception. And clues themselves look different to me, once I have formed a coherent perception from them. Once I have solved a perceptual puzzle, for example, I see it differently. I am committed irreversibly to the emergent coherence; I cannot choose to "unsolve" the puzzle.

Even perception, "the most impoverished form of tacit knowing,"[31] illustrates a number of essential qualities of tacit knowing. Perceiving is revealed to be an achievement, a purposeful and skilled activity which demands effort and risks failure. Persons carry it out on grounds they accept uncritically and cannot formally specify, using standards which they must set to themselves in the act of perceiving. A perception is not the equivalent of the various clues which inform it. It is instead a coherent entity, an emergent meaning, to which the committed perceiver necessarily contributes. Even though the perception conceivably could be mistaken, as in the case of optical illusions, the perceiver holds it with "universal intent,"[32] as something which is truly there, rather than as his own willful (or wishful) projection. The sign of the perceived object's reality is its ability to manifest itself in ways which are not under the perceiver's control. Because he believes himself to have established a contact with something real, he affirms his perception to others, even though their comprehension of the object requires personal commitments on their part similar to the ones he has exercised. For all these reasons, if the ideal of impersonal demonstration were taken strictly, not even knowledge of the reality we call perceptual could meet its rigorous specifications.

Still less could realities of other sorts meet those same specifications. Under objectivism, something is real to the extent that it can be observed with (relative) detachment; thus "the real" is collapsed into "the tangible." Reality, in Polanyi's ontology, is something which "can always manifest itself in still unexpected ways."[33] It is these indeterminate future manifestations which mark reality; it is hardly too much to say that an entity is real to the extent that it exhibits potentials for meanings not yet achieved. Within this orientation, a theory of physics or even a problem in physics may be more real than the physical data which inform either, and a person, who in some senses is a physical object, is more real than physical objects. Polanyi's ontology is hierarchical: physics and chemistry can never explain the functioning of a machine, though physical laws and chemical properties are necessary for a machine to function and can cause it to break down. A living animal, though it requires the machine-like structures of its body in order to live, is capable of achievements not open to a machine. Unlike a machine, an animal has appetitive drives; in seeking to satisfy those drives an animal, unlike a machine, can make a mistake. Of all animals man alone seeks truth, justice, and beauty, under a firmament of standards which he sets for himself and affirms to be true by submitting to their guidance. At the same time, of all animals man is alone capable of falsehood and evil. Each of these higher levels of reality requires a deeper gradient of tacit knowing for its comprehension.

At each level, according to Polanyi, we may speak of *causes* of an entity's failure, causes which may be traced to the subordinate levels which inform that entity: an animal's death may be caused by a chemical imbalance, for example, though that does not reduce an animal's life to the level of chemistry. But we must speak of the *reasons* for an entity's success, reasons which point toward but do not entail the emergent reality the entity achieves, including the kinds of reality that represent the workings of a human mind.[34] Polanyi's is an ontology of which consciousness partakes. Construing consciousness as some disembodied, Cartesian intellect would be a mistake. For Polanyi, consciousness is being in a world, an orientation which his epistemological concept of "indwelling" makes clear. I have said that I use my body as a guide to reality. In Polanyi's language, I "indwell" my body, accepting it uncritically as a generally reliable guide. Brief attention to the integration of other tools will extend the concept of "indwelling" and provide a necessary link to Polanyi's discussion of discovery.

To use a tool is to perform a skilled act, and skills must be learned. When one initially encounters a tool—a probe, say—his attention is focused upon it, and it is useless to him. Through practice, he must develop the skill to use the probe, rendering it subsidiary, an extension of himself. Tools of a discipline encompass not only physical instruments such as probes, but the language currently used and the theories currently accepted within the discipline. All these the aspirant must teach himself to indwell. He must render them subsidiaries, extensions of himself, as he learns to see reality from the point of view which the intellectual framework of his discipline can afford him. This arduous process of coming to indwell is the purpose of an education within any discipline. But a discipline does not consist only of special instruments, language, and theories. Most important to any discipline's effective functioning is the community of persons whose work is grounded in the discipline and upholds it. These persons are convivial;[35] they enjoy sentiments of fellowship generated by their "reverence for a common superior knowledge."[36] These personal affiliations, guided by universal intent, provide a rich, necessary nexus for the stimulation of new ideas and the support of original lines of thought.

Routine work within a discipline, for example one of the hard sciences, may seem to proceed according to strictly specified operations, requiring none of the informal actions so far indicated, including those promoted by conviviality. But an orientation to the routine provides no adequate picture of epistemic change or of striking achievement in any field. Perceiving promising problems and committing their efforts plausibly toward resolutions are actions open only to persons who indwell the discipline's framework, making it part of themselves as a set of sensitive and generally reliable clues toward a real coherence as yet ungrasped. Existing formulations point toward a problem, providing clues to its solution. But a genuine problem is problematic precisely because it resists existing formulations. Thus, to perceive and pursue a genuine problem is the highest and most demanding calling that a member of any discipline can undertake.

The search for a discovery is highly skilled, in ways it would not need to be if methodology were utterly rigorous, precise, and explicit. Guided by his heuristic passion, the scientist pours himself into his search, committing his time, energy, and intellectual efforts, striving with no guarantee of success to see what no one has seen before. The search is hazardous. At each step of the way he guides his own activities, relying on an embodied interpretive framework which he has neither time, skill, nor attention to replicate. He decides on grounds he cannot fully specify to follow certain leads and ignore others, thus accrediting as generally reliable—without formal validation—his own powers of thought and judgment. Because his activities are thus grounded in tacit processes, he risks choosing a problem he will be unable to solve, and he risks being mistaken in thinking he has achieved a discovery.

Furthermore, recall that one's solution of even a perceptual puzzle changes, irreversibly, his view of the clues which point to the solution. To solve a problem is to change, however slightly, the framework which pointed toward the problem but left it problematic, a framework the scientist has rendered part of himself. The discovery

> changes the world as we see it, by deepening our understanding of it. The change is irrevocable. . . . Having made a discovery, I shall never see the world again as before. My eyes have become different: I have made myself into a person seeing and thinking differently. I have crossed a gap, the heuristic gap which lies between problem and discovery.[37]

To engage in inquiry is to risk an existential change, a risk realized to the extent that the heuristic effort seems successful.

Because inquiry is hazardous, communities of peers must judge proffered discoveries. If granted an audience, a scientist tacitly appeals to shared scientific opinion which, because it is informed by its own history, Polanyi calls a "tradition" which provides "the common ground between himself and his opponents."[38]

However, a scientific tradition seeks its own renewal. "Scientific tradition enforces its teachings in general, for the very purpose of cultivating their subversion in the particular."[39] The inquirer cannot convince his peers of his discovery by strictly formal argument within a shared framework, a framework which had left the problem problematic. Instead "revis[ing] and renew[ing] by pioneer achievements the very standards by which his work is to be judged,"[40] he must "meet any opposition of scientific opinion as it *is* by appealing against it to scientific opinion as he thinks it *ought to be*."[41] He must, in short, seek to *persuade* his peers:

> *Like the heuristic passion from which it flows, the* persuasive passion *too finds itself facing a logical gap. . . . [The discoverer's] persuasive passion spurs him now to cross this gap by converting everybody to his way of seeing things, even as his heuristic passion has spurred him to cross the heuristic gap which separated him from discovery.*[42]

As audience, the community must decide whether to be persuaded. And it must decide in the absence of logically compelling proof, partly so that appropriate "verification" of the discovery may eventually be uncovered. To listen sympathetically to another's argument is to submit oneself to risk, in the same sense that an inquirer submits to risk:

> *Proponents of a new system can convince their audience only by first winning their intellectual sympathy for a doctrine they have not yet graspd. Those who listen sympathetically will discover for themselves what they would otherwise never have understood. Such an acceptance is a heuristic process, a self-modifying act, and to this extent a conversion.*[43]

A person who becomes a sympathetic audience risks being misled. He also risks the existential change implied in seeing things anew.

The epistemological reform proposed by Polanyi produces a significant shift in the noetic landscape. His reform does not undermine the operations of objective observation and formal inference, when these are functioning within a context of tacit integrations. But it insists that the explicitness, rigor, and impersonality of any critical methodology give us only a partial picture, at best, of any act of knowing. Knowing is instead an achievement, demanding impassioned efforts and giving no formal guarantee of success. Knowing is rooted in the knower's a-critical acceptance of his own authority and that of his culture, a set of traditional opinions which point toward problems and afford clues to their solutions—as they are part of himself. As Jerry Gill has said, "One must have a 'place to stand'—to attend from—in order to be able to attend *to* anything at all."[44] As man strives for ever more comprehensive meanings, the epistemology of tacit inference accredits his indefinable powers of thought and judgment. In so doing, this epistemology accredits man with the powers of reaching decisions which, while not apodictic, are responsible.

REASONS, INQUIRIES, AND RHETORICS

What distinctive view of human reason does Polanyi's epistemology, with its ontological bearings, point toward? Far from negating formal logic, his epistemology is concerned instead with those actions which underlie or complement formal logic in actual, purposeful use. Still, in Polanyi's view, the major features of human reason contrast with those that formal models have made familiar. Human reason is not an operation on propositions but an action of persons. Reason is not completely explicit. It is not governed by a specified set of unchanging values, with conclusions guaranteed by evidence exhaustively comprehended, or by premises in which the conclusion already is entailed. The goal of reason is not analytic certainty but the achievement of new meaning, the creation of a new understanding of reality—a creation which partakes of that reality. Unlike formal inference, human reason can be mistaken. Unlike formal inference, human reason can achieve discoveries.

For all those reasons, that which constitutes human reason cannot be determined dispassionately by an examination of propositions' entailment or by some other checklist of impersonal and explicit features. Though sets of heuristically useful criteria can be developed, any complete formalization is not only beyond the scope of this paper; it is not finally possible in principle. Indeed, we should speak of human reason*s*. The plural form acknowledges both the multiplicity of inconclusive warrants which humans reasonably advance for holding some belief *and* the fact that reason's actions reveal themselves quite differently when humans address different levels of reality within the contexts that their different communities provide.

Beyond that point it is hazardous to go, not because clues are unavailable but because they may be interpreted too narrowly, especially by readers whose concern lies in the theory of argumentation. Reason is not the equivalent of argumentative discourse. For example, an innocuous greeting between acquaintances hardly constitutes an argument, yet it is an act of reason if it promotes conviviality.[45] A religious creed repeatedly affirmed never leads explicitly to new conclusions, and in certain contexts to request evidence for its premises would be to misunderstand the nature of its statement. Yet a religious creed, Polanyi makes clear, can constitute a reasonable affirmation. So may a poem, though a poem draws us into itself, Polanyi insists, precisely because of the self-contradictory character of its metaphoric mode.[46] A person whose one response in all situations was argument would be a distinctly unreasonable person.

With those cautions borne in mind, however, it may well be that argumentation provides one of the fuller and more public instantiations of human reason. Argument, for Polanyi, is reasoned if it partakes of inquiry. Within it, the speaker's intellectual and moral passions lead him to act with universal intent, before an audience who shares his general commitments. His concern is a vision of some reality, a problem laden with potential meaning or, perhaps more typically, a discovery which he believes himself to have achieved. In either case argument, like inquiry, is called into being by a person who experiences a gap in understanding—a gap which remains despite currently established evidence, values, and logical procedure. Without such a logical gap there would be no need for argument, and none for inquiry. Because of that gap, the arguer must engage in persuasion, inviting his audience in the absence of formal proof to participate in his new way of seeing; he relies on values generally shared, precisely so that those values may be renewed or revised. "When originality breeds new values," Polanyi insists, "it breeds them tacitly, by implication; we cannot choose explicitly a set of new values, but must submit to them by the very act of creating or adopting them."[47] An invitation to a new vision is an invitation to renewed values.

A community must decide whether to join argument, giving audience to a speaker. This decision must be made on grounds that are in part unspecifiable, and the decision may be mistaken. But a community will not and should not attend to a person whose authority it has no reason to respect. If it does attend, it will be in the spirit of inquiry, seeking imaginatively to see some aspect of reality which yet lies beyond its intellectual grasp or any formal methods of proof available to it. As Polanyi says, "explicit logical processes are effective only as tools of a dynamic commitment by which we extend our understanding."[48] Within such a commitment, "the verification of a statement is transposed into giving reasons for deciding to accept it, though those reasons will never be wholly specifiable."[49] An act of human reason, in stretching toward new understanding, involves consideration of reasons as well as conclusions. "The process of examining any topic is both an exploration of the topic, and an exegesis of our fundamental beliefs in the light of which we approach it; a dialectical combination of exploration and exegesis."[50] In an act of reasoned argument, the audience participates with the speaker in that dialectic of exploration and exegesis. In so doing, both employ active powers of human judgment which, though not specifiable, are responsible.

Responsibility does not inhere in criticism alone. Indeed, unbridled criticism would cause any argument to fail in establishing the meaning it sought or even in having that meaning considered. As Polanyi's ontology suggests, the *failure* of any entity is to be explained in *causal* terms drawn from the subordinate levels which that entity embodies. Thus, for example, a machine's failure can be caused by the fatigue of the metals which comprise it; an argument's failure might be caused by the appetites and fears which its proponent undeniably embodies. But neither a functioning machine nor a successful argument is reducible to its subordinate elements. In Polanyi's terms, we must speak of the *reasons* for either entity's success, reasons which are irreducible to the lower levels which inform the entity and from which it has emerged.[51] Polanyi writes: "You can interpret, for example, this essay in terms of the *causes* which have determined my action of writing it down or you may ask for my *reasons* for saying what I say."[52] A rigorously impersonal methodology, if strictly enforced, would reduce all explanation to a causal level. But, "a complete causal interpretation of man and human affairs disintegrates all rational grounds on which man can hold convictions and act on those convictions."[53] Reasons instead are indwellings which interlocutors come to share.

What constitutes human reason for Polanyi are the actions of responsible persons, collectively and individually, in their quests for new meanings which, being real, will reveal themselves indeterminately in the future, and which, being emergent, are not entailed in the clues which point toward them. Good reasons are never anonymous; they receive the personal backing of the speaker who stands behind them,[54] and they seek the personal allegiance of the audience to whom they are addressed. Good reasons are subsidiaries which point toward an emerging meaning, though they never formally entail it. They bear on something beyond themselves, by virtue of a person's integration. Arguments of good reasons are characterized by the impassioned efforts which inform them; they, like successful inquiry, are known by "the gradient of deepening coherence"[55] which their participants experience. Shared by persons of similar commitments, good reasons provide the grounding from which persons seek to enlighten themselves and each other, thereby opening themselves to criticism and to change both epistemic and existential.

Such changes are, irreducibly, rhetorical. Although Michael Polanyi was not a rhetorical theorist, he acknowledged implicitly that there were surprising affinities between the rhetorical tradition and his thought.[56] Those affinities, because he had not expected them, tended in some measure to confirm what his own work had achieved.[57] Certainly, they are striking. Rhetoric, says Aristotle, deals "with such matters as we deliberate on without arts or systems to guide us,"[58] addressing problems which existing "arts and systems" leave problematic. Rhetoric's realm is that of human opinion and decision; any rhetorical theory which is not manipulative or hypocritical assumes that persons can act to form responsible decisions in the absence of compelling evidence or formal demonstration. Rhetorical argument is rooted in communally held beliefs, values, and opinions which, because they are shaped over time, constitute tradition. The enthymematic structure of rhetorical argument often leaves premises unexpressed in the argument itself, and the argument draws on the perceived character of the speaker and on human emotion, as well as on the structure of the subject under discussion. Harold Zyskind claims that "rhetoric has always been an art of reading or posting signs" and that "rhetorical logic . . . is the tendency to discover and complete emerging patterns."[59] Henry Johnstone argues that persons' distinctively human qualities reside in their abilities to persuade and be persuaded[60] and finds that we recognize a truth not by formal demonstration but by its evocative power.[61]

"It is when we have reached the bedrock level," writes philosopher Jerry Gill, "that the logic of persuasion is seen to be that of tacit knowing."[62] In his epistemology of tacit knowing, Polanyi's purpose was not to provide an understanding of persuasive processes but to take seriously the heuristic actions which humans perform and the epistemic changes which they achieve. That persuasion turns out to be irreducible in his epistemology suggests a promising realignment in understanding persuasive acts and those that are epistemic. Some rhetorical theorists have asked whether arguments can claim epistemic status.[63] Even without summarizing their valuable work, it should be easy to see that the answer, when persuasion is measured against an epistemology that is anti-rhetorical, must finally be no. But Polanyi in effect invites us to ask more promising questions: in just what senses does inquiry, which is the ground of epistemic growth, involve actions whose intent must be to persuade oneself or to persuade others? In what senses is rhetorical argument essential, in persons' achievements of meaning? Adequate answers to those questions would give us a fuller and more positive view of rhetorical theory and practice, a deepened view of the relations between rhetoric and invention, and a way of affirming that demagogic appeals, whether under the guise of unwarranted objectivity or unwarranted emotionalism, while among the distinctive failings of rhetorical argument, are not its distinguishing features.

The actions of human reason, whether in inquiry or in argument, are hazardous; the price of reason's transcendent power is the possibility of evil as well as transformation. The point is not that human reason is superior to formal methodologies in some way; the claim is instead that it provides their grounding and is indispensable to their effective use.[64] In a book whose framework is Polanyi's thought, Marjorie Grene poses a challenge which requires all our human powers:

> *The conceptual reform in which we are now engaged must restore our speech about the world to intelligible discourse and the world it aims at describing to significant and coherent form.*[65]

Grene calls us in effect both to exercise and to affirm good reasons. Even if unintentionally, hers is inescapably a call to rhetorical action. The responses to that call can have no ending.

Notes

1. Douglas Ehninger, "A Synoptic View of Systems of Western Rhetoric," *Quarterly Journal of Speech*, 61 (1975), 449.
2. James Wiser, "Michael Polanyi: Personal Knowledge and the Promise of Autonomy," *Political Theory*, 2 (1974), 80–81.
3. Peter T. Koper, "The Rhetoric of Science and the Assault on Ambiguity," *Rhetoric Society Quarterly*, 8 (1978), 28.
4. Karl Wallace, "The Substance of Rhetoric: Good Reasons," *Quarterly Journal of Speech*, 49 (1963), 239–49. Rpt. in *Contemporary Rhetoric: A Reader's Coursebook*, ed. Douglas Ehninger (Glenview, IL: Scott, Foresman, 1972), pp. 74–85.
5. Three valuable orientations to their concerns are the following: Carroll C. Arnold, "Inventio and Pronunciatio in a 'New Rhetoric,' " paper presented at Central States Speech Association Convention, April 8, 1972; Walter M. Carleton, "On Rhetoric as a 'Way of Knowing': An Inquiry into Epistemological Dimensions of a New Rhetoric," Diss. Pennsylvania State University 1975; Walter R. Fisher, "Toward a Logic of Good Reasons," *Quarterly Journal of Speech*, 64 (1978), 376–84.
6. Chaim Perelman, "The New Rhetoric: A Theory of Practical Reasoning," *The Great Ideas Today, 1970* (Chicago: Encyclopedia Britannica, 1971), pp. 273–312, and "The Role of Decision in the Theory of Knowledge," *The Idea of Justice and the Problem of Argument*, trans. John Petrie (London: Routledge & Kegan Paul, 1963), pp. 88–97; Max Loreau, "Rhetoric as the Logic of the Behavioral Sciences," *Quarterly Journal of Speech*, 51 (1965), 455–63; Vasile Florescu, "Rhetoric and Its Rehabilitation in Contemporary Philosophy," *Philosophy and Rhetoric*, 3 (1970), 195–224.
7. As representative of this position, see Lloyd F. Bitzer, "The Rhetorical Situation," *Philosophy and Rhetoric*, 1 (1968), 1–14. For a critique of this orientation, see Malcolm O. Sillars, "Audiences, Social Values, and the Analysis of Argument," *Speech Teacher*, 22 (1973), 291–303.

8. Walter B. Weimer, "Science as a Rhetorical Transaction: Toward a Nonjustificational Conception of Rhetoric," *Philosophy and Rhetoric,* 10 (1977), 20.
9. Michael Polanyi, *Personal Knowledge: Towards a Post-Critical Philosophy* (1958, 1962; rpt. New York: Harper Torchbooks, 1964), p. ix.
10. Marjorie Grene, "Tacit Knowing: Grounds for a Revolution in Philosophy," *The Journal of the British Society for Phenomenology,* 8 (1977), 164. This entire issue of *JBSP* is devoted to articles on Polanyi's thought.
11. Wayne Booth, *Modern Dogma and the Rhetoric of Assent* (Chicago: University of Chicago Press, 1974), p. xvii.
12. Lloyd F. Bitzer, "Rhetoric and Public Knowledge," in *Rhetoric, Philosophy, and Literature: An Exploration,* ed. Don M. Burks (West Lafayette: Purdue University Press, 1978), pp. 67–93.
13. Chaim Perelman, "Polanyi's Interpretation of Scientific Inquiry," in *Intellect and Hope: Essays on the Thought of Michael Polanyi,* ed. T. A. Langford and W. H. Poteat (Durham: Duke University Press, 1968), pp. 232–41.
14. Weimer, "Science as a Rhetorical Transaction." See also Weimer, *Notes on the Methodology of Scientific Research* (Hillsdale: L. Erlbaum, 1979).
15. Michael A. Overington, "The Scientific Community as Audience: Toward a Rhetorical Analysis of Science," *Philosophy and Rhetoric,* 10 (1977), 143–63.
16. Robert Scott, "Review of *Meaning,*" *Philosophy and Rhetoric,* 10 (1977), 123–5.
17. Robert Scott, "The Tacit Dimension and Rhetoric," paper presented at Polanyi Society meeting, Convention of the American Philosophical Association, Chicago, April 29, 1977.
18. Michael Polanyi, "Why Did We Destroy Europe?" *Studium Generale,* 23 (1970), 909–16.
19. Polanyi, *Personal Knowledge,* p. 234.
20. Polanyi, "Why Did We Destroy Europe?" p. 913.
21. Polanyi, *Personal Knowledge,* p. 236.
22. Michael Polanyi, "On the Modern Mind," *Encounter,* 24, (1965), 18.
23. Polanyi, *Personal Knowledge,* p. 230.
24. Michael Polanyi, *The Tacit Dimension* (1966: rpt. Garden City, NY: Doubleday Anchor, 1967), p. 3.
25. For a discussion, from Polanyi's perspective, of how communities constitute and accredit themselves, see Robert W. Norton, "Conviviality: A Rhetorical Dimension," *Central States Speech Journal,* 26 (1975), 164–70.
26. Harry Prosch, "Polanyi's Ethics," *Ethics,* 82 (1972), 91–113.
27. Michael Polanyi, *Knowing and Being,* ed. Marjorie Grene (Chicago: University of Chicago Press, 1969), p. 195.
28. Polanyi, *Knowing and Being,* p. 182.
29. Michael Polanyi, "Logic and Psychology," *American Psychologist,* 23 (1968), 31.
30. Polanyi, *Knowing and Being,* p. 114.
31. Polanyi, *Tacit Dimension,* p. 7.
32. See Polanyi, *Personal Knowledge,* pp. 303, 309.
33. Polanyi, *Knowing and Being,* p. 120.
34. See Michael Polanyi, *The Study of Man* (1959; rpt. Chicago: University of Chicago Press, 1963), pp. 90–94.
35. See Norton, "Conviviality: A Rhetorical Dimension."
36. Polanyi, *Personal Knowledge,* p. 378.
37. Polanyi, *Personal Knowledge,* p. 143.
38. Michael Polanyi, *Science, Faith and Society* (1946, 1964; rpt. Chicago: University of Chicago Press, 1964), p. 52.
39. Polanyi, *Knowing and Being,* p. 67.

40. Michael Polanyi, *The Logic of Liberty: Reflections and Rejoinders* (Chicago: University of Chicago Press, 1951), p. 50.

41. Polanyi, *Science, Faith and Society,* p. 52.

42. Polanyi, *Personal Knowledge,* p. 150; cf. p. 172.

43. Polanyi, *Personal Knowledge,* p. 151.

44. Jerry Gill, "The Tacit Structure of Religious Knowing," in *Logical Analysis and Contemporary Theism,* ed. J. Donnelly (New York: Fordham University Press, 1972), p. 254.

45. See Norton, "Conviviality: A Rhetorical Dimension."

46. See Michael Polanyi and Harry Prosch, *Meaning* (Chicago: University of Chicago Press, 1975), *passim,* especially ch. 4.

47. Polanyi, *Tacit Dimension,* p. ix; see also *Meaning,* pp. 62, 103–104.

48. Michael Polanyi, "The Scientific Revolution," *Christians in a Technological Era* (New York: Seabury Press, 1964), p. 40.

49. Polanyi, *Personal Knowledge,* p. 320.

50. Polanyi, *Personal Knowledge,* p. 267.

51. See Polanyi, *Personal Knowledge,* p. 332; *The Study of Man,* pp. 90–94.

52. Polanyi, *The Logic of Liberty,* p. 22.

53. Polanyi, *The Logic of Liberty,* p. 28.

54. Dallas M. High, "The Morality of Speaking," *Lexington Theological Quarterly,* 5 (1970), 64–75; rpt. as "Language, Life, and Morality," in *Communication: Ethical and Moral Issues,* ed. Lee Thayer (New York: Gordon and Breach, 1972).

55. Polanyi, "The Creative Imagination," *Tri-Quarterly,* 8 (1967), 116.

56. See Samuel D. Watson, Jr., "Michael Polanyi and the Recovery of Rhetoric," Diss. University of Iowa 1973.

57. The first of my two personal interviews took place during "A National Conference on Culture and Crisis: The Social Thought of Michael Polanyi," St. Leonard College, Centerville, Ohio, May 4–8, 1972; the second was a day-long session at Polanyi's home in Oxford, England, on August 1, 1972. Polanyi was patient and, if anything, too generous. Responding to an early dissertation draft, he wrote me, "I do want to tell you that your work is the first attempt at the systematic analysis of my last 20 years in developing my ideas about the nature of human knowledge within its boundless branches" (July 13, 1972). Later he insisted, "My point is that the structure of consecutive levels and the relationship between their different levels penetrates into essential matters" (July 4, 1973). In a brief letter responding to the finished study, Polanyi wrote, "Thank you for your gift which brought me delight, for you and myself, in attendance to your tremendous work. I am glad of this chance to tell you how sorry I was to know that you were [working] without the companionship of others, who would have rejoiced with your works. I hope you will soon be made accessible to such companions, and I will of course be glad to help with it" (September 13, 1973). Few of us experience directly the nurturing conviviality which Polanyi opened to me, conviviality so central to his philosophy and to his person.

58. Aristotle, *Rhetoric,* 1357a, in *The Basic Works of Aristotle,* ed. R. McKeon (New York: Random House, 1941).

59. Harold Zyskind, "Some Philosophic Strands in Popular Rhetoric," *Perspectives in Education, Religion, and the Arts,* ed. H. E. Kiefer and M. M. Munitz (Albany: State University of New York Press, 1970), pp. 378, 387.

60. Henry Johstone, "The Relevance of Rhetoric to Philosophy and of Philosophy to Rhetoric," *Quarterly Journal of Speech,* 52 (1966), 41–46.

61. Henry Johnstone, "Truth, Communication, and Rhetoric in Philosophy," *Revue Internationale de Philosophie,* 23 (1969), 404–9.

62. Jerry Gill, "Saying and Showing: Radical Themes in Wittgenstein's *On Certainty,*" *Religious Studies,* 10 (1974), 290.

63. See Robert L. Scott, "On Viewing Rhetoric as Epistemic: Ten Years Later," *Central States Speech Journal,* 27 (1976), 258–66; Richard Cherwitz, "Rhetoric as 'A Way of Knowing': An Attenuation of the Epistemological Claims of the 'New Rhetoric,' " and James W. Hikins, "The Epistemological Relevance of Intrapersonal Rhetoric," *Southern Speech Communication Journal,* 42 (1977) 207-27.

64. An intriguing book which draws on Polanyi while developing this argument in detail is Hubert L. Dreyfus, *What Computers Can't Do: A Critique of Artificial Reason* (New York: Harper & Row, 1972).

65. Marjorie Grene, *The Knower and The Known* (London: Faber & Faber, 1966), p. 13.

John Stuart Mill's Doctrine of Assurance as a Rhetorical Epistemology

Richard A. Cherwitz
James W. Hikins

Some years ago Douglas Ehninger observed that rhetorics arise "out of a felt need" and are "shaped in part by the intellectual and social environment in which the need exists."[1] Yet in addition to serving as a response to the cultural and intellectual milieu of their period, rhetorics may operate concurrently as points of demarcation for fresh perspectives on recurrent issues. Hence, newer rhetorics "not only corrected a deficiency in the preceding system but encompassed that system to pass beyond it."[2]

It is within the context of this two-fold understanding of the development of particular rhetorics that John Stuart Mill's nineteenth-century treatise, *On Liberty,* appears. Mill's work provides a potential response to one aspect of the intellectual environment of his time, namely, questions in philosophical epistemology; in so doing, the book generates a new perspective from which to view rhetoric's epistemological function. Although not written as a rhetorical treatise per se, nor intended as a direct and explicit response to the epistemological

RICHARD CHERWITZ *is Assistant Professor of Speech Communication at the University of Texas.* JAMES W. HIKINS *is Senior Administrative Specialist at the American College Testing Program, Iowa City, Iowa.*

exigencies confronting nineteenth-century rhetorical thought, *On Liberty* harbors important implications for rhetoric. Specifically, Mill's discussion of the concept "assurance" provides an additional avenue from which to approach a number of nineteenth-century philosophical/rhetorical issues.

RHETORIC AND EPISTEMOLOGY IN THE NINETEENTH CENTURY

The history of rhetoric and philosophy reveals a fundamental relationship between theories of discourse and theories of knowing; for the questions, *What may be said?* and, *How does one know what has been said?* seem, if not inseparable, at least kindred. For example, the distinction between Platonic and Sophistic rhetoric is to be located, at least in part, in the epistemological assumptions upon which each of the two views of discourse were grounded. The former presumed the existence of objective truths which could be known and which must be incorporated in rhetorical discourse. The latter held truth to be a function of the subjective nature of human beings, with the implication that one need not and could not incorporate objective truth in rhetorical discourse. Such diametrically opposed epistemological assumptions unavoidably led to very different conceptions of the nature, scope, and function of the rhetorical art. It is precisely this inherent connection between philosophy and rhetoric that undergirds Ehninger's assertion that the rhetoric of a given period is shaped by the intellectual milieu of the time—one constituent of which is the prevailing epistemology. An understanding of John Stuart Mill's theory of rhetoric, then, may be enhanced by a description of the epistemological climate of his time.

At the close of the eighteenth century, rhetoric had become the art of transmitting objective truths discovered by the other arts and sciences. This view of rhetoric as a managerial art is understandable when one considers the extant epistemologies. Patrick Gardiner describes this climate as one in which "the contents and operations of the psyche lay wholly open to inspection, the results of introspective investigation being such as to afford a paradigm of certain knowledge."[3] Eighteenth-century philosophers believed all that was required for a total victory of reason was to sharpen and adapt empirical methods of inquiry, such as those employed by the sciences. The resulting intellectual optimism of enlightenment science and philosophy provided a solid foundation upon which the discipline of rhetoric could build. With the promise that certain knowledge of practically all aspects of the universe would soon be in hand, it is not surprising that eighteenth-century rhetoricians concentrated on systematizing rhetorical methods whose function was not only to persuade an audience or embellish discourse, but to communicate the objective truths discovered by the scientist and philosopher. As Vincent Bevilacqua suggests, rhetoricians of the eighteenth century regarded the art "as a means of communicating knowledge previously derived by nonrhetorical, empirical investigation. Discovery of the subject matter was, in this respect, beyond the legitimate scope of the art of rhetoric."[4]

It is against this backdrop of eighteenth-century philosophically-based intellectual optimism that subjectivist/relativist views began to emerge. By the end of the eighteenth century, epistemologies based on notions of objective truth were called into question. For example, publication of Immanuel Kant's *Critique of Pure Reason* (1781) at once dashed the hope that *certain knowledge* of the *ultimate constituents of reality* could be obtained through the methods of eighteenth-century empiricism. By viewing the mind as an active participant in the process of perception, Kant contended that our perceptions of reality must necessarily be distorted by the intervention of the mind.[5] With the mind interceding between the objects of reality—what Kant called the *ding an sich* or "thing in itself"—and the perceiving subject, there was no guarantee that our cognitions in any way correspond to reality.[6] It is precisely this intervention of the mind that prompted Kant to distinguish between what he called the noumenal and phenomenal world. The former constitutes the *ultimate* constituents of reality but they are hopelessly obscured by the mind of the perceiving subject in the very process of perception. The latter comprises the world we see through the intervention of mind.

The philosophy of George Hegel and other nineteenth-century figures continued to undermine the objectivist foundations of the previous century. As Robert Solomon has observed, "the story of philosophy in Europe since Kant is largely the story of a war between relativism and absolutism."[7] In particular, Hegel insisted that when one takes stock of the world through the modes of perception, he/she actively participates in shaping the ensuing cognitions. Notions of truth and falsity become displaced by concepts such as "different forms of consciousness."[8]

Given the relationship between rhetoric and philosophy discussed above, and the abandonment of confidence in the objectivist/absolutist epistemologies which had served to ground theories of discourse in the eighteenth century, nineteenth-century rhetoric might have exercised any of several options in response. On the one hand, rhetoric might have *adapted* to the new relativism, generating theories of discourse similar to the Sophistic theories of the classical era. Such an adaptation would have required that rhetoric abandon its eighteenth-century role as the transmitter of *objective* truths. Resulting theories of discourse would have charged the art with the responsibility of transmitting the subjective perceptions of individual rhetors or communities of rhetors for the purposes of informing or persuading others. In Kant's parlance, the resultant discourse would have as its subject matter discussion of the phenomenal world. So conceived, a rhetoric's primary function would be to transmit *opinion* as opposed to objective truth. The epistemology of such a rhetoric would be *doxologic* as opposed to *epistemic.*[9]

On the other hand, rhetoric might have *adhered* to those objectivist epistemologies which continued to grapple with the new subjectivist theories. From this perspective, rhetoric could have reaffirmed its long-standing managerial role as the transmitter of objective truths discovered by the other disciplines. Such a perspective would avoid for rhetoric the label "doxologic," because rhetoric would ostensibly be communicating more than mere subjective perceptions. Because rhetoric in this case is concerned with the transmission of *truths* discovered by the other arts and sciences, it may, in this sense, be described as *epistemic.*

One characteristic common to both the aforementioned doxologic and epistemic rhetorics is that they are dependent on *philosophical* theories of epistemology. That is, they are parasitic on *philosophical epistemology.* A third option for rhetoric in the nineteenth century would have been to abandon the assumption that a theory of rhetoric must be grounded in *either* a traditional objectivist *or* a traditional subjectivist epistemology. Such an approach would involve a uniquely *rhetorical* epistemology. One such uniquely rhetorical epistemology may be found in Mill's *On Liberty,* wherein a conception of rhetoric *as argument* appears within Mill's "doctrine of assurance."

JOHN STUART MILL'S THEORY OF RHETORIC

John Stuart Mill's treatise *On Liberty* reflects a concern for issues in rhetorical theory, yet Mill avoids the term "rhetoric" throughout the work. In place of conventional rhetorical terminology, Mill introduces concepts such as "assurance," "correction," "disputation," "controversy," "completion," and others, all of which, as we note elsewhere, are analogs of contemporary notions in argument theory and thus provide a specific approach to rhetoric.[10] It should be made clear that when we use the phrase "theory of rhetoric" in this essay we are not referring to a broad conception of the art which would include a treatment of the various types of rhetorical discourse. Rather, we are designating a specific mode of rhetorical discourse, namely, *argument,* which exhibits such properties as interaction, bilateralism, initiative and control, self risk, and others. These latter features constitute a particular theory of contemporary rhetoric.[11] Mill's discussion of the doctrine of "assurance," then, and its related concepts, frame a rhetorical theory, whether or not Mill intended *On Liberty* to be a rhetorical treatise.

While our earlier study of Mill's *On Liberty* focused on the work's contemporary implications and permitted us to view the book as a rhetorical treatise, our purpose here is to examine the doctrine of assurance in its nineteenth-century context. Our earlier research left unfinished the task of appraising *On Liberty* vis-à-vis the other rhetorical/philosophical ideas of the time. For the purposes of this essay, our exposition of Mill begins with a synopsis of his rhetorical precepts as outlined in the previous study.

The Doctrine of Assurance

Properly employed, assurance guarantees, insofar as any method of human inquiry can guarantee, that a given belief is true. The doctrine of assurance is comprised of three elements, the first of which may be labeled "access."[12] *Access* allows for the free inspection of any opinion by whoever might care to do so. The concept is stated implicitly by Mill when he writes: "Complete liberty of contradicting and disproving our opinion, is the very condition which justifies us in assuming its truth for purposes of action; and on no other terms can a being with human faculties have any rational assurance of being right."[13] Access operates in its most effective form when one invites others to inspect his/her opinions. "The beliefs which we have most warrant for, have no safeguard to rest on," declares Mill, "but a standing invitation to the whole world to prove them unfounded."[14] Clearly, it was Mill's view that in the search for certain knowledge, whether attainable or not, we may, through this first step in the process of assurance, preclude dogmatism and maximize the likelihood that if errors exist in our reasoning they will be discovered.

While the *potential* of correcting erroneous opinions arises once access has been established, *actual* correction often cannot take place unless one responds to criticism and *defends* the questioned opinion in the face of a rhetorical challenge. The concept of *defense,* then, comprises the second step in the quest for assurance. Mill describes defense thusly: "He who knows only his own side of the case, knows little of that. His reasons may be good, and no one may have been able to refute them. But if he is equally unable to refute the reasons on the opposite side; if he does not so much as know what they are, he has no ground for preferring either opinion."[15]

Even with the processes of (1) offering one's opinions to the inspection of others, and (2) defending one's opinions as rigorously as possible, there is still no guarantee that assurance will be achieved. Such a guarantee can be realized only if the individual profits from access and defense through a third step, viz., *correcting* his/her opinions. The principle of *correction* is detailed by Mill in the following terms: "The steady habit of correcting and completing his own opinion by collating it with those of others, so far from causing doubt and hesitation in carrying it into practice, is the only stable foundation for a just reliance on it."[16] In explaining how it is that correction further facilitates assurance, Mill asserts that it is because "the only way in which a human being can make some approach to knowing the whole of a subject, is by hearing what can be said about it by persons of every variety of opinion, and studying all modes in which it can be looked at by every character of mind."[17]

Inherent within these three elements of the doctrine of assurance is the defining characteristic of Mill's theory of rhetoric; on his analysis, rhetoric functions as both a critical and rational enterprise—its *raison d'etre* is its *constructive* function. Put another way, through rhetoric (argument) *one endeavors to establish the validity of epistemic judgments*.[18] It is just this feature of Mill's theory of rhetoric which provides the basis for a rhetorical epistemology.[19] In the following subsection we show how Mill's doctrine of assurance casts serious doubt on the assessment of philosophical historians who have labeled him a strict empiricist. The importance of this claim will become evident later, when we detail how it is that assurance provides the bridgework linking eighteenth-century empiricism with the new spirit of nineteenth-century thought formulating a uniquely rhetorical epistemology in the process.

Mill's Rhetorical Epistemology: A Mitigated Empiricism

That John Stuart Mill is regarded as a strict empiricist is a notion which pervades the literature of the history of philosophy. John Passmore, for one, includes Mill in his survey of British Empiricism.[20] Sheldon Peterfreund and Theodore Denise describe Mill as "convinced that we must turn to extreme empiricism to adequately account for scientific knowledge."[21] Mill is so regarded chiefly because of his writings in logic and the philosophy of science, most notably his work *A System of Logic,* wherein he develops his famous four canons of induction.[22] In his examination of Mill's philosophical accomplishments, J. B. Schneewind writes that "Mill's *Logic* is in fact by no means neutral with regard to substantive issues. It is the first major installment of his comprehensive restatement of an empiricist and utilitarian position. It presents (sometimes, to be sure, only as 'illustration') a fairly complete outline of what would now be called an 'empiricist' epistemology."[23] Certainly, *A System of Logic* does establish Mill as an empiricist, but one of a special character. In addition, it establishes that Mill is also much in the spirit of eighteenth-century optimism, believing that through the application of the four canons of induction, knowledge about an immutable world of truths is possible.

Unlike eighteenth-century empiricists, though, Mill's concern for truth does *not* depend entirely upon empirical observation. For while the correspondence theory of truth[24] *is*, for Mill, the criterion of epistemological certitude, it operates within a *rhetorical* context as well as an empirical one. Even strictly empirical claims have their ultimate justification rooted in the rhetorical doctrine of assurance. Writes Mill: "If even the Newtonian philosophy were not permitted to be questioned, mankind could not feel as complete assurance of its truth as they now do."[25]

The vitality of assurance-mediated rhetorical judgments for *all* questions of epistemology is spelled out clearly by Mill: "But on every subject on which difference of opinion is possible," he asserts, "the truth depends on a balance to be struck between two sets of conflicting reasons." He continues: "Even in natural philosophy, there is always some other explanation possible of the same facts; some geocentric theory instead of heliocentric, some phlogiston instead of oxygen; and it has to be shown why that other theory cannot be the true one: and until this is shown, and until we know how it is shown, we do not understand the grounds of our opinion."[26]

In speaking about those who might choose to decline the rhetorical challenge, Mill suggests: "Their conclusion may be true, but it might be false for anything they know: they have never thrown themselves into the mental position of those who think differently from them, and considered what such persons may have to say; and consequently they do not, in any proper sense of the word, *know* the doctrine which they themselves profess."[27]

So essential is *rhetorical interchange* for the assessment of knowledge claims that Mill writes: "the source of everything respectable in man either as an intellectual or as a moral being" is "that his errors are corrigible. He is capable of rectifying his mistakes, by discussion and experience. Not by experience alone. There must be discussion, to show how experience is to be interpreted. Wrong opinions and practices gradually yield to fact and argument: but facts and arguments, to produce any effect on the mind, must be brought before it. Very few facts are able to tell their own story, without comments to bring out their meaning."[28] For Mill, then, one's ability to possess knowledge hinges upon the mind's capacity to remain open to criticism; i.e., one's willingness to engage in and profit from argument. Thus, while Mill in *On Liberty* distinguishes the more certain matters which Aristotle called apodeictic (including mathematics and the sciences) from contingent matters (such as questions in politics, religion and ethics),[29] Mill's discussion of assurance formulates an epistemological criterion applicable to both.

How are we to account for the applicability of one criterion to both scientific (apodeictic) matters and probable (contingent) ones? We suggest that Mill, unlike his empiricist contemporaries, viewed all subjects upon which we may inquire as existing on an epistemological continuum; that is, objects of inquiry are not *either* apodeictic *or* contingent, they are merely more or less so.[30] Hence, the rigid distinction between absolute and contingent questions ceases to be useful in the search for knowledge. For regardless of the logical nature of any particular "fact," our assessment of its truth or falsity is, in the final analysis, a function of whether or not our opinions survive the tests engendered within the doctrine of assurance.[31]

Assurance as an Alternative to Traditional Subjectivist and Objectivist Epistemology

Mill's theory of rhetoric, with the doctrine of assurance at its center, provides an alternative to traditional subjectivist and objectivist epistemologies. By asserting that erroneous opinions may be corrected (correction is the final step in the process of assurance), Mill could have avoided the implications of Kantian and Hegelian subjectivity. For while it may be admitted that persons come to see the world through their own individual, subjective perspectives, nonetheless, such selective perceptions could be transcended and subjectivism mitigated through assurance. Phrased differently, Mill's theory of rhetoric suggests that through a rigorous employment of the doctrine of assurance one can surpass his/her individual beliefs, attitudes, and values, even though his/her cognitive apparatus may operate, to a degree, to obscure truth. Hence, the doctrine established for rhetoric a genuine epistemological role, wherein discourse—more specifically, argument—could overcome subjectivity and result in knowledge. Mill's thought in this instance provides a melding between the spirit of eighteenth-century optimism, which viewed objective truth as an attainable goal, and nineteenth-century subjectivism. Mill could admit that the individual thinker was plagued by subjectivism; yet, such a thinker could escape its grasp through the employment of the concept of assurance. Precisely why this is so may be inferred from a comparison of Mill, Hegel, and Kant.

Like Hegel, elements in Mill's doctrine of assurance suggest that the universe is active, as opposed to consisting merely of passive objects which become the focus of our intellectual curiosity. Here, reality itself is seen to impinge upon the totality of our worldview, acting as a corrective when our views of reality do not correspond to it. That reality ultimately impinges, or more precisely, that it is an active constituent in the rhetorical process, is made clear by Mill in his discussion of the suppression of truth—a treatment we earlier labeled Mill's notion of "rhetoric as a preservative."[32] Mill writes: "The real advantage which truth has, consists in this, that when an opinion is true, it may be extinguished once, twice, or many times, but in the course of ages there will generally be found persons to rediscover it, until some one of its reappearances falls on a time when from favourable circumstances it escapes persecution until it has made such head as to withstand all subsequent attempts to suppress it."[33]

Mill departs from Hegel, however, by insisting that the influence of reality is not the impinging of thesis on antithesis with a synthesis as the result. For Mill, reality itself impinges *directly* upon our opinions as a final confirmation or denial of them. Yet such impingement is impossible in the absence of the kind of rhetorical context Mill details in the doctrine of assurance. Commenting on the fulfillment of the three requisite elements of assurance (access, defense, and correction), Mill notes: "we have neglected nothing that could give the *truth a chance of reaching us:* if the lists are kept open, we may hope that if there be a better truth, it will be found when the human mind is capable of receiving it; and in the meantime we may rely on having attained such approach to truth, as is possible in our own day. This is the amount of certainty attainable by a fallible being, and this the sole way of attaining it."[34]

The alternative to traditional subjectivist and objectivist epistemologies also surfaces in a comparison of Mill with Kant. In his theory of synthetic *a priori* judgments, Kant agreed with eighteenth-century empiricists that "all our knowledge begins with experience,"[35] but denied that "it all arises out of experience."[36] Instead of viewing the mind as a Lockean *tabula rasa,* Kant, as we noted earlier, saw it as an active participant in the perceptual process, serving to shape and, *a fortiori, to alter,* the objects of reality *prior* to their becoming cognitions.

The immediate impact of the addition to epistemology of an *active* (as opposed to passive) mind centered on notions of *truth.* As Kant himself put it: "It is not that by our sensibility we cannot know the nature of things in themselves in any save a confused fashion; we do not apprehend them in any fashion whatsoever. If our subjective constitution be removed, the represented object, with the qualities which sensible intuition bestows upon it, is nowhere to be found, and cannot possibly be found."[37]

Obviously, if one were to accept this worldview with its characteristic subjectivist implication, rhetoric would be placed in an untenable position. For Kant, the ultimate constituents of reality comprise the *noumenal* world. Through the very act of attempting to grasp the objects of the noumenal world, the mind distorts reality and, therefore, the only objects humankind can appraise are the *distorted* remnants of the noumenal world, which Kant referred to as the *phenomenal* world. Although we can possess "knowledge" of this latter world, such "knowledge" really amounts to an understanding of the way the world *seems* to be and *seems* to operate. If one could remove all this "knowledge" there would still be a residuum, namely, the ultimate constituents of reality which gave rise to the phenomenal world in the first place. It is this ultimate and objective reality which Kant argues we cannot in any sense know. In this context, the eighteenth-century managerial role of rhetoric as the transmitter of truths gleaned from knowledge of the ultimate constituents of reality would cease to function. Since the mind cannot apprehend the reality of the noumenal world, the only "truth" or "knowledge" it can communicate is that of the phenomenal world—falling short of the goal set by eighteenth-century optimism in the search for true knowledge.

Mill, while accepting the view that man's mind was active, avoided the conclusion that knowledge was, as a result, impossible—a conclusion which Kant, ironically, took for granted. For it does not follow that just because the mind operates upon the world, that, therefore, the objects of the world must be unknowable. Such was the upshot of Mill's discussion of an active universe which impinges upon individuals, acting to correct erroneous opinion. The result of such impingement is the possession of at least partial truth. In Mill's words, "though the silenced opinion be an error, it may, and very commonly does, contain a portion of truth; and since the general or prevailing opinion on any subject is rarely or never the whole truth, it is only by the collision of adverse opinions that the remainder of the truth has any chance of being supplied." Further, contends Mill, "even if the received opinion be not only true, but the whole truth; unless it is suffered to be, and actually is, vigorously and earnestly contested, it will, by most of those who receive it, be held in the manner of a prejudice, with little comprehension or feeling of its rational grounds."[38] In short, through assurance-mediation it is possible to assess not only the more obvious constituents of the phenomenal world, but to speculate about and, to an important degree, verify the ultimate nature of reality.

Mill's theory of rhetoric, then, exposed a clear alternative to traditional subjectivism as espoused in the nineteenth century. For on Mill's analysis, rhetoric, conceived as argument, would assume the role of *discovering* truth, thus affording the art an important new status. Rhetoric need no longer languish in a diminutive position, parasitic on subjectivist philosophical epistemology, nor remain doxologic; rather, rhetoric could find for itself its own epistemological responsibilities.

Mill's theory of rhetoric also provided a viable alternative to traditional objectivist epistemologies. Because rhetoric could now become a means to the *discovery* of new knowledge, the prescriptivist, managerial tasks of the eighteenth century retained their validity and usefulness. Once rhetoric, through assurance mediated disputation, *discovered* the truth on any subject, such truths would require transmission—indeed, they would *demand* it, given the criterion of access, which held that opinions should be widely circulated to permit critical assessment by others. Finally, if opinions survived critical inspection, they might even be elevated to the status of "knowledge," and frame prescriptions. This would in turn preserve the familiar responsibility of the art to propagate such prescriptions, while expanding the role of rhetoric. Mill's conception of rhetoric not only retained an important role for the art, but in the process it also served to expand the function of rhetorical discourse to a point where rhetoric assumed a fundamental office hitherto reserved for the philosopher, namely, the epistemic function of the *discovery* of knowledge. Such a view of rhetoric as more than simply a device of transmission parasitic on traditional objectivist epistemology *might* even elevate the art to a higher level than it enjoyed in the eighteenth century. In Ehninger's words, Mill's treatment of the art "passed beyond" prior systems of rhetoric, becoming "richer in content and more embracing in scope."[39]

In summary, Mill's theory of rhetoric as embodied in the doctrine of assurance provided a clear alternative to both traditional subjectivist and objectivist epistemology. This alternative, while objectivist in nature, differed from the traditional grounding of eighteenth-century rhetorics because it was nonparasitic on *philosophical* epistemology. It was, in essence, a uniquely *rhetorical* epistemology.

IMPLICATIONS

Emerging from the foregoing analysis are several important implications for the field of rhetoric.

Our analysis of Mill's doctrine of assurance indicates that important rhetorical concepts, if not complex theories of rhetoric themselves, may be couched in a nonconventional rhetorical vocabulary. The use of such a nonconventional vocabulary is, we suggest, indicative of the requirement to meet significant changes in the epistemology upon which a particular rhetoric is based, with like changes in the technical terms of the rhetorical art. As we have seen in the case of Mill, such a relationship between rhetoric and epistemology need not be articulated in a conscious attempt to adjust the one discipline vis-à-vis aberrations in the other. It may, as in the instance of *On Liberty,* be merely implicit.

Moreover, a theory of rhetoric, in responding, consciously or unconsciously, to the epistemological milieu of its time, may develop a particular emphasis uncharacteristic of rhetoric conceived as eloquence or persuasion. For example, as we have observed in Mill's *On Liberty,* a rhetorical theory can evolve from a discussion of a particular mode of rhetorical discourse—in this case, argument. So conceived, rhetoric may include within its scope a constructive partnership with those other arts and sciences devoted to the discovery of truth as opposed to its mere transmission.

This view of rhetoric is not only consistent with, but amplifies claims regarding the inseparability of the discovery and propagation of truth. The significance of this contention resides in the analogy between Mill's theory of rhetoric and contemporary notions regarding the epistemic function of rhetorical discourse.

Also implicit in his theory is what we believe to be an important difference between Mill and several of his contemporaries, most notably Richard Whately, Joseph Butler, and John Newman. While all four of these thinkers address issues of direct relevance to the *content* and *structure* of *arguments,* it is only in Mill's discussion of assurance that we find a treatment of *argumentation.* Our claim here is illustrated by Maurice Natanson's distinction among "an argument," "argument as such," and "argumentation." On his analysis, an argument refers to the *content* of any particular dispute we happen to be engaged in at any time, while an argument as such entails the further analysis of the *structure* and *form* of disputes, independent of their content. Argumentation, by contrast, transcends both content and form and refers to the very process or rationale, that is, the very spirit, of engaging in reasoned discourse. Argumentation, therefore, unlike an argument or argument as such, involves more than the mere juxtapositioning of opposites or a study of the structure and form of propositions; it signifies our intentional participation in an enterprise which, by definition, may result in our coming to see the world differently due to the inherently corrective nature of the process.[40] Because argumentation goes beyond content and structure to treat such concepts as human intentions and motives, communication, and audiences, it offers a more amplified analysis of rhetoric *qua* theory of argument than was possible given a rhetorical theory which emphasizes content and structure.

An examination of Mill's concept of assurance vis-à-vis notions of certitude advanced by such theorists as Butler, Newman, and perhaps even Whately, underscores how *On Liberty,* unlike the works of these others, is a treatise on *argumentation* and, hence, suggests a more elaborate rhetoric. To illustrate, Mill's contemporaries are found to engage in an examination of the structure and form of arguments; that is, they are concerned with argument as such. This is exemplified in their discussion of the certainty which obtains from the validity of particular argumentative structures. For example, Butler's exploration of concepts such as "demonstration," "probability," and "presumption" illustrates how certainty is the result of the validity of the *structure* of arguments.[41] Similarly, Newman's treatment of "assent" (e.g., "half-assent," "conditional-assent," and "hesitating assent") also is inherently bound up with the structure, as well as the content of arguments.[42] Likewise, Whately's discussion of types of arguments, "presumption," "burden of proof," and a number of other concepts, while tending to be viewed somewhat more against the backdrop of argumentation, still does not place primary emphasis on this most rhetorical level of argument theory.[43] By contrast, it should be evident from our discussion of Mill's doctrine of assurance that *On Liberty,* with its treatment of such notions as access, defense, and correction, is in large part a discussion of *argumentation.* The conclusion to be drawn from this analysis is that there exists a major difference between "certainty" as employed by Mill's contemporaries and assurance as developed in *On Liberty.* The former purports to achieve indubitability from the validity of the logical structure or inductive method employed by the inquirer. The latter sacrifices veridicality on the grounds that future arguments may be marshalled and interjected into the process of argumentation, thereby invalidating conclusions or opinions initially held. The certainty of Butler, Newman, and Whately thus involves the appraisal of particular, static arguments. The doctrine of assurance is more generally applied, being concerned with the *process* of the search for and preservation of human beliefs and opinions.

A final implication of our analysis frames a challenge for the rhetorical critic. If, as we believe, the doctrine of assurance developed in *On Liberty* reflects Mill's best judgment as to how intellectual investigation should proceed, then one would anticipate that the methodology of assurance would be embodied in Mill's own discourse. Mill, after all, was in the first instance a philosopher who wrote voluminously in such philosophical subdisciplines as ethics, metaphysics, logic, aesthetics, and the philosophy of science. Do Mill's writings illustrate an employment of the doctrine of assurance? An excellent point of departure in answering this question is Mill's debate with his contemporary, William Whewell. This exchange, which continued over the course of several years, might offer the critic ample evidence to confirm or disconfirm Mill's use of the principles of assurance in his own intellectual activity.

A related question would inquire as to the possibility of whether Mill's doctrine of assurance was presented in *On Liberty* for the purpose of completing the task he had begun in *A System of Logic.* In the *Logic* Mill develops a consistent empiricist system of thought. Yet Mill's treatment here is extremely sketchy in terms of how the empirical method is to be employed in investigating the constituents of the world. Perhaps *On Liberty* was meant to serve as an illustration of the manner in which Mill's *System of Logic,* as well as any other variety of investigation—whether scientific, philosophical, social, or religious—could (and should) be employed for the validation of the system being used itself. This speculation would seem to offer a fruitful area for future research.

Conclusion

John Stuart Mill's nineteenth-century work *On Liberty,* ostensibly written as a political treatise, has been shown to offer theorists a wealth of concepts with direct consequences for the rhetorical art. Mill's doctrine of assurance, in providing a uniquely *rhetorical* epistemology, transcended rhetoric's traditional contentment with adopting non-rhetorical epistemologies. His departure from this tradition reveals *On Liberty* to be an important work in the history of rhetoric deserving the continuing scrutiny of rhetorical scholars.

Notes

This research was made possible by a grant as part of the 1979 Karl R. Wallace Memorial Award. The authors are deeply indebted to Douglas Ehninger for his encouragement and critique of the initial draft of this essay. An earlier version of the essay was presented at the Speech Communication Association Convention, Minneapolis, 1979.

1. Douglas Ehninger, "On Systems of Rhetoric," in *Contemporary Rhetoric: A Reader's Coursebook,* ed. Douglas Ehninger (Glenview: Scott, Foresman and Company, 1972), p. 55.
2. Ehninger, "On Systems," p. 57.
3. Patrick L. Gardiner, ed., *19th-Century Philosophy* (New York: The Free Press, 1969), p. 10.

4. Vincent M. Bevilacqua, "Philosophical Influences in the Development of English Rhetorical Theory: 1748–1783," *Proceedings of the Leeds Philosophical and Literary Society, Literary and Historical Section*, 12 (1968), 192.

5. See, for example, Immanuel Kant, *Critique of Pure Reason*, trans. Norman Kemp Smith (New York: Macmillan, 1929), p. 84.

6. Kant, *Critique*, p. 84, passim.

7. Robert C. Solomon, *Introducing Philosophy* (New York: Harcourt Brace Jovanovich, 1977), p. 192.

8. Hegel contended that concepts such as "true" and "false," whether applied to such diverse things as scientific theories or values, were inappropriate. As Solomon indicates, he "wholly endorsed the Kantian thesis that the world is nothing other than the way in which we constitute it. And that means that seemingly opposed philosophies are not really contradictory; they are just alternative views of reality." For Hegel, "there is no reality other than the reality we constitute with our concepts" (pp. 192–93). See George Hegel, *The Phenomenology of Mind*, trans. J. B. Baillie (New York: Harper & Row, 1967), pp. 123–24. See also H. B. Acton, "Hegel, George Wilhelm Friedrich," *The Encyclopedia of Philosophy*, 1967 ed. For an overall view of nineteenth century philosophy and rhetoric, see John Elliot Braun, "The Philosophical Roots of the Nineteenth Century Repose of Rhetoric, With Emphasis on the Idea of Communication in the Thought of Josiah Royce," Diss. University of Michigan 1977; and Gardiner.

9. The distinction between doxologic and epistemic parallels the distinction between opinion and knowledge which has been drawn by philosophers since the Socratic period. Most epistemologists have held that, unlike opinion, knowledge must be comprised of justified true belief. See, for example, A. J. Ayer, *The Problem of Knowledge* (Baltimore: Penguin Books, 1956), p. 35; Roderick M. Chisholm, *Theory of Knowledge* (Englewood Cliffs, New Jersey: Prentice-Hall, 1966), p. 5; and Panayot Butchvarov, *The Concept of Knowledge* (Evanston: Northwestern University Press, 1970), p. 25.

10. Richard A. Cherwitz and James W. Hikins, "John Stuart Mill's *On Liberty*: Implications for the Epistemology of the New Rhetoric," *Quarterly Journal of Speech*, 65 (1979), 12–24.

11. See, for example, Douglas Ehninger, "Argument as Method: Its Nature, Its Limitations and Its Uses," *Speech Monographs*, 37 (1970), 101–10.

12. Cherwitz and Hikins, "Mill's *On Liberty*," p. 17.

13. John Stuart Mill, *On Liberty*, in *Autobiography and Other Writings*, ed. Jack Stillinger (Boston: Houghton Mifflin, 1969), p. 368. All citations from *On Liberty* are from this text.

14. Mill, *On Liberty*, p. 370.

15. Mill, *On Liberty*, p. 385.

16. Mill, *On Liberty*, pp. 369-70.

17. Mill, *On Liberty*, p. 369.

18. We define an epistemic judgment as a statement asserting that something is the case. An epistemic judgment is either true or false.

19. A rhetorical epistemology is a theory of rhetoric which views the central function of the art as the advancement of knowledge claims, i.e., epistemic judgments. Advancement includes both the discovery and transmission of knowledge.

20. John Passmore, "John Stuart Mill and British Empiricism," in *A Hundred Years of Philosophy* (Harmondsworth, England: Penguin Books, 1968), pp. 13–34.

21. Sheldon Peterfreund and Theodore Denise, *Contemporary Philosophy and Its Origins* (Princeton: D. Van Nostrand, 1967), p. 135.

22. John Stuart Mill, *A System of Logic* (New York: Harper & Row Brothers, 1852).

23. J. B. Schneewind, "Mill, John Stuart," *The Encyclopedia of Philosophy*, 1967 ed., p. 315.

24. A correspondence theory of truth holds that a statement (proposition) is true if it accurately reports a state of affairs which exists in the world independently of human beliefs, attitudes, or values. Mill was, similarly, an advocate of the correspondence theory of truth as his thoroughgoing empiricism attests. An exposition of the correspondence theory of truth and its relationship among other competing views is found in Harold H. Titus, *Living Issues in Philosophy* (New York: American Book Co., 1964), pp. 56–69.

25. Mill, *On Liberty*, p. 370.

26. Mill, *On Liberty*, p. 384.

27. Mill, *On Liberty*, p. 385. Emphasis added.

28. Mill, *On Liberty*, p. 369.

29. Aristotle, *Rhetoric* I.2, 1357a. Lane Cooper, trans., *The Rhetoric of Aristotle* (New York: Appleton-Century-Crofts, 1932), p. 11.

30. This statement seems *prima facie* at odds with most contemporary interpretations which view Mill as a strict empiricist. The point to be made, however, is that such theorists have ignored the fact that Mill's empiricism is, as we argue, subject to rhetorical validation. This may account for Mill's practice of introducing in *On Liberty* (supposedly a treatise on political matters) examples from the realm of the empirical sciences, e.g., Newtonian Physics and astronomy, in that the doctrine of assurance serves as a method of validation for *all* systems of knowledge (that is, all enterprises advancing epistemic judgments). See Mill, *On Liberty*, p. 370.

31. Mill's discussion of assurance may be seen as anticipating the currently fashionable contention that rhetoric plays a significant role in scientific inquiry. Representative treatments of the relationship between rhetoric and science appear in Mario Finocchiaro, "Logic and Rhetoric in Lavoisier's Sealed Note: Toward a Rhetoric of Science," *Philosophy and Rhetoric*, 10 (1977), 111–22; Michael A. Overington, "The Scientific Community as Audience: Toward a Rhetorical Analysis of Science," *Philosophy and Rhetoric*, 10 (1977), 143–63; and Walter Weimer, "Science as Rhetorical Transaction: Toward a Nonjustificational Conception of Rhetoric," *Philosophy and Rhetoric*, 10 (1977), 1–29.

32. See Cherwitz and Hikins, p. 14.

33. Mill, *On Liberty*, p. 377.

34. Mill, *On Liberty*, p. 370. Emphasis added.

35. Kant, *Critique*, p. 41.

36. Kant, *Critique*, p. 41.

37. Kant, *Critique*, p. 84.

38. Mill, *On Liberty*, p. 400.

39. Ehninger, "On Systems," p. 57.

40. Maurice Natanson, "The Claims of Immediacy," in *Philosophy, Rhetoric, and Argumentation*, ed. Maurice Natanson and Henry W. Johnstone, Jr. (University Park: The Pennsylvania State University Press, 1965), pp. 10–19.

41. Joseph Butler, *The Analogy of Religion* (Philadelphia: J. B. Lippincott & Co., 1870), pp. 67-75.

42. John Henry Cardinal Newman, *An Essay in Aid of a Grammar of Assent* (Westminster: Christian Classics, 1973), especially pp. 210–58.

43. Richard Whately, *Elements of Rhetoric,* ed. Douglas Ehninger (Carbondale: Southern Illinois University Press, 1963).

On Classes of Inference and Force

Bruce E. Gronbeck

T he substance of rhetoric, and more particularly of argument, undoubtedly is "good reasons," as Karl Wallace so simply put it,[1] but in what sorts of ways can good reasons attach themselves to the contestable propositions of rhetoric and argument? While many basic textbooks in speech and argumentation still teach scholastic syllogisms and nineteenth-century forms of induction, most philosophers of argument probably would agree that the Schoolman's machinery for inference simply cannot account for most examples of everyday inferential reasoning.

Nor, for that matter, can the field of argument's second most popular intellectual skeleton, the Toulmin model, help much, even though it has the extraordinary virtue of descriptive clarity. Most disputes we find in common parlance or even in speculative sciences, in Toulmin's idiom, are "warrant-establishing" rather than "warrant-using." That is, they tend to center on what is the proper or rationalizing warrant or inference to connect data with a claim or proposition one wishes to advance from those data. To make the

BRUCE E. GRONBECK is Professor of Communication at the University of Iowa.

connection, disputants need to discover—i.e. "establish"—a warrant.[2] Because the establishment of warrants demands a relatively sophisticated theory of inferences (more precisely, a theory of "backing" for warrants), and because Toulmin and his co-authors really have not described that theory, we as yet possess no systematic way to talk about the "force" or claim-to-validity of various warrants which fall outside classic mathematical formulae.[3]

Must we either retreat to analyticity or simply discuss warrants vaguely as "general, step-authorizing" statements?[4] I think not. It seems possible to describe technically and practically a whole range of inferences we all draw everyday—more specifically, to clarify the term "inference," to classify inferences into families, and to advance a doctrine of "rules" which explains why families-of-inferences have force in practical discourse. This essay, therefore, will embark on definitional, classificatory, and theoretical forays into the fields of public and professional warrant-establishing argumentation.

THE PROBLEM OF "INFERENCE"

The analysis must begin with words; the most problematic word for our purposes is "inference." It often is used in argumentatively trivial fashions, as are its companion forms "infer" and "inferential process." For example, we sometimes say, "Oh, I don't know, I just inferred it because of the way she acted." In this sentence, "infer" may be taken as synonymous with "guess"; it indicates a lack of positive or adequately grounded knowledge, or a state of unsureness. The notion of inference we are seeking is not analogous to a theory of probability or a psychology.

A second problem confronting us lies in the technical ambiguity of the word. "Inference" sometimes can refer to a product-of-reasoning, and sometimes, to the process-of-reasoning.[5] So, we could say, in parsing Descartes' *cogito ergo sum*, that *"ergo sum"* is an inferred statement somehow produced from *"cogito,"* or we might aver that *"ergo sum"* is a claim inferred from *"cogito"* by virtue of a generalization (i.e. an "inference" or "inferential process") concerning thinking animals and being. To return to Toulminian concepts, inferences can be either claims or warranting procedures. Indeed, perhaps Toulmin was exceedingly clever when he assiduously avoided using the word at all except to denigrate notions of mathematical validity.[6]

In spite of its ambiguities, I do not wish to avoid "inference," because I am interested in the idea of "force" understood strongly. The idea of *logical coercion* will be important in this essay. The problem can be restated in this manner: Toulmin has, more or less, taken a permissive position with regard to validity and inference, saying in effect that a warrant (or inference) "allows" a claim to be advanced. Inferential processes are seen primarily as *justificatory*—in his words, as "a 'license to argue from grounds to a conclusion.' "[7] I shall argue that we can talk productively about inferences as *argumentative demands,* which, if understood by competent interlocutors involved in a dispute, force conclusions and require adherence. As we shall see, the "force" of one particular inferential process is not necessarily identical to that of all other inferential processes—i.e. "force" can be considered a variable construct. Yet all of the patterns we shall examine have at least one feature in common: they all involve some discernible degree of force or coercion, making them potentially powerful engines in both public and private argumentation. Figure 1 represents the forms of argument we are investigating (p. 88).

Thus, the focus is on sets of rules which produce powerful connections between statements in argumentative contexts. In the words of Frank Ramsey: "The human mind works essentially according to general rules or habits; a process of thought not proceeding according to some rule would simply be a random sequence of ideas; whenever we infer A and B we do so in virtue of some relation between them."[8] The first question to be approached is *"In what ways, i.e., by what sorts of rules, can arguers interrelate two or more statements inferentially?"* The second question is *"From what sources do each group or family of rules gain force in our lives?"*

THREE CLASSES OF INFERENCE

Everyday Inferences

In exploring inferential rules and inferred statements, let us begin by examining some innocent-looking sentences which serve as data or grounds for arguments:

1. "This is a tree."
2. "This is a good road."
3. "Susan is an aunt."
4. "How do I get to Sampson's Drugstore?"
5. "Jones promised to pay Smith five dollars."

From the first statement, "This is a tree," had it been uttered by someone, we normally would infer another: "The speaker's sense-perceptors are reporting to him a cluster of sense-data we call a 'tree.' " That is, we would infer that the speaker is offering us a report of

Figure 1: Schematic Representation of Inferences, Inferential Processes, and Their Force

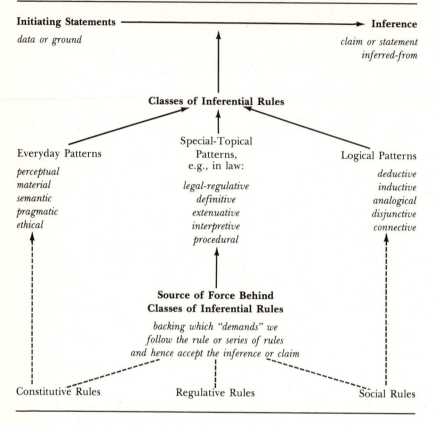

Initiating Statements ————————————————→ Inference

data or ground   *claim or statement*
                                                       inferred-from

Classes of Inferential Rules

Everyday Patterns   Special-Topical   Logical Patterns
                           Patterns,
perceptual   e.g., in law: *deductive*
material   *legal-regulative*   *inductive*
semantic   *definitive*   *analogical*
pragmatic   *extenuative*   *disjunctive*
ethical   *interpretive*   *connective*
                           procedural

**Source of Force Behind
Classes of Inferential Rules**

*backing which "demands" we
follow the rule or series of rules
and hence accept the inference or claim*

Constitutive Rules   Regulative Rules   Social Rules

experiences in the world. We can call this inference a *perceptual inference.* The warrant or inferential rule we could cite, if pushed to defend our inference, might run something like "Unless a speaker's senses are playing tricks on him, unless he is lying, unless he misunderstands the English word 'tree,' etc., we are obligated to accept a speaker's observational reports as accurate perceptions." One might be uncomfortable, perhaps, calling mere perceptual processes "inferences" and "inferential rules," and I suspect such statements as can be derived from "This is a tree" are of little interest argumentatively,[9] but at least we would not be doing the language a grave injustice were we to identify the second statement as one inferred from the first via the perceptual inferential rule.

Our statement (2)—"This is a good road"—potentially generates a few more problems. What with the bedeviling word "good" in it, some might want to make an evaluative issue out of inferences we could draw. I would not, however. When someone says to me, "This is a good road," *ceteris paribus* I infer another statement: "This road is straight, well surfaced, not too heavily traveled, and perhaps scenic." That is, I take the speaker's use of the term "good," not as an evaluative judgment of Interstate 80, but as a shorthand method for listing properties of it. Such an inference can be called *material implication,* meaning that some uses of words such as "good" are contextually conventionalized, i.e., have agreed-upon referents in certain situations. Those conventions can, if necessary, be stated as inferential rules—"In reference to 'roads' in this context, the word 'good' counts as properties $a_1, a_2, \ldots, a_n$."[10]

The step from "This is a good road" to "Susan is an aunt" may seem minuscule, but it is not. From the statement "Susan is an aunt" I am *obliged,* if I have sufficient acquaintance with English, to infer a second statement, "Susan has at least one nephew or niece." Both "This is a good road" and "Susan is an aunt" coerce inferred claims because of word usage, but in the first case we are citing contextual conventions which I legitimately may choose to accept or deny. That is, I could, without violating our language or committing a logical faux pas, simply like or prefer crooked, unsurfaced, heavily traveled, and/or ugly roads. If, however, I accept the statement "Susan is an aunt" but then reject the inference that she has at least one nephew or niece, I most certainly ought to be accused of misunderstanding or mocking the English language. This third sort of inference, then, is a *semantic inference,* justifying itself by the ways all people of a culture use referential words.[11]

The fourth sentence, "How do I get to Sampson's Drugstore?", moves us into very different linguistic territory, into one of the contemporary extensions of philosophical work by Ryle, Wisdom, Austin, and Searle.[12] From that sentence I am able to infer a series of others: "The speaker does not know where Sampson's Drugstore is," "The speaker wishes me to answer," "The speaker (perhaps) wants to get to Sampson's Drugstore," etc. From the question I am able to infer statements concerning the speaker's motives, habits-of-mind, desires to communicate with me,[13] etc., because of our usual interpretations of the interrogative sentence form and the fact of direct address. This series of *pragmatic inferences,* when such questions are asked seriously, are important sorts of inferences in human relations, and, ultimately, in argument. Based on an inferential rule which might run roughly like "When speakers ask direct questions, they usually have motive x, desire y, lack of knowledge z, etc., depending upon the context," psychological or pragmatic rules represent the culture's method for engaging others in informational or argumentative exchanges. The demand inherent in them is impelling.

Finally, the statement "Jones promised to pay Smith five dollars" is the sample statement employed by John Searle to demonstrate the derivation of an "ought" or ethical statement from an "is" or descriptive statement.[14] The statement and its relatives are especially interesting to those who study speech acts and their illocutionary aspects. Rooted in "Jones promised to pay Smith five dollars," Searle argued, are implications relative to Jones' ethical responsibilities. Jones' act of promising—his use of that word (or any other of the commissive verbs in English)—ethically obligates him, thereby implying another statement, "Jones ought to pay Smith five dollars." (Searle's derivation actually involves a five-step inferential process.)[15] Now, one may want to term this inference a special case of our third (the semantic) form, but I prefer not to because of the potentially grave moral responsibilities such statements incur. To say that Susan has no nephews or nieces after one has said "Susan is an aunt" is to raise havoc with words, as when Jack Douglas humorously entitled a book *My Brother Was An Only Child*. But, to say "I, Jones, will not pay Smith five dollars" after one has said "I, Jones, promise to pay Smith five dollars" is to call into question one's personal integrity—to lie, to destroy one's credibility. Such *ethical inferences* strike to the very core of obligatory social understandings.

Perceptual, material, semantic, pragmatic, and ethical inferences are undoubtedly used commonly, without thinking. The inferred-from statements are perceived as immediately apparent because this class of inferences is the product of our acculturation, of education in our fellow beings' linguistic, mental, and behavioral customs. We all take recourse to each (except perhaps the first) rather matter-of-factly when arguing.

Special-Topical Inferences

The second general class of inferences may be termed "special-topical." They are tied to particular topics or to ways of arguing which are peculiar to a field or discipline; in Toulmin's terms, these are "field-variant" inferences—employed by professional lawyers, social scientists, and the like.

By way of illustration, let us inspect law and five exemplary pieces of data (the following are not intended to represent every possible legal situation, but will be sufficient to ground this analysis):

6. "Citizen Smith has committed acts x, y, and z."
7. "Citizen Smith has committed act x but not act y."
8. "Citizen Smith has committed act x, which is illegal under Law 123, but legal under Law 456."

9. "President Smith has committed acts x, y, and z."
10. "Citizen Smith has committed Crime A, but his rights were violated during arrest/arraignment/trial/etc."

From statement (6), "Citizen Smith has committed acts x, y, and z," I am able to argue "Smith ought to be judged guilty of Crime A" if I supply a warrant such as "Law 123 declares acts x, y, and z illegal." Such a rule can be termed a *legal-regulative inference* because its focus is upon a series of behaviors regulated explicitly by statutory law. A more complicated but somewhat similar inference is involved with statement (7), "Citizen Smith committed act x but not act y." We arrive at the conclusion, "Citizen Smith ought to be charged with Crime B," via the warrant, "Law 123 demands one demonstrate that act y was done to prove a person guilty of Crime A, but that act x was done to prove a person guilty of Crime B." (To make more sense of the example, substitute "first degree murder" for "Crime A," and "manslaughter" for "Crime B.") As in inference (6), the appeal is made to statutory law, but in this case, we have a *definitive inference* because the focus of the argument is upon an interpretation of a behavior, and not the behavior itself.

We advance one step further argumentatively in the case of statement (8): "Citizen Smith has committed act x, which is illegal under Law 123 but legally obligatory under Law 456." One moves in this case to the conclusion "He ought not be found guilty," via the warrant "Smith was under a legal obligation to commit act x," in much the same way defenders of President Richard Nixon did during the House Judiciary Committee's impeachment hearings, by explicating conflicting laws.[16] The argument represents a specialized form of *inference from extenuating legal circumstances*. It is somewhat similar to the situation faced in sentence (9), "President Smith has committed acts x, y, and z," where, via the warrant, "The founding fathers intended such acts to constitute 'high crimes and misdemeanors,'" we arrive at the conclusion, "President Smith ought to be charged with 'high crimes and misdemeanors' (i.e. be impeached)."[17] This inference is comparable to the definitive inference noted earlier, in that the arguer is in a sense defining. In addition, it has affinities with the inference from extenuating legal circumstances, as it is concentrating upon special aspects of statute-construction. Yet, it differs from both inasmuch as the inference per se takes its force from an interpretation-of-intent. Hence, it is *interpretive*, rather than definitive or extenuative. It appears regularly in arguments from constitutional sources or *assumptisi*.

Finally, consider statement (10): "Citizen Smith has committed Crime A, but his rights were violated during arrest/arraignment/trial/etc." To reason from these data to a conclusion ("Smith ought not be found guilty"), we move from the strictly rule-governed sorts of inferences we have been discussing into the disarrayed universe of legal ideology. To give this argument coherence and force, we must supply a warrant which says "'Proper' legal procedure is the mainstay of this culture's system of justice"—a warrant which parallels classical commonplaces for arguing the "spirit" vis-à-vis the "letter" of the law. Thus, in this argumentative unit we have a general, *procedural-constitutional inference,* one which takes whatever force it can generate from societal values built into either an abstract document (the Constitution of the United States) or the social consciousness of a people. It is not, strictly speaking, based upon either statute or interpretation-of-intent; like many constitutional inferences, it draws its power from legal abstractions, conjointly with (the disputant hopes) the values held sacred by an adjudicant.[18] Hence, its coercive power tends to vary from one constitutional theory to another, and thus from one advocate to another; it has determinative force, however, for its adherents.

While we have not fully unpacked these legal inferences, it should nonetheless be clear that each—regulative, definitive, extenuative, interpretive, and constitutional—has a quality in common with all of the others: each is based upon a specialized rule. Human acts are not inherently "crimes"; rather, acts are termed or imputed to be "crimes" on the bases of essentially artificial, stipulated rules we call "laws." Such legal rules are codified in treatises ("rules of evidence") which define acceptable inferential processes; a lawyer must employ such inferential rules when moving from testated data to conclusionary judgments. Likewise, in the social sciences, similar rules are codified in books on statistics and experimental design, in concepts appropriate to a scientific paradigm (e.g. currently, "random numbers," "degrees of probability," "levels of significance," etc.). To argue as a lawyer or as a scientist, one must work inside a highly conventionalized system given power by a host *institution.*

Logical Inferences

Before commenting further, let us briefly consider a third set of data:

11. "All crows are black."
12. "Crow *A* is black, crow *B* is black, . . . crow *n* is black."
13. "The acorn contains the potentialities for oak trees."
14. "In situation *x* we should do *A,* or in situation *y* we should do *B.*"
15. "A funnel cloud is a sign of an approaching tornado."

Because such crows and acorns crop up in virtually every textbook on logic, we need spend little time on them. From statement (11), "All crows are black," I am entitled to infer another statement, "Crow *A* is black," by virtue of a *deductive inference* (classification) and an inferential rule, "What is true of the whole is true of the parts." Statement (12) is a usual set of data necessary for accepting the conclusion, "All crows are black," via an *inductive inference* (generalization) based on rules for sampling populations. Statement (13) regarding acorns, with the aid of an *analogical rule* ("Similar causes produce similar effects"), allows us to argue the conclusion, "Likewise does the boy foreshadow the grown man." With statement (14) as a disjunctive major premise, we move, once we know we have situation *x*, to the conclusion, "We should do *A*," via a *disjunctive inference*. And, finally, depending upon the fallibility or infallibility of the sign, we move to the conclusion, "A tornado is approaching," by means of a *connective inference* (e.g. "Experience shows that tornadoes *x* percent of the time follow funnel-shaped clouds"), the kind of inference which is used in arguments from cause or from sign.[19]

These logical inferential patterns are familiar, yet highly problematic. Their coerciveness seems markedly variable; deductive inferences are extremely "strong," for example, while analogical rules are only as good as the case we can make for similarities between elements in the analogy. A second problem lies in specifying the source of "logic's" force. Are logical rules innate to human cognition? Are they purely artificial, prescriptive rules impressed upon "educated" citizens? Or, are they, as Wittgenstein argued, merely analytical conveniences, and hence useful but ultimately "empty"?

With these questions we are driven to consider, as noted earlier, fundamental questions concerning the "force" of inferential processes—that is, the features of such statements and reasoning processes which *demand*, to varying degrees, that we accept any of them as making serious claims upon our assent. The notion of "demand" at work here is akin to the notion of "prima facie" case in both interscholastic debate and legal dispute: just as a prima facie case comes as an agitating force, demanding response, action, or acquiescence to its claims, so, too, do argumentative inferences make serious claims upon those at whom they are aimed.

TYPES OF RULES WHICH BACK INFERENCES

Generally speaking, inferences gain their force in our lives by appeals to "rules." Basically, a rule is a statement which guides or constrains mental or physical acts; a rule can be reduced to a sentence in the form, "In circumstances *X, Y* is (is not) required or permitted."[20] While any number of taxonomies of rule-types have been articulated by philosophers of language and action, three general classes of rules deserve our attention.

A *constitutive rule* is a statement which defines or comprises an activity. The "rules of the game" are of this type. Indeed, games essentially are a series of operationalized constitutive rules (e.g., "If a player's king is not in check and yet the player cannot move any of his or her pieces, the game shall be deemed a stalemate"). The "rules of grammar" are of the same genus; statements regarding the proper and improper semantic and syntactic operations required to "speak English" or "write German" fit this category. Constitutive rules, therefore, in an odd but accurate sense, are *in fact* the activity or behavior itself. As John Searle notes, the prototypical form of a constitutive rule is "*X* counts as *Y*"; that is, "Having all of your pieces frozen, unable to move, counts as a stalemate," or "A subject and predicate count as an English declarative sentence, "etc.[21]

A *regulative rule* is a kind of imperative which tells us what we ought to do in certain circumstances. Prototypical regulative rules are driving laws, the rules of parliamentary procedure, directives for borrowing money, the steps in a religious liturgy, and the like. They are distinguished, for our purposes, by two of their features. First, they are superimposed upon an activity, in order to control or routinize it. Thus, one can drive an automobile with a bit of mechanical knowledge and some psychomotor skill; but, one cannot drive legally without adherence to traffic laws. Second, their power often is derived from legitimizing institutions. Driving laws are set down by state agencies; monetary policies flow from local, state, and national banking institutions; and religious liturgies are formulated in statements regarding church worship issued by institutionalized religion.[22]

This brief distinction between constitutive and regulative rules is important for our discussion of inferences. The first—the everyday—class of inference seems rooted in constitutive, i.e. linguistic, rules. The perceptual inference depends upon the referential meaning of the word "tree"; the material inference relies upon a contextualized usage of the word "good" as applied to roads;[23] the semantic inference has power because of the meaning of the word "aunt," while the pragmatic

inference draws from our syntactic rules for interrogative constructions; and, as noted, the ethical inference is coercive because of the
obligations attached to such illocutionary verbs as "promise."

This family of everyday inferences thus is grounded in language
itself, in the very vehicle of cerebration and communication. Although
uninformed or insane people, liars, poets, and others twist and torture
literal language, we could not judge them uninformed, insane,
dissembling, or whatever *without knowing the constitutive rules;* these
exceptions "prove" the rules.[24] Such rules gain their coerciveness,
perhaps, from a principle called by Isabel Hungerland "The principle
of attending to the Circumstances of Communication" or "The
presumption of normalcy in the act of stating," or from what H. P.
Grice labels as "conversational implicature."[25]

What, then, of the second class of inferences, the special-topical
rules? Earlier, we saw that laws' regulative, definitive, extenuative,
interpretive, and constitutional inferences all were based on "specialized" rules. These rules generally are regulative. The modes of
inference we commonly find in such fields as law and social science
represent agreed-upon regulative rules which specify what can and
cannot be argued (i.e. inferred) from something else. Lawyers and
scientists belong to highly trained cults of communicators working
within their own institutional frames, their own regulated rules of
inference.

Families of special-topical inferences have been sanctified by the
elites and their institutions in various epochs. Each family of
special-topical inferences is a special paradigm,[26] a way of thinking
about and acting toward the world. The inferential rules of the cult
dwell in a *sanctum sanctorum* which can be entered only by the
initiated—by those with legal or scientific training, by those who can
"talk law" and "do science" properly. Stephen Toulmin goes so far as to
suggest we do a "populational analysis" and map out the "intellectual
ecology" of particular epochs or institutions in order to understand
how knowledges are governed by the rulers of powerful, professional
communities.[27]

Although "artificial" and "superimposed," regulative rules nevertheless make strong claims upon us. They guide the culture's
institutional practices and thus affect the way every citizen must "think"
when entering the field governed by the rules. Ultimately, therefore,
the regulative rules backing special-topical inferences can be thought
of usefully as *institutional rules.*

We now are left with the third class of inferences—logical
connectives. Are they backed by constitutive, regulative, or some other
kind of rule? While connectives have been regarded as constitutive by
the scholastics and as regulative by some twentieth-century anthro-

pologists,[28] there is profit in exploring another class of rules to explain logical inferential processes. We shall enter the field of *social rules*.[29]

Broadly, a social rule is a teachable guide to social interaction in specific contexts—a guide employed by persons to acculturate, to advise, to direct, or to sanction the verbal and nonverbal behavior of others. A social rule, therefore, can take numerous forms, as in "We do not (i.e. a member of this culture does not) speak to superiors until we are spoken to" (acculturative rule); "I suggest you don't interrupt him until he's through speaking" (advisory rule based on custom); "Don't eat oatmeal with your hands" (directive rule based on "manners").[30]

Social rules, hence, take many different forms; but, no matter the form, to Raymond Gumb they all have five basic characteristics: (a) they are teachable; (b) they can be misapplied, and hence are used to judge competency; (c) they are reflected in the "behavioral regularities of the social group," and hence can be emulated even without verbal specification; (d) they have normative power, and thus are used to justify and criticize others' behaviors; and (e) they can be followed by agents who know them (i.e. applied as well as misapplied).[31] To assert, then, that logical inferential processes are backed by social rules is to aver that *they gain their force, not from institutionalized authority or language per se, but from one's experience with fellow culture-mates in particular situations.* In support of this position, we must examine, at least briefly, "arguing" as a kind of speech act and "reason-giving" as an inferential activity.

Generically, there is agreement on a series of statements characterizing "arguing" as a species of discourse. (1) Arguing involves the assertion of a proposition and reasons why others ought to accept it. (2) Arguments are bilateral communicative activities, and hence involve a "taking-account-of" another person holding a presumably incorrect or defective view. (3) Arguers adhere to an "equal time" standard, one which says others have a right to examine one's reasons and reasoning. (4) When people choose to argue, they at least implicitly commit themselves to a notion of "rationality," that is, commit themselves to some form of reason-giving and to an examination of their reasoning processes by another. (5) The "rules" for arguing tend to vary from context to context: parliamentary situations demand specific and highly ritualized rules; candidate debates and religious disputations likewise have predetermined formats; even familial disputes often are characterized by specifiable ways of discoursing argumentatively.[32]

To put this all another way, people participating in or watching an argument have sets of general and specific expectations; and, many of those expectations are situation-bound. Further, we even may say that "reason-giving" and "inferring" as intellectual processes also tend to be situation- and/or role-bound. So, in my roles as parent, son, husband, and neighbor, I assume varying relations to those significant others, employ varying modes of language when arguing with them, and even analyze and discuss problems with them via particular argumentative forms. I argue one way with my children, another way with my wife, and a third way with my neighbor. The same is true of my professional roles, where I am called upon to serve as educator, consultant, scholar, political activist, etc. "Building a case" in my classroom is quite different from building a case for a cocktail party tête-à-tête. In all such roles, I will be judged "competent" to the degree that I adhere to commonly accepted forms and adapt those forms in situationally appropriate ways.[33]

Conversely, I understand the arguments advanced by others within a set of expectations, and perhaps even within inferential parameters peculiar to some context. So, when my spouse argues, "All right-thinking citizens will vote for Candidate X for the school board," in spite of the linguistic form she has chosen I know from experience in our relationship that she is *not* advancing a generalization based on nose counts as a major premise for a categorical syllogism; yet, I know she is drawing an inference which is sensible in our association. Formally, she has not advanced a deductive claim; her full argument probably would be better diagrammed as an analogical claim ("Candidate X is very much like Candidate Y"; "You voted for Candidate Y last time, with much satisfaction"; "Therefore, you ought to vote for Candidate X this time"). Our husband-wife context "tells" me the form, warns me not to accuse her of hasty generalization, and provides her inference with force.

While we may be taught technically the abstracted forms for deductive, inductive, analogical, disjunctive, and connective inferential patterns, we can apply those forms only in particular contexts, and *those contexts control the "rules" I am to apply when judging argumentative forms, validity, appropriateness, and force:*

(a) *Forms.* The forms of argument, along with their "special words" (all, some, none, if-then, either-or, like, etc.), are neither innate psycholinguistic constructions nor mere institutionalized constraints, but rather are products of socialization which have been acquired by members of a culture through interaction with others. I am expected to use them so as to be engaging in proper "rule-conforming behavior" while arguing with others.[34]

(b) *Validity.* Standards of validity or correctness, however, lie not so much in the logical form as in the rules for interpreting someone's use of a particular form in a particular context. An argument which "looks like" an inductively derived generalization in some contexts may actually be a hidden analogy, and vice versa. Validity, in social intercourse, seems to lie in judgments given relevance by the context and by understandings or conventions accepted by the interlocutors.

(c) *Appropriateness.* The question of appropriateness—"May I use this inferential process in connecting these data to this claim?"—then becomes a matter of "rule-applying" or "rule-reflective" verbal behavior.[35] As a disputant in a particular context, I should know the range of permissible forms from which I may draw, and then I must select consciously the forms which "apply" to a particular problem (e.g., a school board election) and the inferential rules which "reflect" standards usually used in settling this sort of problem (e.g., for whom to vote). Appropriateness, then, is determined partially by context, partially by mutually agreed-upon standards-for-judgment, and partially by the problem area.

(d) *Force.* In the case of logical patterns of inference and their applicability to social argumentation, then, an argument has force in a dispute insofar as (1) it conforms to reasoning patterns sanctioned by my society, (2) it is understood to be valid within the conventionalized agreements of the participants, and (3) it is appropriate to the context, the judgmental standards, and the problem at hand.

If, as a disputant, I can construct so-called logical arguments so as to meet these three conditions, I fully expect them to make serious demands upon my opponent. If my argument somehow fails in one or more of these conditions, it will lose its coerciveness *even though* it is in perfect syllogistic or analogical form. The crucial condition, in such disputes, is the appropriateness test: if a given pattern is deemed inappropriate to a particular context, all of its force dissipates. So, if I attempt to convince a friend to become a Lutheran by pointing to all of the good people who are Lutherans, I should expect that form to have no force because he and I know we agree that questions of religion and morals are not subject to inductive procedures; an inductive inference is inappropriate to the question at hand within our social framework.

Logical connectives and their use in argumentation, in summary, never can be separated from contexts, persons, and problem areas. That is because they are backed by social rules—interpersonal agreements as to their form, validity, appropriateness, and hence force.

Concluding Thoughts

In the heart of this essay, we have explored three general classes of inference—everyday, special-topical, and logical warrants—and have examined briefly three sorts of rules (constitutive, institutional, and social) which might explain how such inferences gain force in our argumentative lives. A good reductionist, of course, might wish to collapse these three categories into one, bravely declaring that all "rules" ultimately are social rules and hence all inferential families are intermarried. To the extent that we view language as a social instrument and institutions as social agencies, the reductionist position is easily defended. Yet, statements about Susan's auntness are quite different from statements about crow's blackness; and statements derivable from codified institutional regulations have only surface characteristics in common with those forwarded at cocktail parties. Further, maintaining the separateness of these three classes of inference may well have certain heuristic values as we go about the business of talking about and teaching argument and "good reasons."

Several important implications flow from the preceding analysis:

(1) The ageless philosophical question—*Is argumentation a logical or a psychological process?*—has been recast. Argumentation, as viewed here, is both logical and psychological activity, because these perspectives have been subsumed under a more general ethnographical one. In suggesting that various families of inferences make varying demands upon us because they are backed by at least three classes of rules, this essay urges an anthropological-phenomenological thesis which drives us beyond logical formalism and psychologism. The work on sociolinguistic conventions, begun by Schutz, Husserl, Searle, Hall, Hymes, and Evans-Pritchard, can and should be combined by specialists in argument to more fully explore the cultural bases of argumentative categories, forms, and appeals. The rules-paradigm enjoying so much interest in linguistic philosophy and general communication studies also needs to be more particularly focused on argumentation.[36]

(2) The scholar-theorist working within the confines of such assumptions, in particular, should begin by building taxonomies of situations. While considerable work has concentrated on types of rules,[37] less has been directed toward outlines of contexts—especially social situations. Rules are situated, disputants are situated, and hence all questions of force or argumentative demand ultimately are situation-specific. Without an ecology of situation, we never will be able to do more than offer prototypical analyses such as this one, and never will fully comprehend the variability in the force of particular inferential patterns.

(3) The rhetorical critic likewise faces new challenges from this view. The kinds of inferences we have reviewed, I think, can be seen in speeches as diverse as Antiphon's "On the Murder of Herodes" and discourses delivered in the House Judiciary Committee hearing on Articles of Impeachment. The rhetorical critic, seeking to explicate *logoi*, certainly has had help from Aristotle and his successors in identifying dominant appeals and premises. But that critic, in

attempting to describe relationships between premises and advisory conclusions, has had less assistance from discussions of the syllogism (or even the Toulmin model) in full or truncated forms. With more careful chartings of the constitutive, institutional, and social rules being observed by speakers, the critic ought to be better able to describe reasoning processes by reference to the respective densities of forms and rules in particular discourses, and to comment upon the force of such forms in actual contexts.[38]

(4) This view also has strong implications for questions concerning the ethics of argument, as Gronbeck and Ehninger have urged.[39] If notions of obligation and responsibility are grounded in language-use and its conventions, then we have returned to a utilitarian kind of Aristotelian ethic, wherein one discovers *ethos* in a speaker's statements uttered at particular times, an ethic which ought to reveal him or her *during the act of discoursing* in thus-and-so a place as a person of good sense, good will, and good morals. *Ethos,* once more, becomes message-bound and situation-specific, with judgments of integrity based on tests of interpersonal validity and appropriateness. Judgments concerning a speaker's veracity and responsibilities can be made by observing the relationships among propositions, conventionalized agreements among disputants, and contextual cues allowing for the use of substantive inferential processes in specific arenas of discourse.

(5) And finally, this essay makes an important demand upon teachers of argument. In stressing the social, rule-governed nature of inferences and their force, it drives the teacher out of abstract speculation and into social interactions. It urges that argument be taught, not only with rationalistic models, but within social-institutional paradigms. It preaches the examination of public exchanges in law, social science, politics, journalism, social milieus, etc. Public argumentation admittedly embodies a hodge-podge of forays, stances, promises, disappointments, and "short-cuts" in "reasoning." Even in that cacophony, however, there appear to be operative rules worth unearthing and critiquing. Especially when we move beyond the idiosyncratic rules of interpersonal dispute, we are talking about practical argumentation which makes the differences in quality of life, which nudges a culture along its way through time and space. Unless we guide our students through the swamps of public decision-making, context by context, we are being less than useful to them.

It is inference—the connective, the leap—which distinguishes argument and arguing from other forms of discourse and discoursing. It is to inferences that we must turn our attention, for in them are theoretical, critical, ethical, and pedagogical questions of fundamental importance.

Notes

An earlier version of two sections of this paper was presented at the Central States Speech Association Convention, Kansas City, 1975.

1. Karl R. Wallace, "The Substance of Rhetoric: Good Reasons," *Quarterly Journal of Speech,* 48 (1963), 239–49.
2. See Stephen Toulmin, *The Uses of Argument* (1958; Cambridge: Cambridge University Press, 1964), pp. 120–22, 184–85. Cf. Gidon Gottlieb, *The Logic of Choice; An Investigation of the Concepts of Rule and Rationality* (New York: Macmillan, 1968), esp. pp. 33–34. Gottlieb reviews Ryle's (see n. 12) notion of "inference-licenses": statements which "license" or "allow" a person to do or say something in a particular context. Gottlieb's attempt to move beyond a sense of permission to a sense for that which is "required" and "obligatory" (p. 34) does not place the same stress on the sources or forces of inference as I do.
3. Toulmin and his most recent co-authors certainly talk about "backing," and offer a good many examples (especially of what we shall call "special-topical" warrants), yet do not propose a systematic theory of backing, one which deals with relationships between classes of inference. See Stephen Toulmin, Richard Rieke, and Allan Janik, *An Introduction to Reasoning* (New York: Macmillan, 1979), esp. pp. 57-61.
4. Toulmin et al., *Introduction,* p. 44. More specifically, most philosophers of reasoning will agree that inferring factual conclusions from factual data is a matter of employing analytical logics, that is, the classic logics of deduction and induction, in one or another of their forms. Such logics, in and of themselves, are analytical (built on tautologies); that conclusion we have lived with since eighteenth-century empirical philosophy and more particularly since Ludwig Wittgenstein *(Tractatus Logico-Philosophicus,* trans. D. F. Pears and B. F. McGuinness [1922; new trans. London: Routledge & Kegan Paul, 1974], esp. arts. 6.1–6.1224 [pp. 59–62]). The Wittgenstein position, however, said nothing about deriving *particular* conclusions from premises or about deriving *normative* conclusions from valuative premises. It was a concern over particular conclusions which led Gilbert Ryle and others in the "other minds" controversy to discuss "rules" vis-à-vis inferences, and it was an attempt to find models of normative or advisory or justificatory inferences which created a large group of twentieth-century "ethicists." For a review of the major schools of contemporary ethicists, see, among others, W. D. Hudson, *Modern Moral Philosophy* [Garden City: Doubleday 1970].
5. The "process-product" distinction has been the subject of recent discussion within the field of argumentation. See Wayne Brockriede, "Characteristics of Arguments and Arguing," *Journal of the American Forensic Association,* 13 (1977), esp. 129–30; Daniel J. O'Keefe, "Two Concepts of Argument," *Journal of the American Forensic Association,* 13 (1977), esp. 127; Charles Arthur Willard, "A Reformulation of the Concept of Argument: The Constructivist/Interactionist Foundations of a Sociology of Argument," *Journal of the American Forensic Association,* 14 (1978), 121-40; and various essays in *Proceedings of the Summer Conference on Argumentation,* ed. Jack Rhodes and Sara Newell (Falls Church: Speech Communication Association, 1980). That distinction urges that we view argumentation both as a "product," a "thing" separable from the people "doing" the arguing, and as a "process," specifically a communication process in which the interlocutors and their strategies are the focus of interest. In part, then, because the product-process distinction touches upon questions of rationality and inference, subjectivity and objectivification, etc., this essay impinges upon those concerns, although it should be

noted that I am using the words "product" and "process" quite differently from the ways the words are used by Brockriede et al.

6. See especially Toulmin, *Uses,* pp. 113–22, 147–210. Even Gottlieb, as well as other so-called "informal" logicians, avoids the word "inference" because it is associated primarily with "analytical" rather than "substantive" reasoning processes. See Gottlieb, esp. pp. 16–17, 33-35.

7. Toulmin et al., *Introduction,* p. 45. They trace the idea of warrants back to royal warrants, licenses, and permits.

8. Frank P. Ramsey, "Truth and Probability," in *Pragmatic Philosophy: An Anthology,* ed. Amelie Rorty, Anchor Books (Garden City: Doubleday, 1966), p. 347.

9. The question of perceptual inferences and what to call them is discussed in Jack Ray and Harry Zavos, "Reasoning and Argument: Deduction and Induction," in *Perspectives in Argumentation,* ed. Gerald R. Miller and Thomas R. Nilsen (Glenview: Scott, Foresman, 1966), esp. pp. 52–55.

10. For enlarged discussions of material logics, see R. F. Atkinson and A. C. Montefiore, " 'Ought' and 'Is': A Discussion," *Philosophy,* 33 (1958), esp. 39–41 (for Montefiore's position); Paul Edwards, *The Logic of Moral Discourse* (Glencoe: The Free Press, 1954), pp. 106, 120, 161–62; and Kurt Baier, *The Moral Point of View: A Rational Basis of Ethics* (Ithaca: Cornell University Press, 1958), pp. 47–106.

11. For a fuller discussion, see Max Black, "Saying and Disbelieving," *Analysis,* 13 (1952), 25–33. An additional observation should be made: In this example, we are perilously close to an analytical argument—perhaps even no "argument" at all. In other instances, however, and especially when we are dealing with more abstract concepts, the agitational aspect of the construction is clearer. For example, as data we might take the statement, "America is a democracy," and as our semantic rule the statement, "The idea of 'democracy' includes notions of 'free speech,' " so as to produce the claim, "America must guarantee free speech." The inferential process here is identical to the one dealing with Susan and auntness; the force has the same fountainhead. The claim, however, is one that *matters*—and one certainly that is the product of synthetic argument—especially in disputes over antigovernmental attacks, pornography cases, and the like.

12. For a fuller exposition of the so-called "speech act" school of ordinary-language philosophy, see Gilbert Ryle, "Systematically Misleading Expressions," *Proceedings of the Aristotelian Society* (1931/32) and his *The Concept of Mind* (London: Barnes & Noble, 1949); see also John Wisdom, *Other Minds* (London: Basil Blackwell, 1952); J. L. Austin, *How To Do Things With Words* (Cambridge: Harvard University Press, 1962); Austin, *Philosophical Papers* (Oxford: Clarendon Press, 1961); Anthony Flew, *Logic and Language* (First Series, 1951, Second Series, 1953; rpt. Garden City: Doubleday, 1964). A second, somewhat distinct group of philosophers, rather than focusing upon the operations of the human mind, began to examine systematically the contexts or situations in which language is used. See P. H. Nowell-Smith, *Ethics* (Baltimore: Penguin Books, 1954) and R. M. Hare, *The Language of Morals* (New York: Oxford University Press, 1964). Two works bridging the concerns of these perspectives are John Searle, *Speech Acts* (Cambridge: Cambridge University Press, 1969), and John Searle, *The Philosophy of Language* (London: Oxford University Press, 1971). Much of what I am trying to say here is a gentle extension of these philosophers' ground-breaking conceptions. For a more recent contribution to the philosophy of speech acts, see Richard L. Lanigan, *Speech Act Phenomenology* (The Hague: Martinus Nijhoff, 1977).

13. This position is defended most strongly by Wisdom in *Other Minds.*

14. See John Searle, "How to Derive 'Ought' from 'Is,' " *Philosophical Review,* 73 (1964), 43–58.

15. Searle's five-step derivation is an attempt to cast this inferential process into formal notation. Carl Wellman, however, argues that this same sort of reasoning usually occurs in a much simpler, two-step process: "Jones ought to pay Smith five dollars because he promised to do so." He terms this "conductive" reasoning, where, in informal discourse, a series of circumstances is assembled by an arguer to support in *a priori* fashion a particular claim about a particular situation. To Wellman, a conductive argument is neither deductive nor inductive, and not subject to tests for validity, for additional circumstances might intercede between the because-clause (here, the promise) and the claim (the 'ought-to-pay' conclusion)—e.g. a later forgiveness of the debt, some extenuating circumstances, etc. Wellman's ideas are interesting, although because of their nonformal basis we lose the sense of "logical coercion" I seek here. But, see Carl Wellman, *Challenge and Response; Justification in Ethics* (Carbondale: Southern Illinois University Press, 1971), pp. 51–83.
16. This essentially was the form of argument offered by Representative David W. Dennis (Indiana) with regard to the issue of IRS files, and by Representative Charles Wiggins (California) with regard to wiretapping. Both acts were construed as legal in one context, illegal in another. See U. S. Congress, House of Representatives, *Debates on Articles of Impeachment; Hearings of the Committee of the Judiciary, 93rd Cong., 2nd Sess.* (Washington, D.C.: GPO, 1974), pp. 398, 392.
17. See, e.g., the speeches by George Danielson (California) and William Hungate (Missouri) relative to the second article of impeachment and to definitions of "high crimes and misdemeanors," in *Debates on Articles . . .*, pp. 337–38, 338–39.
18. And, one should add, those inferences normally go beyond "written" law, as in the case of defendants' rights, which in this country were outlined by Supreme Court decisions through broad interpretations of "due process."
19. Technically, of course, arguments from cause and arguments from sign are quite different beasts, because an argument from cause moves from a specifiable "cause" to a specifiable "effect," while an argument from sign moves from a specifiable "effect" to a specifiable "condition" which might have brought about that "effect." Thus, blood on a conspirator's toga is one of the several conditions (along with access, motive, etc.)—i.e. one of several "signs"—a disputant would use to argue that the conspirator killed Julius Caesar. Still the best discussion of arguments from cause and sign, perhaps, is that of Richard Whately in his *Elements of Rhetoric,* 7th ed., ed. Douglas Ehninger (1846; rpt. Carbondale: Southern Illinois University Press, 1963), Chap. II, art. 3, "Signs," esp. pp. 53–57. I lump arguments from cause and sign together, nevertheless, because the connectives are quite similar; both rely upon experience or popular maxims as inferential statements.

    A second technical distinction likewise should be noted: I have distinguished between deductive and inductive inferential processes primarily on the direction of intellectual "movement"—from general to specific vs. from specific to general. More commonly, we now distinguish between the two forms with reference to truth conditions. I certainly accept this latter distinction, but herein have relied upon a description of "movement" to keep my discussion of all forms of inference parallel in their development. See, however, Howard Kahane, *Logic and Philosophy; A Modern Introduction* (Belmont: Wadsworth, 1969), esp. pp. 3–5.
20. See Gottlieb, *Logic of Choice,* esp. p. 40.
21. See especially the first two chapters of Searle, *Speech Acts.*
22. Although the distinction between "constitutive" and "regulative" rules can be attacked primarily on the ground that any given rule has both constitutive and regulative features, I wish to maintain a distinction for its heuristic value—it allows me to separate for inspection and analysis secondary features such as families of inference and force.

23. Because judgments of a road's goodness may well be rooted in specific contexts, one legitimately could argue that the rule we are dealing with here is *regulative,* more particularly, stipulative. The translation of the rule then would read: "I hereby stipulate that 'goodness' in roads will consist of smoothness, straightness, etc." To make that stipulation, further, one would have to counterargue that the statement "Goodness in roads counts as $a_1, a_2, \ldots, a_n$" makes less sense than the translation. In the constitutive position, on the other hand, we are not dealing with the question of "proper inferential rule" at all; we are dealing, rather, with personal preference, which has little or nothing to do with contextual meanings of the word "good" (i.e. "goodness" in roads is normally assumed to be a property of a taste-community—a "culture"—or a context). So both a regulative and a constitutive approach can be taken toward material inferences. I, obviously, *prefer* the constitutive position.

24. This idea is developed fully in C. K. Grant, "Pragmatic Implication," *Philosophy,* 33 (1958), 303–24.

25. Isabel C. Hungerland, "Contextual Implication," *Inquiry,* 3 (1960), 211–58; H. P. Grice, "Logic and Conversation," in *Syntax and Semantics, Vol. 3: Speech Acts,* ed. Peter Cole and Jerry Morgan (New York: Academic Press, 1975), pp. 41–58. It is developed more fully—so as to be construed as a fourth class of inferences—by Douglas Ehninger in his "On Inferences of the 'Fourth Class,' " *Central States Speech Journal,* 28 (1977), 157–62.

26. Thomas S. Kuhn, *The Structure of Scientific Revolutions,* 2nd ed. enl. (Vol. II, Foundations of the Unity of Science Series, 1962; rpt. Chicago: University of Chicago Press, 1970).

27. Stephen Toulmin, *Human Understanding* (Princeton: Princeton University Press, 1972), I, 261–318. David Gauthier takes a different tack: he terms special-topical inferences "the *methodology of practice,*" that is, rules-for-appraisal which apply to "substantial" rather than "merely formal" questions. Even though his stress is more on inferential techniques than is Toulmin's, they both make the same point I do; the kinds of inferences being treated in this second class differ significantly from both "everyday" and "logical" rules. See David P. Gauthier, *Practical Reasoning; The Structure and Foundations of Prudential and Moral Arguments and Their Exemplification in Discourse* (Oxford: Clarendon Press, 1963), esp. pp. 95–99.

28. For a historical overview of the innateness argument—normally traced back to Aristotle's *Organon* with its "laws of thought" approach to logical operations, see Thomas Gilby, *Barbara Celarent; A Description of Scholastic Dialectic* (London: Longmans, Green, 1949). The cultural determinism argument—that all modes-of-thinking, including inferential reasoning, are grounded in regulations sanctioned by social units—is promoted in Émile Durkheim and Marcel Mauss, *Primitive Classification,* trans. and ed. Rodney Needham (1903; Chicago: University of Chicago Press, 1963), esp. p. 81. Current thinking about rules—especially social rules—steers a middle, "constructivist" course between psychological and cultural determinism.

29. A full defense of the "social rules" position would demand a relatively complete analysis of the ways in which reality is constructed socially, of the ways in which subcultures develop procedures for practical reasoning and action context by context, and of the varied methods groups employ for dealing with deviant behavior (in this case, "bad" reasoning). (See n. 36.) Rather than list all exemplar scholarly sources for such a defense here, I will note only that I have gathered together references to these materials in other places: Bruce E. Gronbeck, "The Rhetoric of Political Corruption: Sociolinguistic, Dialectical, and Ceremonial Processes," *Quarterly Journal of Speech,* 64 (1978), 155–72, and "From Argument to Argumentation: Fifteen Years of Identity Crises," in *Proceedings of the Summer Conference,* (see n. 5), esp. pp. 16–19.

30. This list of rule-types I adapt from Max Black, *Models and Metaphors* (Ithaca: Cornell University Press, 1962), pp. 109–15, and Gottlieb, *Logic of Choice*, pp. 37–38. These are broad interpretations of social rules, in contradistinction to the narrower focus of, say, Georg Henrik von Wright, *Norm and Action; A Logical Inquiry* (New York: Humanities Press, 1963), esp. pp. 6–7. He understands "rules" more as Searle defines "constitutive rules." For von Wright, "norm" is the broad concept, and "rules" the narrower one. Along with Black and Gottlieb, I go the other way. For a current listing of rule-taxonomies, see Susan B. Shimanoff, *Communication Rules: Theory and Research*, Vol. 97, Sage Library of Social Research (Beverly Hills: Sage, 1980), esp. Chap. 4.

31. Raymond D. Gumb, *Rule-Governed Linguistic Behavior* (The Hague: Mouton, 1972), pp. 37–44. If Gumb discusses rules' social power, Gottlieb describes their technical aspects: "The principle components [of rules] are: (1) an indication of the circumstances in which the rule is applicable; (2) an indication of that which ought, or may, or must be, or not be, concluded or decided; (3) an indication of the type of inference contemplated, whether under the rule it is permitted, required, or prohibited; (4) an indication that the statement is indeed designed to function as a rule or inference-warrant." See Gottlieb, *Logic of Choice*, pp. 39–40.

32. I draw these characteristics from Douglas Ehninger, "Toward a Taxonomy of Prescriptive Discourse," in *Rhetoric in Transition: Studies in the Nature and Uses of Rhetoric*, ed. Eugene E. White (University Park: Pennsylvania State University Press, 1980), pp. 92–94, and from Douglas Ehninger, Alan H. Monroe, and Bruce E. Gronbeck, "Public Argumentation and Advocacy," Chapt. 21 in *Principles and Types of Speech Communication*, 8th ed. (Glenview: Scott, Foresman, 1978). Cf. Grice on implicature (n. 25).

33. Such differences in rules and roles become even more radical, of course, as one moves from one society to another; anthropologists since Durkheim and Mauss' classic discussion (n. 28) have conclusively documented extreme variation in concepts of time, space, and logical connective. Variations in social structures and communication patterns led Edward Hall to assert his thesis that "communication is culture and culture is communication." See Edward Hall, *The Silent Language* (Fawcett Premier Books, 1966; rpt. New York: Doubleday, 1959).

    My general view of social construc*tionism* is influenced heavily by Peter L. Berger and Thomas Luckmann, *The Social Construction of Reality* (Garden City: Doubleday, 1966); my understanding of construc*tivism* corresponds to positions advanced in such review essays as C. Jack Orr, "How Shall We Say: 'Reality is Socially Constructed Through Communication?' ", *Central States Speech Journal*, 29 (1978), 263–74, and, more apropos to this essay, Charles Arthur Willard, "A Reformulation . . . ."

34. This concept is developed as one concept in a seven-fold taxonomy of rule-types by Stephen Toulmin, "Rules and Their Relevance for Understanding Human Behavior," in *Understanding Other People*, ed. Theodore Mischel (Oxford: Blackwell, 1974), pp. 185–215. This concept along with the rest of the taxonomy is reviewed and critiqued by Shimanoff, *Communication Rules*, pp. 119–22.

35. Toulmin, "Rules"; Shimanoff, *Communication Rules*, pp. 119–22.

36. For relevant pieces by Alfred Schutz, E. E. Evans-Pritchard, and Edmund Husserl, see Mary Douglas, ed., *Rules & Meanings; The Anthropology of Everyday Knowledge* (Middlesex, Eng.: Penguin Books, 1973). Dell Hymes's overview essay, "Sociolinguistics and the Ethnography of Speaking," in *Social Anthropology and Language*, ed. Edwin Ardener (New York: Tavistock Publications, 1971), pp. 47-93, is most helpful. The work of ethnomethodologists, as has been suggested, is especially appropriate. See Harold Garfinkel, *Studies in Ethnomethodology* (Englewood Cliffs: Prentice-Hall, 1967), and Roy Turner, ed., *Ethnomethodology; Selected Readings* (Baltimore: Penguin Books, 1974).

37. For several, see Shimanoff, *Communication Rules,* pp. 119–22.
38. To view one rhetorical critic searching for alternative methods of inference, see Carroll C. Arnold, "Explicitly 'Argued' Content" and "Implicit Content," Chapters III and IV in *The Criticism of Oral Rhetoric* (Columbus: Charles E. Merrill, 1974). The same impulse for finding rhetorical relevance in inference patterns and connectives is visible in Richard Weaver, "Edmund Burke and the Argument from Circumstance," "Abraham Lincoln and the Argument from Definition," and "Some Rhetorical Aspects of Grammatical Categories," in his *The Ethics of Rhetoric* (Chicago: Henry Regnery, 1953), pp. 55–84, 85–114, and 115–42.
39. Douglas Ehninger's strongest statement on this subject is found in "Serious Speech, Pragmatic Implication, and Ethics," (paper presented at the Speech Communication Association Convention, Chicago, 1974). Cf. Bruce E. Gronbeck, "From 'Is' to 'Ought': Alternative Strategies," *Central States Speech Journal,* 19 (1968), esp. 39.

A final thought: I have been concerned particularly with rules a disputant can invoke to provide arguments with force. But, what if the argument nevertheless is ignored by an opponent? Within the rules-paradigm, obviously, we would *not* say that that person is "illogical" or, from a psychological viewpoint, is "impervious to persuasion." Rather, one would have to talk about possible sanctions which can be brought to bear on social "rule-breakers." Those who in some fashion fail to respond to a forceful, proper, rule-governed argument would either (1) be expected to answer in kind, i.e., counter with another "proper," rule-based argument, or (2) be prepared for any number of possible social consequences. Such consequences might run from mild scorn to social opprobrium to, in extreme cases, social ostracism. In the case of (1), the argumentative process obviously continues until some sort of resolution occurs. In the case of (2), arguing as a decision-making process has been destroyed, and penalties invoked. For an interesting analysis of such penalties, see Erving Goffman, *Asylums* (Garden City: Doubleday, 1961).

Cicero's *Topica:*
A Process View of
Invention

Donovan J. Ochs

Scholars of argumentation theory
generally agree that the classical conception of topics as a means of
inventing proofs, while teachable, was essentially mechanical, sterile,
and poorly suited to nonforensic discourse. Indeed, the demise of
topical systems of invention in the rhetorics of the modern era can be
explained by even a hasty reading of the topics as tabulated in the *de
Inventione*. Whatever the relationship between invention as taught in
the Roman schools of rhetoric and invention as practiced by the orators
in the Forum, the topics of the *de Inventione* can hardly be termed other
than mechanical. The question motivating this essay, however, is one of
historical puzzlement. Would a mature Cicero, as a veteran of the
Forum and Assembly, author of treatises both philosophical and
rhetorical, prescribe a mechanical system of invention for a valued
member of his own profession? A close reading of the *Topica* suggests
several answers.

Donovan Ochs is Professor of Speech and Director of the Rhetoric Program at the University of Iowa.

The *Topica*,[1] Cicero's last literary effort in rhetoric, can be dated from July of 44 B.C. (*Ad Fam.* vii. 19). Despite the fact that Cicero claims to be reproducing Aristotle's *Topica* from memory for his friend, Trebatius, the resemblance is slight. The lists of topics which Aristotle gives in his *Topica* are primarily premises and these premises number in the hundreds. The topics presented by Cicero in his *Topica* are less numerous and are not given as premises; instead, Cicero devotes the major portion of his treatise to an explication of the formal *loci*. This emphasis no doubt is a result of the fact that while Aristotle's *Topica* was written to assist the dialectician, Cicero seems concerned with both the dialectician and the rhetorician. The a priori task of both is the acquisition of material for argument. H. M. Hubbell recognizes this distinction when he observes in his introduction to the work:

> It must be noted that the Topica *deals with more than topics of argumentation . . . what emerges is a miniature treatise on Invention, and it seems clear that Cicero is adapting, perhaps from memory, some later Hellenistic treatise.*[2]

I agree with Hubbell that the *Topica* is, in fact, a treatise on *inventio*. If this were a treatise solely devoted to dialectic, discussion of causes, *genera,* and the parts of an oration would be out of place. That the work itself should be titled *Topica* is not, however, unusual. *Inventio* is generally defined as the locating of either true or probable proofs, and since topics are the means by which "true and probable proofs" are located, the title must be taken to mean that the major emphasis is placed not on *inventio,* but on the role of *loci* in *inventio.* Also, Cicero seems to attempt a blending of dialectic and rhetoric in his last two rhetorical treatises, the *de Partitione Oratoria* and the *Topica.* In both he addresses sections to *proposita,* theoretical unlimited questions often referred to as theses. The realm of dialectic encompasses theses; and in his *Topica* Cicero seems to imply (and occasionally state, *cf.* 1.3, 9.41, 12.53, *et passim*) that the topics of which he writes are as much the tools of the rhetor as the dialectician.

DEFINITION OF LOCUS

As a prelude to his definition of *locus* Cicero asserts that the Stoics rendered only partial service to the theory of argumentation. Although invention and evaluation of proofs comprise the two main tasks of the suasive effort, the Stoics, he says, "have studiously pursued the way of evaluation by means of that science *(scientia)* which they call dialectic."[3]

This body of evaluative knowledge, however, must be complemented by a topical art.[4]

Cicero's initial distinction is followed immediately by his general definition:

> *Just as invention is easy when the place of those things that are concealed is designated and delineated, so too, when we wish to track down some proof we ought to know the topics; for that is what Aristotle labeled those residing places, as it were, from which proofs are drawn. Thus it is possible to define a topic as a residing place of proof, that is, argumentative knowledge which renders a doubtful matter credible.[5]*

While this definition approximates that given in the *de Partitione*, an important and illuminating addition is made. All of Cicero's previous definitions indicated that a *locus* is, at one and the same time, a place in which proofs are stored and a place from which something may be drawn. In this statement, however, the characteristic of a topic as something which contains a reasoning process *(ratio)* shifts the meaning. The previous concept of a topic as a container of something inert is now changed. Topics, considered as a receptacle for something akin to an ongoing, nonstatic process, can only be found in the *Topica*. At this stage of Cicero's theory, topics take on a dynamic character beyond their earlier role as mere containers.

The crucial definition occurs at 2.8,

> *Itaque licet definire locum esse argumenti sedem, argumentum autem rationem quae rei dubiae faciat fidem.*

As a noun, *sedes* denotes that on which someone sits, i.e., a bench, chair, seat, etc. By extension, the word also came to mean one's residence or dwelling place. Cicero's metaphoric definition of a topic as a *spatially designated* area, indeed, does retain the concept of topic-as-container in the ordinary sense that anything located in a space both circumscribes and is, in turn, circumscribed. The appositive phrase, *argumentum autem . . .* , however, extends and clarifies not the notion of proof, but the metaphoric use of *sedes*. Were this not so, *argumentum rationem* would be cast, quite properly, in the genitive case.

What, then, does the appositive phrase suggest? The noun, *ratio*, carries multiple meanings, i.e., a computation, respect, course, etc. For Cicero the word usually refers to knowledge (δοχά), that is, knowledge as opinion which is held on reasonable grounds. Therefore, I argue that Cicero considers topics to be categories, types, or kinds of thinking processes. As methods or processes for attaining argumentative knowledge, topics aim not at certitude, but credibility *(fides)*.

Intrinsic Topics

In the *Topica* Cicero divides *loci* into intrinsic and extrinsic categories and lists topics under each heading. I shall first compress his discussion into a diagram and then use this diagram as a guide for further analysis.

Topics

Intrinsic *loci* (inherent in the nature of the matter being discussed).[6]

Extrinsic *loci* (not connected with the nature of the matter being discussed).

1. Definition *(definitio)*
2. Division *(enumeratio)*
3. Etymology *(natatio)*
4. Circumstances
   a. Conjugates *(conjugata)*
   b. Genus *(ex genere)*
   c. Species *(ex forma)*
   d. Similarity *(ex similitudine)*
   e. Difference *(ex differentia)*
   f. Contraries *(ex contrario)*
   g. Adjuncts *(ex adjunctia)*
   h. Antecedents *(ex antecedentibus)*
   i. Consequents *(ex consequentibus)*
   j. Contradictions *(ex repugnantibus)*
   k. Causes *(ex causis)*
   l. Effects *(ex effectia)*
   m. **Comparison with greater events** *(comparatione maiorum)*
   n. Comparison with events of less import *(minorum)*
   o. Comparison with equal events *(parium)*[7]

1. Testimony *(ex auctoritate)*

Each of the eighteen intrinsic *loci* here listed is treated twice. Cicero's first discussion extends from section 8 to section 24. The second treatment of intrinsic topics is protracted and designed for the stated purpose of explaining each *locus* in greater detail.[8] In order to provide an illustration of Cicero's method of presentation, I shall excerpt his several discussions of "similarity," since it is worked out in relatively better detail than most. The conclusions I wish to draw will become more apparent after we see how Cicero treats a given *locus*.

Cicero first introduces us to the formal topic of "similarity" in this way:

> [We can reason] from similarity in this manner: If a man inherits a house which is deteriorated or in a state of disrepair, he is not obligated to

refurbish it any more than he has an obligation to replace a bequeathed slave, if the slave has died in the interim.[9]

Later in the *Topica* "similarity" is explained in detail:

Next comes similarity which has far-reaching ramifications, but it is of more use to orators and philosophers than to you [a lawyer]. Even though all the topics are capable of supplying proofs for every sort of dispute, yet some topics are more prevalent, some more restricted, in certain disputes. For this reason, then, know well the classes of topics. The questions themselves will guide you as to when to use each class. There are proofs from similarity which result in credibility by means of many comparisons. For example, if a guardian ought to be trustworthy, and a business associate and a trustee, and an executor [should be endowed with the same virtue], so also an agent should be trustworthy. This [proof], arriving at credibility by many comparisons is called induction, which the Greeks label, 'ἐπαγωγή. This type is frequently used by Socrates in his dialogues. Another class of proof from similarity derives from comparison as when one item is compared to one item, or an equal is compared to an equal. . . . Hypothetical examples of similarity also have suasive force. . . In this kind of topic it is permitted for orators and philosophers to make the speechless speak, the dead come to life, the impossible possible, for the sake of augmenting or lessening what is said.[10]

What can be said about Cicero's conception of topics upon the basis of these two excerpts? First, we may observe that by a "thought process" Cicero would seem to have us understand a "relational pattern." The pattern of "similarity," for instance, is not given a definition. Instead, we are left in the first instance with an example in the form "If situation A and its legal implication, then situation B and its contested implication." The pattern might be stated as the mathematical ratio $A:C = B:x$, in which the known or uncontested quantities are A, B, and C. To the degree that a listener accepts or recognizes the elements of likeness between A and B, or to the extent that a listener grants the existence of such similarity, to that degree the pattern will evoke credibility.

From the way in which Cicero used the word "similarity" as a descriptive label, we might call this label the "container." Of far greater importance, however, is the content or "thing contained." Within the container of "similarity" is the relational pattern "If A is *like B*, then C is *like x*." Cicero (or whatever possible Hellenistic source he was using) has extended Aristotle's concept of a rhetorical topic as a "container in which is contained the relationship between premises." This change is one of degree, not of kind. Cicero is now stating that a topic (i.e., a formal topic) contains a relationship—a formal, modal pattern. This topical relationship can exist between premises—the Aristotelian concept—and, moreover, the same relationship also can exist between terms, court decisions, historical examples, and the like.

The implications of this shift in emphasis can be seen by comparing Aristotle's twenty-eight τόποι with Cicero's *loci*. For Aristotle, the τόποι produced enthymemes, and the enthymemes Aristotle uses to illustrate his τόποι are short, concise, and not readily suited for amplification. Cicero, by focusing primarily on the element of relationship, expands the scope and range of each *locus*. His topics are suited for oratorical amplification because his notion of relational patterns does not restrict an orator to deal only with premises.

Cicero's *sedes argumentorum,* likewise, can be used to formulate rhetorical proofs. In particular, since the relationship is the key component, Cicero's *loci* are capable of providing the architectural structure for the entire *confirmatio* or *refutatio* as parts of an oration. The *Pro Milone*, for example, is basically a "comparison" of the two men involved.

It should be clear that Cicero has widened the scope and increased the possibilities of the topics by stressing the kinds of relationships into which speech materials may be cast. Nonetheless, he shares essentially the same point of view as does Aristotle concerning the purpose of *loci*.

Let us again consider the topic of "similarity." Its purpose is to secure credibility, and further, to secure credibility from one's auditors by invoking this modal thought pattern which they, themselves, have frequently used. Even if, as probably happened all too frequently in the Roman courts, a jury was unable to understand all the facts of a case, they would tend to believe the advocate who put the facts into a familiar mode of analogical reasoning.

In the second quotation concerning "similarity" Cicero provides four subcategories for the *locus:* one of these types is "many comparisons," which he labels "induction"; a second is "equal compared to equal"; the others, "real" and "hypothetical" examples. All of these subtypes can properly be called formal *loci*, because all four derive their suasive impact from the main pattern of "similarity."

The pattern is readily seen operating in the subtypes of "many comparisons," and "equal compared to equal." Similarity in the other two forms is not so apparent. The *locus* of "real" examples, however, can be shown to fit the pattern of "similarity" when we remember that for Cicero a topic contains a relationship, and that this relationship can exist between terms, premises, court decisions, historical events, examples, and the like. The range of the termini for such a relationship seems bounded only by the orator's mental and imaginative powers. The relationship, however, remains constant, regardless of the comparative breadth of the termini in any given case of "similarity."

Thus, "real" and "hypothetical" examples in Cicero's view, can be used as termini in the relationship of "similarity."

Now that we have examined in some detail one of the eighteen *loci*, it remains to show how typical of the rest this single example is. In Cicero's initial presentation of the eighteen *loci* none is defined in the traditional manner of genus joined to specific difference. Each *locus* is illustrated by means of an example, just as "similarity" was. The logical form of these illustrative examples is interesting. Some are given as Aristotelian syllogisms. E.g., Cicero's example of "definition" is phrased: "Civil law is a system of equity to insure property rights for the citizens of a state. Knowing this system is useful. Therefore, the science of civil law is useful."

Examples given for "enumeration," "etymology," "genus," "contraries," and "causes" follow the same syllogistic structure as "definition." Other topics use an example framed as an hypothetical or disjunctive syllogism. "Conjugates," "species," "similarity," "difference," "adjuncts," "antecedents," "consequents," "contradictions," "effects," as well as the three types of "comparison," are so framed.[11]

Two points can be made on the basis of Cicero's illustrations of the eighteen *loci*. First, he knew and could use categorical and hypothetical syllogistic structures. Second, Cicero does not explicitly comment on what the nature of these relational patterns might be. His definition suggests that they are ways of reasoning; his examples suggest that he views them as processes for evoking belief. Whether he understood the topics sufficiently well to articulate their nature is a moot question. Several centuries later, his commentator, Boethius, did specify them.[12]

THE MAXIMAL PROPOSITIONS OF THE FORMAL TOPICS

Cicero himself does not state the topical maxims, and whether or not he realized that his topical relationships were, in fact, based on logical maxims is not important here. Cicero's commentator, Boethius, however, (ca. 475 A.D.) wrote a work entitled *De Differentiis Topicis*, in which he explains with painstaking detail the role of maximal propositions. Something more than passing comment must be given to Boethius' treatment of these maxims because, as one scholar recently observed, his treatise "became the source for medieval topical doctrine."[13]

Boethius describes in this manner the maximal propositions which underlie Cicero's formal topics:

The residing place of a proof [Cicero's definition of a topic] can be known partly by the maximal proposition, partly by the difference existing between the maximal propositions. Since there are some propositions which are known through themselves and nothing else exists by which they can be proven, these are called maxims and principles.[14]

In addition to being known through themselves and being incapable of proof, maximal propositions can be called topics for the following reasons:

The universal and maximal propositions are called topics because they contain other propositions and through them a conclusion becomes consequent and sound. And just as place contains within itself the quantity of a body so these propositions which are maximal hold within themselves all the force and consequence of the conclusion itself.[15]

The allied concept of the difference between maximal propositions also can be called a topic:

Moreover the differences of the maximal propositions are called topics, differences which are derived from these terms that constitute the question which must be discussed.[16]

In other words, the maximal proposition for the topic of "definition" differs from that of "genus" or "species." The maxim of the topic of "definition" warrants an inference between terms in which a definition occurs, whereas the maxim for "genus" or "species" warrants an inference in a proposition where the concepts of "whole" and "part" occur.

Maximal propositions, in short, are warrants for making an inference, and they are uncontested since they are knowable in themselves. Maximal propositions are distinguished from one another on the basis of the difference existing between the terms of a given question or proposition.

Maximal propositions, as licenses to make inferences, in the sense described by Boethius, underlie each of Cicero's *loci*. Although Cicero does not openly declare that we can argue from "similarity" because of an underlying maxim, the elaborate discussion which he provides for the topic of "similarity" has validity only insofar as one accepts as tenable the maxim "If that which is shared similarly [in two situations] is not characteristic, neither can that which is questioned be characteristic."[17]

We can translate this inference-warrant into one of Cicero's examples in this way:

The accepted situation: a man has no obligation to replace a bequeathed slave if the slave has died in the interim.

The unresolved situation: a man inherits a house that is in dire need of repair.

The question: Is he legally bound to repair this inherited house?

The unstated maxim or inference-warrant: In both situations what is shared similarly is the unusable condition of the two pieces of property. If an opponent denies that the unusable condition is "characteristic" in each of the situations, he thereby challenges the existing law about inherited slaves and is forced to show that the unusable conditions are other than similar (i.e., different, disparate, etc.).

An orator, therefore, can use these formal topics either by knowing the maximal propositions[18] or the labels which suggest the maxims (i.e., the names of the *loci,* "definition," "similarity," and the rest). The very fact that Cicero relies on illustrations instead of defining each *locus* suggests that he prefers to have his student learn a model of each relationship. Both learning methods—knowing the maximal propositions and knowing a model for each *locus*—achieve an identical end, namely a suasive and credible proof in which an inference can be made on the basis of a logical maxim.

Such, then, is the nature of Cicero's treatment of the eighteen intrinsic topics. They are suggestive formal patterns to use in argumentation, and they derive their suasive force from the logical maxims on which the patterns themselves rest. As distinct families of such patterns, *loci* are differentiated on the basis of the kinds of relationships that can be shown to exist between terms, premises, situations, etc.

SPECIAL TOPICS

Cicero also provides special *loci* in the *Topica.* These special loci are designated as "extrinsic," and they are described in this way:

Therefore, this argumentation which is said to be devoid of artistry resides in testimony. I define testimony as everything which is taken from some external matter to win credibility. Not every sort of person has impact as an authority. To win credibility, influence [attached to the person] is sought. Either one's nature or circumstances give rise to influence. Influence from one's nature resides in greatness of virtue, from circumstances, in many components: natural ability, wealth, age, good fortune, skill, experience, necessity, sometimes even a confluence of fortuitous events. People think that natural abilities and wealth and character that have been demonstrated repeatedly for a number of years is trustworthy. Sometimes [this kind of trust] is probably incorrect, but the opinion of the common people is hardly able to be changed, indeed, all those who either plan, or evaluate or think [use the same] principle.[19]

Each of the "components" of testimony—natural ability, wealth, etc.—is treated summarily in the sections immediately following this quotation. Whether Cicero is assuming that Trebatius knows of other traditionally taught extrinsic proofs or whether he is purposely disregarding physical evidence is difficult to determine. Testimony, however, is the only special topic treated.

The special topic of testimony resembles the eighteen intrinsic *loci* in two ways. First, both categories are divisible into "families" of topics. Just as "similarity" includes allied topics, so too does "testimony." Second, both classifications of topics have the same purpose—that of securing credibility. Here, however, the similarity ends. Intrinsic *loci*, when used as patterns of reasoning, evoke credibility largely on the basis of the maxim contained within the pattern. The orator has a variety of patterns available to him once his materials are before him. With the extrinsic *loci*, on the other hand, his available choices are narrowed, since the number of men in any society who fit all the qualifications for influence (i.e., natural ability, wealth, age, good fortune, etc.) is small. The presumption on which Cicero is working seems to be that the more components of influence an orator can bring forth to warrant the credibility of the source, the greater the probability of winning belief from the audience.

The suasive force of an intrinsic topic derives from the maxim underlying each relationshp. The suasive impact of the extrinsic *loci*, however, ultimately must rest on "what kind of person the listeners believe the author of the evidence to be." Although the extrinsic topic of testimony, in actual practice, tends to be subject to a host of whimsical opinions and vagaries, it cannot be dismissed entirely from an orator's arsenal. Knowing that an audience will believe testimony which originates from a man of "ability," "wealth," "age," "good fortune," and the rest, the orator will use these elements as guiding criteria for the selection of testimony and also as special topics for researching his case. As special topics for research, however, the labels of "wealth," "age," etc., must be changed into the questions "How influential is witness A?", that is, "how wealthy?", "how old?"

SUMMARY

From the foregoing discussion I conclude that the *Topica* is the most lucid Ciceronian statement of formal and special *loci*. Cicero is primarily concerned with those thought patterns by which men customarily reason. His illustrations and examples serve to focus attention on the *loci* as enunciated rather than on *loci* in the process of construction. Yet, the process is quite apparent in his illustrations.

The *a priori* requirements for enunciating a proof would seem to be (1) some method for acquiring, researching, or recollecting the material, (2) some method for structuring the material in ways that make inferences possible, (3) some criteria for evaluating the structures, (4) a method for enunciating the proof. Cicero emphasizes the second and fourth steps almost to the exclusion of the others.

Why this exclusion? Many answers are possible. Perhaps Cicero was giving only partial attention to his work. Perhaps the death of his daughter and his divorce, as well as the publication of his philosophic treatises, had dampened his interest in prescriptive analysis. Within a year's time he published the *Consolatio, De Finibus, Academicae Quaestiones, De Natura Deorum, De Divinatione, De Fato, De Amicitia, De Senectute* and *De Gloria.* The *Topica* was wedged between drafts of his treatise, *De Officiis*. Perhaps the source from which he claims to be remembering contained the same flaws. Perhaps, in addressing his treatise to a fellow lawyer he did not feel the need to expand the topics as they might be used by dialecticians. Had he tried, he would necessarily be forced to enunciate the maximal propositions in any discussion of formal topics for arguing a thesis.

Conjectured reasons aside, the *Topica* presents a methodology for inventing matter and form for an oration that is considerably less mechanical than that offered in the *De Inventione*. Although the evidence adduced here is incomplete and circumstantial, Cicero, most probably, did not view the topical system as a mechanical method. Instead, he seems to understand its active, dynamic character, but fails to address, clearly and concisely, its rhetorical nature.

Notes

1. I am using Wilkins' edition of the text as it appears in the Oxford series. English translations are available in the Bohn series and in the Loeb series by Hubbell. See Augustus S. Wilkins, *Rhetorica* (Oxford: Clarendon Press, 1902–03); Charles Duke Yonge, *The Orations of Marcus Tullius Cicero* (London: H. G. Bohn, 1852); Cicero, *Topica,* trans. Henry M. Hubbell (Cambridge: Harvard University Press, 1949). I have found two dissertations extremely helpful: Johann Joseph Klein, *Disertatio de*

Fontibus Topicorum Ciceronis (Bohn, 1844) and Maximilian Wallies, De Fontibus Topicorum Ciceronis (Halle, 1878). Casper Hammer, Commentatio de Ciceronis Topicis (Landaue, 1879), is a worthwhile commentary. Boethius' Commentariorum on Cicero's Topica may be found in Migne, Patrologiae Latinae (Paris, 1891), 44, cols. 1041–1216. Hammer has incorporated the relevant observations which Boethius makes. I have not been able to secure a copy of Hugo Jentsch, Quaestiones de Aristotele Ciceronis in Rhetorica auctore (Gubunae, 1874) which purportedly demonstrates that Cicero did not even read Aristotle's Topica.

2. Hubbell, Topica, p. 378.

3. Cicero, Topica, 2.6: "Judicandi enim vias diligenter persecuti sunt ea scientia quam διαλεκτκήν appellant." Since Cicero immediately distinguishes this "science" from the topical "art," I think we can posit that he is de-emphasizing dialectic in his essay.

4. Cicero, Topica, 2.6: "Inveniendi artem quae τοπική dicitur."

5. Cicero, Topica, 2.7–8: "Ut igitur earum rerum quae absconditae sunt demonstrato et notato loco facilis inventio est, sic, cum pervestigare argumentum aliquod volumus, locos nosse debemus; sic enim appellatae ab Aristotele sunt eae quasi sedes, e quibus argumenta promuntur. Itaque licet definire locum esse argumenti sedem, argumentum autem rationem quae rei dubiae faciat fidem."

6. Cicero, Topica, 2.8. As far as I am able to discover, Aristotle originates this division of άτεχνοι; and ἔντεχνοι; (cf. Aristotle, Rhetorica, trans. John H. Freese [New York: G. P. Putnam, 1926], 134b35). By "inherent in the nature of the matter," I understand the relationships that can be found among the material data.

7. I have placed in parentheses the Ciceronian word(s) to facilitate any cross-referencing which the reader may wish to do.

8. Cicero, Topica, 4.26.

9. Cicero, Topica, 3.15.

10. Cicero, Topica, 10.41. I have omitted the examples which Cicero provides not only to compress the excerpt but also to remove the rather complicated legal applications.

11. Cf. Hubbell's note a, Topica, pp. 422–23. Stoic influence on Cicero's logical notion of syllogistic forms is clearly indicated.

12. Boethius, Commentariorum, 1185a.

13. Otto Bird, "The Formalizing of the Topics in Medieval Logic," Notre Dame Journal of Formal Logic, 1 (1960), 140.

14. Boethius, Commentariorum, 1185a.

15. Boethius, Commentariorum, 1185d–1186a.

16. Boethius, Commentariorum, 1186a.

17. Boethius, Commentariorum, 1190d.

18. These maxims can be easily obtained in either Boethius' or Hammers' commentaries. A complete listing of the maxim and an explanation-application of each would be needless repetition.

19. Cicero, Topica, 19.73.

The Theory of Expression in Selected Eighteenth-Century Rhetorics

Eric Wm. Skopec

In a series of essays culminating in
his keynote address to the 1978 Doctoral Honors Seminar, Professor
Douglas Ehninger described a view of rhetoric in which individual
treatises were seen to be representatives of coherent systems of
thought. Initially, he developed the view as a means of organizing the
"treatises usually studied in courses in the history of rhetoric . . . into
some sort of viable framework."[1] His subsequent work emphasized the
use of systems theory as a solution to some problems in the philosophy
of rhetoric, and he proposed abandoning the "persistent search for a
single master characteristic" or "defining property" which denotes
rhetoric in all its forms. Instead, he suggested, we should recognize the

ERIC WM. SKOPEC *is Assistant Professor of Speech Communication at Syracuse University.*

existence of many rhetorics, each uniquely adapted to the environment in which it functions.[2] Finally, in his address to the seminar, he described the use of systems theory as an organizing principle directing the conduct of historical research. In his view, "the central task of the historian of rhetorical thought is to explore the nexus between theories of communication and the intellectual, cultural and socio-political environments in which those theories arose and flourished.[3] This is our "natural task" because all systems of rhetoric are "embedded" in an intellectual environment and studies which ignore this fact are devoid of interest. He writes:

> *Bereft of their intellectual, cultural, and socio-political environments, accounts of what rhetoricians have written or said in times past are reduced to the level of annals. Instead of being history in the true sense of the word, they are arid catalogues of names, dates and passages; a record of who said what, when, under the influence of which predecessors and with what effect on those who followed.[4]*

Allusions in the final lines of this claim represent a measured condemnation of philological, biographical, and history-of-ideas perspectives commonly employed in historical research. Systems theory is the recommended alternative and it differs from the others in two particulars.

First, a systems perspective employs a "macroscopic" perspective and defines research problems with reference to broader units of analysis. The units are rhetorical systems constituted by "any organized, consistent, coherent way of talking about" practical discourse. A system may be found "not only [in] the rhetoric embodied in a single treatise, but also the rhetoric embodied collectively in the treatises of a given place or period."[5] Such a unit extends "over an entire genus of treatises [and] submerges differences and details so as to call forth the common characteristics of rhetorical systems as organized wholes—the parts of which they are composed, the joints at which they are articulated, and the weaknesses to which they are prone."[6] In contrast, traditional perspectives generally select "microscopic" phenomena for analysis. These are concepts or doctrines found in single texts or a series of texts by a single author or school. Exploring these topics may involve secondary reliance on other materials, but the research problems are defined with reference to a very limited number of documents.

Systems historiography also differs from conventional frames in selecting the context within which rhetorical phenomena are explained. Here again, nonsystems perspectives typically choose a far narrower and more precisely defined body of material. For example, textual studies generally take a single document to be the context for explaining its components. Biographical studies employ the works by a single author as the context, and studies of rhetorical schools expand the range to works composed by members of the school. Influence studies employ works with which the author in question was known to be familiar; and history-of-ideas studies examine sequential expressions of concepts or ideas. In contrast, systems historiography calls for the historian to take the total intellectual environment in which ideas were presented as the explanatory context. The context for explanation of a system is nothing less than the total "intellectual, cultural and socio-political environment" in which the rhetorical system functioned. Naturally, exposition will be more selective, but the selection is made for convenience of reporting—not as a means of limiting the interpretive context.

As described, systems historiography has a unique ability to isolate rhetorical phenomena obscured by other historiographic procedures. It also provides a more comprehensive explanation of some theories by directing attention to a broad range of contemporaneous developments which might otherwise be thought irrelevant. The purpose of this essay is to demonstrate the historiographic value of systems theory by explicating a rhetorical system which has previously been unreported. I argue that a select group of eighteenth-century theorists who defined rhetoric as fine art constitute a *sui generis* system, and explore the contextual developments which made this view viable in its own era. In conclusion, I suggest that recognizing the existence of this system offers insight into the demise of rhetoric in the nineteenth century.

THE EXPRESSIONIST SYSTEM

The rhetorical system here described is represented by the writings of a diverse group of theorists who defined rhetoric to be a "fine art" and considered it to be closely related to those arts which produce material objects. Table I lists some of the more prominent participants in this system. Each thought rhetoric could be best understood by focusing attention on the characteristics it shares with the arts listed in the final column of the table.

These enumerations imply that the products of rhetoric (speeches and some forms of literature) are to be judged by aesthetic criteria, and these criteria were understood to reflect the ability of an art work to appeal to unique mental faculties. In fact, the ability to appeal to an aesthetic sense intermediate between mental activity and physical sensation was taken to be the common feature of the arts and several

Table 1: Rhetoric and the Fine Arts

(1)	**Charles Perrault** *Le Cabinet des Beaux Arts* (1695)	Eloquence, Poetry, Music, Architecture, Painting, Sculpture, Perspective, and Mechanics. Of these, the first three are "set to one side" because they deal with "purely spiritual matters and are expressed by the spoken word and by the voice."
(2)	**Jean Baptiste DuBos** *Critical Reflections on Poetry, Painting, and Music* (trans. 1748)	Eloquence and Declamation are compared to Poetry, Painting, and Music.
(3)	**Anonymous** *The Polite Arts* (1749)	Poetry, Painting, Music, Architecture, and Eloquence.
(4)	**Edmund Burke** *A Philosophical Inquiry into the Origin of Our Ideas of the Sublime And Beautiful* (1756)	No explicit list of the fine arts, but draws examples from Music, Painting, Architecture, Gardening, Poetry, and Eloquence.
(5)	**Alexander Gerard** *An Essay on Taste* (1759)	Music, Painting, Statuary, Architecture, Poetry, and Eloquence.
(6)	**James Burgh** *The Art of Speaking* (1761)	Eloquence, Poetry, Painting, Sculpture, Music, and "the other elegancies."
(7)	**Henry Home, Lord Kames** *Elements of Criticism* (1762)	Lists only Poetry, Painting, Sculpture, Gardening, and Architecture, but makes frequent references to Eloquence.
(8)	**Thomas Reid** Unpublished lectures on the Fine Arts (1764-1780)	Eloquence, Music, Painting, Sculpture, Gardening, Architecture, Landscaping, Poetry, and Acting.
(9)	**William Cockin** *The Art of Delivering Written Language* (1775)	Speaking and Reading are compared to Music; "Polite Speaking" is an art of improving nature classified with Music, Dancing, and Gardening.
(10)	**Anselm Bayly** *The Alliance of Music, Poetry, and Oratory* (1789)	Criticizes the accepted union of Music, Poetry, and Painting, and argues that Music, Poetry, and Oratory are the true sister arts.
(11)	**Immanuel Kant** *Critique of Judgment* (1790)	Arts of Speech including Rhetoric and Poetry; Formative Arts such as Sculpture, Architecture, and Painting; Arts of Sensory Modulation consisting of Music and the Art of Color; and Combined Arts containing Theater, Song, Opera, and Dance.

theorists defended the union of apparently dissimilar arts on this ground. Mark Akenside, in describing the faculties of aesthetic perception as "certain powers which seem to hold a middle place between the organs of bodily sense and the faculties of moral perception,"[7] echoed Joseph Addison's claim that "the pleasures of the imagination, . . . are not so gross as those of sense, nor as refined as those of the understanding."[8] Thomas Reid capitalized on a distinction between mind and body to order his entire theory of knowledge and art.

> The sciences divide into two grand branches[.] One that is employed about mater [sic] and another that is employed about mind. But as these two objects matter and mind have certain connections and relations one to the other . . . ; so there is a large branch of human knowledge founded upon these connexions [sic]. And to this branch belongs all that is scientific in the fine arts.[9]

The extent to which this system differs from its predecessors is evident when we recall that, in traditional classifications, rhetoric, logic, and grammar are united as "arts of composition" or "arts of discourse." These phrases presuppose taxonomies of knowledge in which use of language and emphasis on rational thought processes are assumed to be fundamental attributes of the arts. Aristotle's declaration that "rhetoric is the counterpart of dialectic" is the recorded origin of this premise and the principle was maintained by the scholastic curriculum uniting the three arts as the trivium. Even writers who sought to liberate mankind from the Aristotelian legacy retained taxonomies treating Rhetoric, Logic, and Grammar as proximately related arts. For example, the impact of Ramus' reforms was to eliminate redundancy among the arts so that comprehensive preparation for discourse required instruction in all three.[10] Similarly, Francis Bacon reduced knowledge to four intellectual arts: inquiry, examination, custody, and tradition. Rhetoric proper is located within tradition, and the division which establishes its boundaries repeats the order of the trivium. Tradition is broken into the organ of discourse, the subject of Grammar; the method of discourse, the object of Logic; and the illumination of discourse, the province of Rhetoric.[11] Bacon's taxonomy proved extremely popular during the eighteenth century,[12] and even overshadowed Thomas Hobbes' equally comprehensive division. However, Hobbes also predicates a substantial union between the arts of discourse. In his taxonomy, absolute knowledge is the product of sense and memory while "science" is conditional knowledge displaying the consequences of what is known absolutely. Science is subdivided into Civil History and Natural History, and the latter is the ultimate genus of discourse. Several divisions of Natural History bring

Hobbes to consequences from the qualities of men which include consequences from passions and from speech. Consequences from speech give rise to the arts of Poetry, Rhetoric, Logic, and Justice.[13]

These traditional classifications emphasized rational processes as the fundamental features which unite the arts of discourse. Appeals to passions and emotions were regarded as secondary or nondefining characteristics by theorists in the Aristotelian mold. In contrast, by uniting rhetoric with the plastic arts, the expressionist system made material expression of mental phenomena the defining characteristic of the art. This switch elevated the importance of nonrational, emotional processes because all mental phenomena were seen to have equal status. Coleridge summarized this view by noting that the principal function of the arts, "like poetry,[is] to express intellectual purposes, thoughts, conceptions, [and] sentiments that have their origin in the human mind."[14] For theorists participating in this system, comparing Rhetoric to Logic and Grammar was seen to be uninstructive and irrelevant. More was to be learned, they believed, by exploring the similarities between Rhetoric and Music, Drama, and plastic arts such as Painting, Sculpture, and Architecture. The characteristic these diverse arts were said to share was EXPRESSION. For example, Cockin's *Art of Delivering Written Language* (1775) notes that there is something in Music which affects the hearer beyond measure and then explains:

> *In practical music this commanding particular is called Expression; and as we find certain tones analogous to it frequently coalescing with the modulations of the voice which indicate our passions and affections (thereby more particularly pointing out the meaning of what we say) the term is usually applied in the same sense to speaking and reading.*[15]

Of course, many earlier theorists had recognized expression of emotions as an accompaniment of discourse, but none had made such expression the ultimate purpose or defining attribute of the art. Moreover, none had outlined a rhetorical system in which expression is the dominant concern.

FOUNDATIONS OF THE SYSTEM

In ascribing systematic characteristics to the rhetorics described here, I am extending standard literary histories by suggesting the emergence of an expressionist aesthetic doctrine nearly a century earlier than is commonly recognized. The accepted view is that 1800 is "a good round number . . . by which to signalize the displacement of mimetic and pragmatic by the expressive view of art in English criticism."[16] Scholars defending the accepted view correctly note that the theory of expression did not receive systematic explication in print prior to Kant.[17] However, they fail to recognize that constituents of the doctrine had been explicated in works by theorists who had little interest in art, *per se,* but who so shaped the intellectual climate of the era that no theorist could ignore their writings. The constituents to which I refer are the Cartesian mind-body distinction, generally accepted claims about natural language, and moral theories emphasizing the role of emotion and sentiment in producing belief and arousing action.

By the midpoint of the eighteenth-century, these constituents had been discussed in an array of writings including theoretical treatises, synoptic reviews, and digests intended for casual readers. No member of the literary public could miss even off-handed references to these doctrines, and most readers would recognize their implications for Rhetoric even when unstated. These constituents of expressionist theory were widely accepted and altered the intellectual climate of the era. Traditional statements about Rhetoric were repeated but no longer provided the guiding assumptions for speculation about discourse. The resulting Rhetoric of expression was part and parcel of the emerging Romantic movement. An adequate account of developments during this period requires attention to the constituents of the expressionist aesthetic.

Mind-Body Interaction

Systematic development of expression as an aesthetic concept in the modern sense required careful distinction between internal and external phenomena. Prior to the seventeenth century, these phenomena "were so blended together that it was impossible to say where the one ends and the other begins."[18] Descartes' distinction between mind and body brought an end to the early confusion and, in the process, furnished the essential foundation for subsequent theorists. Descartes observed that mind and body appear to share no common attributes and may be conceptually distinguished from one another on that basis. Moreover, the essential or defining attribute of each is different; this fact alone justifies maintaining that they are radically different sorts of existence. He wrote:

> But although any one attribute is sufficient to give us a knowledge of substance, there is always one principal property of substance which constitutes its nature and essence, and on which all the others depend. Thus extension in length, breadth and depth, constitutes the nature of corporeal

substance; and thought constitutes the nature of thinking substance. For all else that may be attributed to body presupposes extension, and is but a mode of this extended thing; as everything that we find in mind is but so many diverse forms of thinking. Thus, for example, we cannot conceive figure but as an extended thing, nor movement but as an extended space; so imagination, feeling, and will, only exist in a thinking thing.[19]

While the concepts, mind and body, could be distinguished from one another, it was obvious to most theorists following Descartes that neither actually exists independent of the other. This fact gave rise to a secondary problem of determining the relationship between these forms of existence. Several alternatives were explored. Hobbes and Hartley maintained that mental phenomena are merely particular consequences of physical activity while Berkeley and Hume argued that physical objects are mere illusions resulting from the mind's attention to its ideas. Neither of these extremes were widely accepted, and most members of the literary public agreed with Thomas Reid's assessment: denying the uniqueness of mind and body is absurd and an affront to common sense.[20]

The common philosophical view was that mind and body exist simultaneously in each person and that these two aspects of the individual are in a constant state of interaction. Support for this view was found in the fact that mental phenomena produce physical changes—as embarrassment produces a red face—and physical events such as illness affect mental processes. This combination of mental and physical aspects of man was seen to be an unavoidable consequence of human nature which could not be fully explained, but which had important consequences for the fine arts. The pleasures of the soul, Montesquieu argued, are distinct from those of the body and the perfection of art consists in manipulating physical representations to give maximum pleasure to the soul. He wrote:

The way in which we are constituted is entirely arbitrary. We could have been made as we are or differently; but if we had been made differently, we would have felt differently; an organ more or less in our machine would have produced a new eloquence, a new poetry; a different make-up of the same organs would have produced still another kind of poetry.[21]

Use of physical representation to express mental phenomena was made possible by the interaction between mind and body. Positing such interaction had important implications for theories of all the arts of expression, and it produced two consequences of unique importance to Rhetoric. First, some writers recognized the interaction between mind and body in the presentation of effective messages. DuBos maintained that the "chief merit of a declaimer, is to move himself" because "the internal emotion of a speaker throws a pathos into his tone and gesture which neither art nor study are able to produce."[22] Although anticipations of this belief include a number of classical sources such as Cicero, Quintilian, and Horace, simple attribution overlooks the special currency given the doctrine by eighteenth-century theories of human nature.

The second unique consequence of this doctrine resulted from its conjunction with analysis of human sensory apparatus. Perception was taken to be a process in which each sensory modality produced distinct mental contents. Locke and the empiricists called these contents "ideas" or, in Hume's detailed analysis, "ideas and impressions." Reid and kindred theorists preferred to call such contents "conceptions."[23] In both cases, an auditor's response to art was understood to depend on the mental contents created by his perception of the object. The number and impact of the contents created was seen to be a function of the number of sensory modalities addressed. In this regard, eloquence was believed to be pre-eminent because the number of sensory modalities invoked by the speaker gave him unrivaled access to the mind of his auditor. "There is no earthly object," James Burgh maintained, "capable of making such various, and such forcible impressions upon the human mind, as the consummate speaker."[24]

Natural Signs

The second component of the emerging expression theory of art resulted from analyses of linguistic signification. Language was seen to be an image of the mind and figurative speech was seen to be particularly indicative of an individual's feelings. Joseph Priestley aptly summarized the emerging theory in the following passage.

> *Figurative speech . . . is indicative of a person's real feelings and state of mind, not by means of the words it consists of, considered as* signs of separate ideas, *and interpreted according to their common acceptation; but as* circumstances *naturally attending those feelings which compose any state of mind. Those figurative expressions, therefore, are scarce considered and attended to as words, but are viewed in the same light as* attitudes, gestures, *and* looks, *which are infinitely more expressive of sentiments and feelings than words can possibly be.*[25]

Words were taken to be "artificial signs," and many writers were fascinated by the relationship between mental images and linguistic signs. However, an even more significant development was systematic attention to nonverbal forms of expression. Francis Bacon had observed that the "lineaments of the body do disclose the disposition and inclination of the mind in general [and that] . . . the countenance and parts . . . do further disclose the present humor and state of the mind and will."[26] Bacon was confident that the correspondence between physical features and mental dispositions "was no less comprehensible by art" than other phenomena, but believed that then current learning was deficient and marked this as an area for further study.

Coincidentally, Descartes observed that inherited lore concerning the passions was defective;[27] the combined recommendations of Bacon and Descartes were sufficient to call forth a number of efforts to catalogue the emotions and to describe their effects. Although of limited theoretic interest, such catalogues were well received and provided the materials with which subsequent rhetoricians worked.[28] There was general agreement concerning the potential of the human constitution for signification. James Burgh maintained that "every part of the human frame contributes to express the passions and emotions of the mind,"[29] and other theorists offered more precise enumerations. For example, Henry Home, Lord Kames, began by distinguishing between voluntary and involuntary signs, and further subdivided voluntary signs into arbitrary and natural varieties. Signs of the countenance were divided into those which are "temporary, making their appearance with the emotions that produce them, and vanish with these emotions," and permanent signs which display long-term dispositions or tempers. All involuntary signs were said to be natural with the enumeration including tones of voice, "attitudes or gestures that naturally accompany certain emotions," and expressions "displayed upon the countenance" such as smiling and frowning.[30]

The designation "natural" for signs of this type carries a double sense in the prevalent descriptions. On the one hand, it was used to distinguish such signs from those of human invention. In this sense, natural signs are contrasted with words which are called "arbitrary" or "instituted," and with writing which is said to be even further removed from natural processes. On the other hand, "nature" was said to be the active agent in composing such signs. "Nature," Burgh explained, "has given to every emotion of the mind its proper outward expression."[31] The popularity of natural endowment is evident in the fact that it appealed to empiricists who maintained that all knowledge has its origin in experience and to others who claimed that essential components of human knowledge are known prior to experience. According to the empiricists' version, the capacity for signification is incidental to human nature and the expressive capacity arises from the fact that all individuals are constituted according to the same principles. Individuals learn to recognize natural signs in the activities of others through experience with their own physiological processes.[32] In the anti-empiricist view, natural signs are the direct product of natural intervention and their signification is known prior to experience. For Kames, the operation of such signs must be ascribed to "the original constitution of human nature" because their meanings could not be determined from experience.[33] Thomas Reid's position is equally strong and his doctrines are somewhat more explicit. He described these signs by saying that the "connection between sign and signified is not only established by nature, but discovered to us by a natural principle, without reasoning or experience." He maintained that all men understand this language without instruction and its operation appears to be akin to reminiscence. The ability to interpret such signs is "latent in the mind." We intuitively recognize them in others and understand their meaning without deliberation.[34]

Distinctions between the strong and weak versions of this theory were of minor concern to the rhetoricians of the era because both maintained that such signs were particularly efficacious in the expression of emotion. DuBos explained this characteristic as follows:

> *Words must first excite those ideas, whereof they are only arbitrary signs. These ideas must be ranged afterwards in the imagination, and form such pictures as move and engage us. All these operations, 'tis true, are soon done; but it is an uncontestable principle in mechanics, that the multiplicity of springs always debilitates the movement, by reason that one spring never communicates to another all the motion it has received. Besides, one of these operations (that which is performed when the word excites the idea it signifies) is not done by virtue of the laws of nature; but is partly artificial. Those objects therefore, which are exhibited to us . . . by natural signs, must certainly operate with greater expedition.*[35]

This greater expedition in addressing the emotions was of particular significance to the rhetoricians of the day because prevailing theories of belief and motivation emphasized the role of the passions in directing conduct.

Belief and Motivation

The theory described here viewed material expression of mental phenomena through artificial and natural signs to be an essential operation of Rhetoric and the other fine arts. However, it also recognized that the quality of expressions affects the reactions of an audience. Although the ability to produce audience reaction was not seen to be a characteristic attribute as it was in communicative and pragmatic theories of art, this ability is seen to be a natural attendant of an orator's expressions. Historically, this coincidental association of expression with audience response is important because it helps to explain the transition from classical to romantic theories of discourse.

The significance of expression and emotional arousal in romantic literary theory is well known, and intrusions of such theory into rhetorical works are now suspect. Under the influence of Romanticism, Rhetoric is said to have abandoned its interest in pragmatic communication and to have suffered as a consequence. Witness David Kaufer's juxtaposition of classical and romantic theories:

> The views of Classical and Romantic theories approximate the very extremes of idea types. Ancient theorists—tending to ground rhetoric in transparent cultural norms, identify language with the enforcement of these norms, and neglect the possibilities of language in personal expression—offer a theory of language "locked into" the observer's perspective. Much of Romantic rhetorical theory, on the other hand, carries opacity assumptions to the extreme . . .—leaving it to the single perceiver to define rhetorical situations from an idiosyncratic perspective, disparaging the instrumental function of language, and raising self-expression to the highest social art.[36]

The neat contrast between instrumental and expressive views of discourse is commonplace, but its applicability to eighteenth-century rhetorics is marred by the failure to recognize that then prevailing theories of human motivation made the appropriate expression of emotion the surest means of accomplishing persuasive objectives.

Marking the connection between moral theory and Rhetoric, Francis Hutcheson argued that "upon this moral Sense is founded all the Power of the orator."[37] Not all theorists subscribed to Hutcheson's particular moral sense theory, and alternatives included the theory of sympathy articulated by Adam Smith, claims of divine inspiration defended by conservative clergy, and the enlightened self-interest advanced by David Hume.[38] However, disagreements between these rival camps concerned the origin of moral distinctions while the observations used to test each theory were generally accepted. Or, as Hume observed in a cryptic footnote to the *Treatise,* "there is such uniformity in the general sentiments of mankind, as to render such questions of but small importance."[39] These general sentiments represented a theory of belief and motivation to which most rhetoricians assented and which is evident in their rhetorics. The important tenets of this theory include (i) the belief that the operations of reason alone are insufficient to explain human nature and conduct; (ii) recognition that under certain conditions observers experience strong emotional responses to the situation of others; (iii) acknowledgment that emotional response is a strong impetus to belief; and (iv) admission that emotional responses are a primary source of action.

Collectively, these observations concerning human behavior and motivation imply that appropriate expression of emotion by an orator would cause the hearers to feel a like emotion and to respond as if it were their own. Thomas Sheridan explained such expression by saying that "persuasion is ever its attendant, and the passions own it for a master."[40] G. P. Mohrmann has demonstrated that the presumed persuasive efficacy of expression was "a philosophical justification for the elocutionary theory [and] had widespread currency during the eighteenth century."[41] The following examples show that theorists who are not thought of as elocutionists also subscribed to the theory of expression.

Both verbal and nonverbal forms of expression were thought to be capable of arousing the passions. Verbal techniques of expression depend on description of the objects naturally suited to arousing each passion. Hugh Blair's account of this process is particularly well stated.

> To every emotion or passion, Nature has adapted a set of corresponding objects; and, without setting these before the mind, it is not in the power of any Orator to raise that emotion. . . . The foundation, therefore, of all successful execution in the way of Pathetic Oratory is, to paint the object of that passion which we wish to raise, in the most natural and striking manner; to describe it with such circumstances as are likely to awaken it in the minds of others.[42]

Similarly, George Campbell recognized the persuasive force of both verbal and nonverbal forms of expression.

> A person present with us, whom we see and hear, and who, by words, and looks, and gestures, gives the liveliest signs of his feelings, has the surest and most immediate claim upon our sympathy. We become infected with his passions. We are hurried along by them, and not allowed leisure to distinguish between his relation and our relation, his interest and our interest.[43]

The origin of Campbell's theories is a matter of historical controversy, but the pervasiveness of this theory is indicated by the fact that it was championed by both radical empiricists and defenders of common sense. David Hume observed that "the principles of every sentiment, [are] in every man; and, when touched properly, they rise to life, and warm the heart."[44] Hume's most capable critic, Thomas Reid, explained the persuasive efficacy of expression as follows:

> The great force of Eloquence is chiefly to be resolved into sympathy. We perceive the sentiments and Emotions of the Speaker, and when they appear Just and proper, We are seized with the same by a kind of contagion. As in Musical Chords the Vibration of one produces a similar Vibration in another which is in concord with it; so it is in human Minds. Every passion in the Speaker that appears just and proper produces by sympathy a like passion in the hearers.[45]

Finally, the significance of expression is apparent in the growing rhetorical interest in sublimity. The sublime was said to transport an individual outside himself, and some rhetoricians believed effective expression overwhelmed the auditor. The following passage describes the anticipated consequences of truly sublime expression.

> *True eloquence does not wait for cool approbation. Like irresistable beauty, it transports, it ravishes, it commands the admiration of all, who are within its reach. If it allows us time to criticise [sic] it is not genuine. It ought to hurry us out of ourselves, to engage and swallow up our whole attention; to drive everything out of our minds, besides the subject it would hold forth, and the point, it would carry. The hearer finds himself as unable to resist it, as to blow out a conflagration with the breath of his mouth, or to stop the stream of a river with his hand. His passions are no longer his own. The orator has taken possession of them; and with superior power, works them as he pleases.*[46]

Conclusion

This essay describes a rhetorical system which is distinguished by the fact that its participants united rhetoric with the fine arts and maintained that its definitive characteristic is external expression of internal phenomena. Recognizing the existence of this system directs attention to diverse writings in which the components of a formal expressionist aesthetic were described nearly a full century before they were presented in a single coherent treatise. The evidence at hand is too slender to claim an explicit causal relationship between emergence of this system and developing attitudes toward discourse. However, it is clear that some rhetoricians came to regard eloquence as a form of aesthetic expression, and I believe the consequences of this attitude for Rhetoric are evident in two developments.

First, the treatment of the classical canons during the closing decades of the eighteenth century is fully consistent with the expressionist attitude. With both verbal and nonverbal forms of expression valued, the canons related to style and delivery flourished while speculation concerning invention and disposition languished. The rationale for this occurrence is apparent in the emergence of an expressionist perspective. As an art of expression, Rhetoric is charged with displaying the thoughts, feelings, emotions, and sentiments which are already present in the mind of an orator. Since mental contents need not be anxiously searched after, means of discovery are unimportant. Similarly, the order of ideas or conceptions in the mind is determined by natural principles so artificial patterns of organization are unnecessary. In fact, the universality of human nature implies that the order in which a speaker conceives a series of ideas is the order in which an auditor can most readily process the message. Mechanical schemes of organization reduce effectiveness by employing an "unnatural" order.

The second development is the rapidity with which Rhetoric became an object of opprobrium during the nineteenth century. By the close of the eighteenth century, the expressionist system had been impressed on the popular mind but the Rhetoric of expression remained viable only so long as the assumptions supporting it remained popular. The fate of Rhetoric during this era exactly parallels the fate of the constituents described above. During the nineteenth century, speculation concerning the mind-body problem came to be seen as a dead end—formally, a "pseudo problem" or "unresolvable anomaly"—and philosophers turned to more fertile fields. Theories of natural language faltered when observers were unable to identify universal expressions uninfluenced by culture, and the philosophic underpinnings of the doctrine were crushed by the weight of John Stuart Mill's attack on intuition and Common Sense in his *Examination of Sir William Hamilton's Philosophy* (1865). Finally, the proliferation of faculties required to explain mental experiences brought faculty psychology into disrepute and moral sense theories were swept aside with the rest. "When one no longer finds a need for faculty psychology, the need to search for a moral faculty goes too," and subsequent philosophers have elected to study the logic of moral judgments instead.[47] With the passing of the assumptions supporting it, the Rhetoric of expression ceased to be valued. Thomas DeQuincey's estimate of the accepted notion of Rhetoric during the third decade of the nineteenth century displays the consequences. The aim of expression, he said, was seen to be "something separate and accidental in the *manner*," so that the promises of Rhetoric are "impostures wherever its pretensions happened to be mighty, and . . . trifles wherever they happened to be true."[48]

Notes

An earlier version of this essay was presented at the second biennial congress of the International Society for the History of Rhetoric, Amsterdam, The Netherlands, 1979. The author expresses his appreciation to Professor Paul Ried of Syracuse University whose thoughtful comments facilitated this expansion.

1. Douglas Ehninger, "A Synoptic View of Systems of Western Rhetoric," *Quarterly Journal of Speech,* 61 (1975), 448.
2. Douglas Ehninger, "On Rhetoric and Rhetorics," *Western Speech,* 31 (1967), 242. The same argument is advanced in "On Systems of Rhetoric," *Philosophy and Rhetoric,* 1 (1968), 131–44.

3. Douglas Ehninger, "The Promise of Rhetoric," in *H TEXNH*, eds. Richard Leo Enos and William E. Weithoff (Falls Church, Va.: Speech Communication Association, 1978), p. 7.

4. Ehninger, "The Promise of Rhetoric," pp. 7–8.

5. Ehninger, "On Systems of Rhetoric," p. 131.

6. Ehninger, "On Systems of Rhetoric," p. 131.

7. Mark Akenside, *Pleasures of the Imagination* (1744) in *The Poetical Works of Mark Akenside,* ed. Alexander Dyce (London: N.P., 1834), p. 83.

8. Joseph Addison, *Spectator,* no. 411 (1712), in *The Works of Joseph Addison,* ed. George Washington Green (Philadelphia: J. B. Lippincott & Co., 1883), VI, 324.

9. Reid's manuscripts are now housed in the Birkwood Collection at the University of Aberdeen Library (Aberdeen, Scotland). This citation is from Birkwood Ms. 2131.7 (I)(12).

10. Wilbur Samuel Howell, "Ramus and English Rhetoric: 1574–1681," *The Quarterly Journal of Speech,* 37 (1951), 299–310; and *Logic and Rhetoric in England: 1500–1700* (Princeton: Princeton University Press, 1956), pp. 146–72.

11. Francis Bacon, *The Advancement of Learning,* II, xvi–xviii. A most helpful commentary on this point remains Karl R. Wallace, "Bacon's Conception of Rhetoric," *Speech Monographs,* 3 (1936), 21–48.

12. Ephriam Chambers, *Cyclopaedia: or an Universal Dictionary of Arts and Sciences* (1728) set the standard for several generations of encyclopedic works. He begins with a formal catalogue of knowledge following Baconian lines, but anticipates expressionist theory by dividing knowledge of human activities into internal arts such as Logic, and external arts. The external arts deal either with real objects as in Chemistry, or with symbolic objects. Symbolic objects include words, the objects of Grammar; armories, the objects of Heraldry; fables, the objects of Poetry; and tropes and figures, the objects of Rhetoric. (Cited from the 3rd edition; Dublin: Richard Gunne *et al.,* 1740, I, iii.) Chambers' work was in its third edition within twelve years, and other authors borrowed from it extensively. Composing the "Preliminary Discourse" to the *Grand Encyclopedia,* D'Alembert relied heavily upon Chambers, and D'Alembert's version was itself plagiarized by Temple Henry Croker in his "Preface" to *The Complete Dictionary of Arts and Sciences* (1764).

13. Thomas Hobbes, *Leviathan,* ed. Herbert W. Schnieder (Indianapolis: The Bobbs-Merrill Company, Inc., 1958), pp. 75–77.

14. Samuel Taylor Coleridge, "Poesy or Art," quoted in M. H. Abrams, *The Mirror and the Lamp,* (New York: W. W. Norton & Company, Inc., 1958), p. 48.

15. Abrams, *Mirror and Lamp,* p. 82.

16. Abrams, *Mirror and Lamp,* p. 22.

17. The qualification, "in print," is particularly important here because Thomas Reid developed a coherent expression theory of art which he articulated in his unpublished lectures at Glasgow throughout the 1770's. For description of his manuscript remains and examination of his aesthetic doctrines, see my articles, "Thomas Reid's Rhetorical Theory: A Manuscript Report," *Communication Monographs,* 45 (1978), 258–64, and "Thomas Reid's Fundamental Rules of Eloquence," *The Quarterly Journal of Speech,* 64 (1978), 400–408. Peter Kivy maintains that Reid was the only eighteenth-century theorist to entertain "something like the 'classical' expression theory," but his argument is unconvincing. See Kivy, "Thomas Reid and the Expression Theory of Art," *The Monist,* 61 (1978), 167–83.

18. Thomas Reid, *The Works of Thomas Reid,* D. D., ed. Sir William Hamilton (Edinburgh: MacLachlan and Stewart, 1863), I, 274.

19. Rene Descartes, *The Philosophical Works of Descartes,* trans. Elizabeth S. Haldine and G. T. Ross, (Cambridge: At the University Press, 1931), I, 240.

20. Reid, Birkwood Ms. 2131.6 (I)(1), pp. 22–23.

21. C. de Montesquieu, *Encyclopedia: Selections,* trans. Nelly S. Hoyt and Thomas Cassirer (Indianapolis: The Bobbs-Merrill Company, Inc., 1965), p. 342.
22. Jean-Baptiste DuBos, *Critical Reflections on Poetry, Painting, and Music,* trans. Thomas Nugent (London: John Nourse, 1748), I, 337.
23. Primary texts include John Locke, *An Essay Concerning Human Understanding,* 2 vols., ed. Alexander Campbell Fraser, (New York: Dover Publications, Inc., 1959). David Hume, *A Treatise of Human Nature,* ed. L. A. Selby-Bigge (Oxford: At The Clarendon Press, 1888); and Thomas Reid, *Essays on the Intellectual Powers of Man,* ed. Baruch Brody (Cambridge: The M.I.T. Press, 1969).
24. James Burgh, *The Art of Speaking* (London, 1761), p. 29.
25. Joseph Priestley, *Course of Lectures on Oratory and Criticism,* ed. Vincent M. Bevilacqua and Richard Murphy (Carbondale: Southern Illinois University Press, 1965), p. 77. Alexander Gerard's thoughts parallel Priestley's; see Gerard, *An Essay on Taste,* ed. Walter J. Hipple, Jr. (Gainesville: Scholars' Facsimiles & Reprints, 1963), pp. 48–49.
26. Francis Bacon, *The Advancement of Learning,* in *The Works of Francis Bacon,* eds. James Spedding, Robert Leslie Ellis, and Douglas Denon Heath (London: Longman and Co., 1859), III, 368.
27. Rene Descartes, "The Passions of the Soul," in *Descartes: Philosophical Writings,* ed. Norman Kemp Smith (New York: The Modern Library, 1958), p. 265.
28. The following from Monsieur LeBrun, *The Conference of Monsieur LeBrun,* translated from the French (London: John Smith, 1701), p. 7, is a good illustration of such works:

    > ADMIRATION is a surprize *[sic]*, which makes the Mind consider with Attention those Objects which seem rare and extraordinary: And this Surprize is sometimes so strong, as to drive the Spirits towards the place from whence the Impression of the Object is received; and being so much imployed *[sic]* in considering this Impression, that there remain no Spirits to pass through the Muscles, the Body thereby becomes immoveable as a Statue.

    Such descriptions were not taken lightly. This treatise includes forty-three carefully executed engravings illustrating the effects of the various emotions and a description of the physiological processes associated with each.
29. Burgh, *The Art of Speaking,* p. 13
30. Henry Home, Lord Kames, *Elements of Criticism,* II (Edinburgh: A. Kincaid & J. Bell, 1762), 119–20.
31. Burgh, *The Art of Speaking,* p. 12.
32. This position was espoused by Condillac as a means of explaining language without resorting to innate ideas. He adopted this rather complex position as a means of defending Locke's theory of knowledge from the challenge of those who observed the apparent universality of certain linguistic phenomena, and he explained the apparent commonality as follows:

    > This language is natural to all individuals of the same species; nevertheless, all need to learn it. It is natural to them, because if a man who has not the use of words shows with a gesture the object he needs, and expresses by other motions the desire that his object gives birth to in him, it is, . . . a result of his constitution. But if this man had not observed what his body does in such a case, he would not have learned to recognize the desire in the movements of another. He would not therefore be capable of intentionally doing the like in order to make himself understood. This language is not, therefore, so natural that it is known without being learned.

    Quoted in Isabel F. Knight, *The Geometric Spirit: The Abbé de Condillac and the French Enlightenment* (New Haven and London: Yale University Press, 1968), pp. 155–56n.
33. Kames, *Elements of Criticism,* II, 145.
34. The quoted passages are from Reid, *Works,* I, 122 and II, 665.

35. DuBos, *Critical Reflections*, I, 323.
36. David Kaufer, "Point of View in Rhetorical Situations: Classical and Romantic Contrasts and Contemporary Implications," *The Quarterly Journal of Speech*, 65 (1979), 175.
37. Francis Hutcheson, *An Inquiry into the Original of Our Ideas of Beauty and Virtue* (1725), in *Collected Works of Francis Hutcheson*, prepared by Bernard Fabian (Hildesheim: Georg Olms Verlagsbuchhandlung, 1971), I, 237.
38. The principal texts have been collected by L. A. Selby-Bigge, *British Moralists* (Oxford: Clarendon Press, 1897). Useful commentaries include James Bonar, *Moral Sense* (New York: The Macmillan Company, 1930); Dwight Daiches Raphael, *The Moral Sense* (London: Oxford University Press, 1947), and David Fate Norton, "From Moral Sense to Common Sense: An Essay on the Development of Scottish Common Sense Philosophy, 1700–1765," Diss. University of California at San Diego 1966.
39. David Hume, *Treatise on Human Nature*, ed. L. A. Selby-Bigge (Oxford: Clarendon Press, 1888), p. 547n.
40. Thomas Sheridan, *Discourse*, ed. G. P. Mohrmann (Los Angeles: Augustan Reprint Society, 1969), p. 17. Sheridan is here quoting from his own *British Education* (1756).
41. G. P. Mohrmann, "The Language of Nature and Elocutionary Theory," *The Quarterly Journal of Speech*, 52 (1966), 116–24.
42. Hugh Blair, *Lectures on Rhetoric and Belles Lettres* (London: W. Strahan, 1783), II, 192. For a general account of the importance of description in eighteenth-century theories, see Gerard A. Hauser, "Empiricism, Description, and the New Rhetoric" *Philosophy and Rhetoric*, 4 (1972), 24–44.
43. George Campbell, *The Philosophy of Rhetoric*, ed. Lloyd Bitzer (Carbondale: Southern Illinois University Press, 1963), p. 90.
44. David Hume, "Of Eloquence," in *Of the Standard of Taste and Other Essays*, ed. John W. Lenz (Indianapolis: The Bobbs-Merrill Company, Inc., 1965), p. 69.
45. Reid, Birkwood Ms. 2131.5 N.
46. Burgh, *The Art of Speaking*, p. 29.
47. Elmer Sprague, "Moral Sense," *The Encyclopedia of Philosophy* (1967).
48. Thomas DeQuincey, *Selected Essays on Rhetoric*, ed. Frederick Burwick (Carbondale: Southern Illinois University Press, 1967), pp. 82 and 81.

Richard Whately's Theory of Rhetoric

Ray E. McKerrow

Richard Whately's treatises on the arts of discourse *(Elements of Logic, Elements of Rhetoric)* have been major influences on twentieth-century perceptions of "reasoned discourse." Their influence recently has waned in the face of an increasing preoccupation with intersubjective theories of communication. Since the latter diminish the role of external standards for the conduct of disputes, there is less perceived need to rely on systems which advance ratiocinative models of rhetoric. But the lessening of Whately's influence, particularly at the present moment, also stems from misunderstandings regarding his approach to rhetoric. The purpose of this essay is to revise current impressions of the nature of Whately's views on logic and rhetoric and, in the process, to argue for the continuing importance of his conception of discourse.

Wayland Maxfield Parrish[1] and Wilbur Samuel Howell[2] view Whately as a disciple of Aristotle; Douglas Ehninger[3] asserts that this perspective overlooks Whately's obvious links to eighteenth-century presuppositions about human nature. However, Whately is neither the

RAY E. McKERROW is Associate Professor and Chairperson, Department of Speech Communication at the University of Maine at Orono.

Aristotelian he is assumed to be nor is his theory simply the natural extension of Campbell's *Rhetoric*. In brief, these are the views that require alteration in order to appreciate Whately's contribution "in a new light."[4] The reorientation of our understanding of Whately's rhetoric will assume the following form in this essay: (1) the context in which Whately produced the initial drafts of the *Logic* and *Rhetoric*, (2) the principal philosophical assumptions upon which both rest, (3) the relationship between, and use of, logic and rhetoric, and (4) implications for contemporary perspectives on the conduct of discourse.

THE EDUCATIONAL CONTEXT

The classical tradition prevailed at Oxford's Oriel College during Whately's tenure as student and teacher. Aristotle, the acknowledged master among the ancients, was the chief source for instruction in Logic, Moral Philosophy, and Rhetoric.[5] However, this did not mean that Aristotle's theories on these subjects could be transplanted into the modern world without change. In a remarkably perceptive discussion of the culture-bound nature of rhetorical theory, Whately observed in his 1810 Prize Essay that while the Ancients remained "our best instructors. . . . their authority we may surely respect, without paying implicit obedience to their laws: and some portion of their genius we may hope to imbibe, without falling into a servile imitation of their manner."[6]

This realistic approach to using materials from the ancients as they might apply to modern problems was underscored by a common-sense approach toward the relation between abstract theory and practical affairs. This, as Mark Pattison illustrates, was particularly true with respect to the study of logic. Noting the reaction against the technical, verbal style of the earlier Scholastic period, Pattison observed that "Whately, with great naturalness and originality, applied common sense to elucidate the old logic, and breathed life into the dry bones of Aldrich. . . . The ethics [Aristotle's] were now discovered to be an eminently practical treatise; so far from being a string of syllogistic technicalities written in good Greek, they came home. . . . and told us of the commonest things we were doing every day of our lives. . . . Common sense was the only interpreter."[7] Whately's 1810 essay and Pattison's observations suggest a pragmatic rather than an academic approach to the study of logic and rhetoric: the examination of precepts is to be conducted with a view toward their practical application in everyday affairs.

Principal philosophical positions

Consistent with the nonspeculative, pragmatic emphasis in education, Whately abjured philosophical niceties in favor of plain, unadorned advice, whether the subject related to civil liberties, transporting prisoners to New South Wales, educating children, or preparing arguments. Nevertheless, four philosophical assumptions can be gleaned from his various essays and tracts. These will be discussed under the headings of realism, relativism, nominalism, and empiricism. All four have a significant impact on the nature and use of the principles of rhetoric and logic.

Realism

Whately's pragmatic approach towards logic and rhetoric was dictated by a philosophy of realism. Although he never pretended to be a philosopher, or to write above the level of lay readers, Whately adhered to a perspective that could best be classified as realism: an uncritical acceptance of the objects of experience as real.[8] The arguments Whately advanced on behalf of this and other philosophical subjects are similar in many respects to Reid's common sense philosophy, at least insofar as that philosophy viewed objects in the physical world as real and argued for the existence of first principles as natural constitutions of the mind. Three major points of similarity are present between the philosophy of Whately and Reid: a belief in an active mind, the rejection of the Lockean theory of ideas, and an endorsement of "active powers" of the mind, including a belief in the innateness of a moral faculty.[9]

The active nature of the mind, a thesis in direct contrast to Aristotle, Locke and Hume, is premised on the mind's ability to engage in a variety of activities—remembering, determining causality, comparing objects, etc.—in direct proportion to their presence as faculties of an individual mind. Likewise, Whately's rejection of Locke's theories of ideas, and the subsequent decision to speak of "notions," is consonant with Reid's own arguments.[10] Referring to Locke's theory as "a metaphysical theory built on a figure of speech," Whately noted that "when we speak of 'inclinations', 'motives' . . . *operating* on the *mind* we are not literally stating the fact; (as Locke seems to have imagined in his system of ideas. . .) for all these are not *distinct things existing in the mind* but states or conditions of the mind itself."[11] The term "idea" simply refers to "thoughts" or "notions," not to *objects of thought.*

The endorsement of active principles is clearly indebted to Reid's **principal disciple, Dugald Stewart.** Whately acknowledges the use of

Stewart's ordering of powers in discussing affective states which might be appealed to in the process of persuasion.[12] Finally, the belief in an innate moral faculty, though not unique to Reid or Stewart, is nonetheless consonant with Whately's decision to employ the latter's listing of active powers. As Whately observed: "We have, indeed, a certain moral faculty implanted in us which is intended to help us to the distinguishing of right and wrong: this, like all our other faculties, is capable of improvement, and liable to corruption."[13] True to his common sense leanings in matters philosophical, Whately is unconcerned with whether the moral faculty is irreducible to other faculties, as Stewart argued, or is called by other names. What is important for an ordinary person is the knowledge that there is a moral faculty, and that it functions as a judge of human action.

Nominalism

Even a cursory reading of the *Logic* is sufficient proof of Whately's nominalistic bias. Beginning with the thesis, undoubtedly derived from Stewart, that language is the instrument of thought, Whately departs from Aristotle's moderate realism and Locke's conceptualism.[14] Consistent with his pragmatic acceptance of the physical world (denominated realism above), Whately rejected the existence of physical objects standing for such words as "genus" or "species," regarding these as abstract, collective terms referring to several discrete physical beings. A passage in the *Logic* clearly indicates his acceptance of nominalism: "no 'common terms' have, as the names of Individuals ['singular terms'] have, any *real thing existing in nature* corresponding to each of them . . . (as the Sect of Realists maintained) distinct from each individual."[15] The nominalistic bias was consistent with the pragmatic approach Whately took: a chair is physically real, the word "chair" does not have any thing present in the mind; it is not an object of thought, but merely a word for an object. Words are vitally important for thought to occur, for without them there would be no possibility of thinking or reasoning. To say they are more than instruments, or have a real quality themselves, was absurd in Whately's view.

Relativism

This final principle is, in many respects, the most significant, as it affects Whately's interpretation of essence, probability, and the truth. The nature of relativism can be seen in Whately's interpretation of Aristotle's doctrine of essence. Following his acceptance of nominalism, Whately argued that the Aristotelian predicables have no "real" probability as a province of rhetoric, but he did alter radically the premises on which it operates: "whereas Aristotle was concerned with an objective, quantifiable sense of probability, Whately emphasizes each individual's sense of that which 'usually happens.' The claim that is made about the probability of an event is a statement about the speaker's belief."[22]

Finally, Whately endorsed Bishop Butler's view on the knowledge man may possess. Butler's creed, "probability is the guide of life"[23] governed Whately's view of truth: God alone possesses absolute Truth; man's vision is relative to his understanding and experience. Whately affirmed in his 1822 *Bampton Lectures* that "practically speaking, all truth is relative," and went on to illustrate his observation: "That which may be to one man a true statement of any doctrine, may be, in effect, false to another, if it be such as cannot but lead him to form false notions; and that which gives him, if not a perfectly correct notion of things as they are, yet the nearest to this that he is capable of, may be regarded as, to him, true."[24] With respect to the truths of religion, only God knows whether the miracles reported in the Gospels actually took place. The "certainty" man can achieve is premised on his perceptual and reasoning powers. While there may exist a high probability in favor of the miracles, the "truth" is only morally certain, its acceptance a psychological commitment to believe.

Empiricism

Although Whately was not an empiricist in the sense of Locke, Hume, or Campbell, he was nonetheless committed to observation and investigation as means of obtaining data about the "truth" of events. Knowledge, for Whately, was derived from three sources: *nonreferential* (mathematical demonstration), *referential* (empirical) and *a priori* (antecedent conjecture).[25] The latter is employed in a non-Kantian sense, as Whately's illustration indicates: "That any endowed or otherwise *prevailing* religion is likely to have among its nominal followers a large proportion of the irreligious and of the indifferent, is what any man of sense would antecedently conjecture, and is confirmed by daily experience."[26] In the presence of other experience, one presumes to know how an event might transpire. In effect, *a priori* knowledge is equivalent to "educated guesses" while referential knowledge has direct recourse to experience without the benefit of prior information. Whately's discussion of the process by which the mind acquired knowledge of the external world is dependent on Dugald Stewart: sensation, perception, and conception provide the foundation for referential and *a priori* knowledge.[27]

existence, they refer instead to the mind's conception of the quali
objects. Whately contended in the *Elements of Logic* that "our mo
conceiving, and of expressing our conceptions, have reference
relations in which objects stand to our own minds; and are influ
in each instance by *the particular end we have in view.* That, accordir
accounted a part of the Essence of any thing, which is essential
notion of it formed in our minds."[16] That is, man reasons by recou
common terms. These terms are applied relative to the mind's pu
in knowing; they do not simply reflect whatever exists in the e>
world. Qualities inhere in individual objects, but are importar
with respect to the mind's object in perceiving those qualities. '
Navigator, for example, "the *polarity* of the Magnet is the es
quality"; while to the Manufacturer "the *attracting* power of the N
is the essential point."[17]

Just as an object's essence is relative to the perceiver, so to
"probability" be perceived in a similar manner. The imp
relativism on probability can be discerned through an initial ana
the relative nature of certain terms. Whately agreed with Hun
"*no matter of fact* can be mathematically demonstrated; though it
proved in such a manner as to leave no doubt on the mind.'
proof that results is relative to the position of the observer, it is
"certain" than any other matter of fact may be. The "certa
psychological, not logical. Whately described the difference
following passage: "I have no more doubt that I met such and
man, in this or that place, yesterday, than that the angles of a t
are equal to two right angles: but the *kind* of certainty I have (
two truths is widely different; to say, that I did *not* meet the man
be false indeed, but it would not be any thing *incon*
self-contradictory, and *absurd,* but it would be so, to deny the equ
the angles of a triangle to two right angles."[19] Likewise, th
"contingent" always is used *"relative to our knowledge"* of the e
question.[20] The interrelation between "certain" and "contin;
dependent on the situation:

> We say, "*it is certain that a battle has been fought:*" "*it is certain*
> *moon will be full on such a day:*" . . . *meaning, in these and in*
> *cases, that we are certain or uncertain respectively; not indica*
> *difference in the character of the events themselves, except in ref*
> *our knowledge respecting them; for the same thing may be, at the sc*
> *both certain and uncertain, to different individuals; e.g., the life*
> *at a particular time, of any one, is certain to his friends on*
> *uncertain or contingent, to those at a distance.*[21]

This perspective yields a subjective sense of probability, quite
Aristotle's. As has been argued elsewhere, Whately did n

Ray E. McKerrow

THE ARTS OF DISCOURSE

The philosophical presuppositions outlined above form the intellectual background of Whately's view of logic and rhetoric. *Realism* entails a pragmatic, as opposed to theoretical, approach towards the use of the arts of discourse; *nominalism* underlies the analysis of language and underscores the importance of clarity in the choice of terms; *relativism* provides a subjective perspective on the nature of contingency, thereby allowing man's grasp of truth to be predicated on his knowledge and experience; finally, *empiricism* commits Whately to the world his realism posits without question (data is essential in the construction or reinforcement of one's claims). Absent from this reconstruction of the underlying philosophy is any sense of finality or permanence accorded the arguments being advanced. Since man's position is not equivalent to God's, the most he can hope for is to approach truth through sound reasoning. It is to this end that Whately presented the essential elements of "reasoning," considered broadly as the arts of logic and of "argumentative composition" or rhetoric. The following discussion of these arts considers the nature of logic, its relationship to rhetoric, the context in which both are used to promote conviction, and their role in prompting action.

Mary Prior's description of the *Logic* as a *moral metalogic* is an apt summation of Whately's desire to revitalize interest in the study of the methods of reasoning.[28] In addition to stressing the practical value of logic, Whately brought his own independence of mind to bear on the details of the science. While borrowing heavily from Aldrich's *Compendium*, the major logic treatise in use at the time, Whately departed on several occasions from that work's formulations. Whereas Aldrich only briefly mentioned "analytic" and "synthetic" modes of organizing, Whately satisfied the empirically minded John Stuart Mill by using these modes as the major divisions of the *Logic*.[29]

Although "Aristotelian" in the sense that it draws its impetus for the discussion of logic from Aristotle, the *Logic* bears the imprint of numerous accretions to that philosopher's initial efforts. As G.E.M. Anscombe suggests, from "the sixteenth to the nineteenth centuries a mutilated and incorrect version of Aristotle's nonmodal syllogistic theory, cumbered with nonsensical accretions not to be found in him, was presented as the whole of logic, a finished science."[30] Chief among the additions were Whately's assumption (shared by earlier writers) that the *dictum de omni et nullo* (whatever is predicated universally of any class of things may be predicated of any member of that class) was *the* principle underlying syllogistic thought. The first explicit recognition that the *Dictum* was a universal rule did not occur until the fifth century A.D. in Boethius's translation and commentary on parts of Aristotle's *Organon*.[31] Whately's acceptance of nominalism also was a departure from Aristotle's conception of logic. Finally, the "psychologisms" prevalent in the *Logic*—conceiving, judging, reasoning—did not become a dominant part of that science until the Port Royal *Art of Thinking* (1662).[32] These departures, and those noted in a study of Whately's assessment of Campbell's critique of logic, indicate that the *Logic* is more properly considered as a *neo-Aristotelian* treatise.

It also is inappropriate to consider the *Logic* as representative of the "old" logic, in opposition to the "modern" logic of Bacon and Campbell.[33] Howell's disjunctive approach ignores several aspects of Whately's *Logic* which cross the gap created by the characterization of "old" and "modern." The major features of significance for the present essay are (1) logic's relation to truth and (2) its role in the discovery of new knowledge.

The *Logic,* contrary to Howell's belief, does not view truth and consistency as "completely equivalent concepts."[34] Instead, the function of logic is to assess the consistency between and among propositions irrespective of their actual truth. Logic "teaches you only to throw the argument into regular form,"[35] hence it does not tell the advocate whether the premises are *"fairly laid down"* but only whether the conclusion *"follows fairly from the Premises [sic]."*[36] The determination of the truth of the premises is a function of arts outside the domain of logic. The disjunction between truth and consistency is a tacit recognition of the importance of empirical observation in supporting "matters of fact." The truth of the conclusion will only be as strong as the support for the truth of the individual premises brought to the argument. Thus, logic serves as an aid to the organization or "management" of the materials of discourse.

Consistent with the foregoing, logic does not function as the primary vehicle for the discovery of new knowledge. As Whately noted in his response to Campbell's critique of the utility of the syllogism, logic never should have been presumed to fulfill an investigative function.[37] Agreeing with Bacon and Campbell that the scholastics had misused logic, Whately nonetheless scored the "Baconian inductivists" for going too far in their rejection of syllogistic reasoning. The chief utility of such reasoning was premised on the assumption that it was the *sole* mode of thinking: the rules of logic were merely formalized accounts of the mind's natural operation in sorting data and reaching conclusions. Whately disagreed with Mill's defense of inductive logic on the ground that we do not reason *by* such a system, but instead *from* the data it provides. Induction is a prior inventional tool, not to be confused with the rigor of the reasoning process itself.[38] In response to

Mill's claim that "not only *may* we reason from particulars to particulars without passing through generals, but we perpetually do so reason,"[39] Whately argued that such a process was impossible, as the mind was led naturally to combine individual items of experiences into like groupings, and to reason from these general classes in assessing the relevance of subsequent items. More specifically, he noted that: "When anyone talks of *'particular* instances', he should be asked 'Instances of *what?'* 'Will instances of Gales of wind enable us to reason about Poor Laws?' . . . No; they must be, we are told, instances of the same *kind:* in other words, belonging to the same *Class;* and the name of a Class is a *general* term; which is just what I have been saying."[40]

Whately did allow for a sense of "discovery" aside from that provided by induction alone. Distinguishing between "logical discovery" and "physical discovery" or induction, Whately noted that, through a unique combination of propositions already known to the mind, one might generate new conclusions and thereby advance knowledge. This process was particularly evident in abstract reasoning in fields such as mathematics, where the dependence on physical reality was far less.[41]

In essence, Whately did not object to inductive processes, but to the elevation of those measures to the equivalent status of the rules of logic. While such measures guiding investigation may be helpful or even essential, their presence could not offer the same rigorous assessment of the consistency between propositions. Thus, it was one thing to engage in investigation; it was quite another to label the process "logic."

As his pragmatism would imply, Whately did not envision the advocate presenting arguments in strict, formal fashion. The syllogism was not intended for "common discourse"; one should "keep the knowledge of it . . . as a test when (analyzing) any argument."[42] As a further indication that the strict syllogism does not dominate ordinary conversation, Whately noted that the proper logical order of an argument may differ substantially from its most effective order so far as presentation is concerned.[43]

The relationship between logic's province and that of rhetoric is clearly delineated by Whately. Logic functions as a *judge* of arguments: it analyzes the relationships between premises, irrespective of their truth value. Rhetoric *invents* arguments, not in terms of seeking raw data, but in terms of assembling facts into the categories provided by the typology of arguments. This difference is further evidenced by Whately's statement that whereas logic is concerned with the *form of expression,* rhetoric is concerned with the *relations that exist between the subject matter of the premises and that of the conclusion.*[44] The separateness of the two functions, in the midst of a clear dependency, is set forth by

Whately in the following excerpt from an unpublished manuscript predating the *Logic* and *Rhetoric:* "Logic has nothing to do with fine writing; eloquence and even ordinary neatness of expression are quite out of its province; though of course they *are necessary to be* added in practice. Logic furnishes only the framework—the bare skeleton, as it were, of your argument, the flesh and skin must be laid on afterwards. This skeleton need not be kept exposed to sight, but it is of the first consequence that it should be accurately constructed."[45] This statement, which is almost a carbon copy of a passage found in Copleston's *Examiner Examined* (1809),[46] suggests that if the foundation consists of premises whose truth is nondemonstrable, then the ground on which the foundation is laid must first be secured by a thorough-going investigation. Without the firmness supplied by consistent reasoning, the "building" which rhetoric finishes will be weak and capable of being overrun by incisive counterarguments. Hence, rhetoric's ultimate dependency on logic is assured.[47]

Throughout the *Logic* and *Rhetoric,* Whately set forth a system for generating sound reasons as bases for calls to decision and action. Arguments, whether from cause or sign, may be tested for validity by recourse to the standards of logic. The *Rhetoric*'s "rules" for the creation and presentation of arguments are not intended to be rigid or inflexible. Instead, they function as guides to the development of discourse and may be abandoned whenever greater advantage results from a different approach.[48] What may not be abandoned is the central function of logic in judging consistency and of rhetoric in assessing the substantive relation between propositions (i.e., in producing arguments from sign, cause, etc.). The probative force of the discourse is dependent on the skill with which the arguments have been constructed as well as on their inherent "truth" value. In any case, the advocate normally will fall short of proving his claim in an absolute sense.

Whately's relativism assures the centrality of probability in most, if not all, arguments being advocated. Even in reference to ecclesiastical concerns, the evidence and argument approach moral as opposed to absolute certainty. While the arguments may be *valid* with regard to their form, their efficacy will be dependent as well on the strength of the substantive relationship (as an argument from cause or sign) and the relative degree of truth of the propositions themselves. The recipient of such arguments responds with a psychologically-grounded sense of certainty: the claims may be refuted, but their strength leads one to accept them as bases for action.[49] This discussion is not meant to obscure rhetoric's function in managing the materials of discourse. Rather, it is intended as a clarification of the end product of such management: a set of "good reasons" sufficient to produce belief in a questioning subject. Whately's treatment of testimony as a species of sign reasoning further clarifies the content within which management operates and supports the foregoing analysis of the efficacy of arguments.

The assumption which legitimizes testimony as a sign—a reason for knowing that an event has occurred—is that the testimony would not have been given unless it reflected accurately the existence of the event.[50] Only if this assmption can be confirmed, by analyzing the honesty and integrity of the witnesses, can one accept the testimony as a sign of the event's existence. The placement of testimony in this context is a result of Whately's relativism—our knowledge of events is based either on direct experience or on supportable *signs* that the event occurred. If there is testimony to the effect that miracles occurred, and if these reports are given by honest witnesses (reluctant witnesses would provide even stronger support), then there exist "good reasons" for accepting the claim as true.

Thus, testimony provides "morally certain" evidence that the event in question actually happened. Because of our relative knowledge of past events, we can never know with absolute certainty that particular actions did take place as the Jews and Apostles attest (the miracles could be a complete fabrication); hence, we must be content with our own investigation into the integrity and value of the testimony history offers. This is one of the main points of Whately's pamphlet, *Historic Doubts Respecting the Existence of Napoleon Bounaparte* (1819).[51] Designed to illustrate, among other things, that "what is *unquestioned* is not necessarily unquestionable," *Historic Doubts* presents three specific tests for assessing testimony. These tests are: (1) whether the witnesses have access to the event, (2) whether they have any interest in concealing facts or in propagating untrue statements, and (3) whether or not they agree in the testimony given. Whately applied these tests of *credibility* to the newspaper accounts of Napoleon's exploits and, on determining the weaknesses present in them, concluded that it is possible for any narrative, however circumstantial the evidence is for its truth, "*to be nevertheless an entire fabrication.*"[52] He went on to argue that if this is true the chances of truth arising from newspaper accounts are actually less than the chances of truth arising from the Apostles' accounts of Christ's miracles. Surely, he argued, if people believe in the existence of Napoleon, they have even stronger grounds for believing in miracles.

Besides argument from testimony, Whately illustrated the function of arguments from experience and from analogy.[53] The latter form aptly illustrates the convergence of his commitment to nominalism and to empiricism. Whately advised his readers that Biblical analogies were used to convey practical knowledge, but worried that the terms used in the analogies would be taken too literally. Following Reid and Stewart, the Archbishop recommended changing the terms of analogies lest readers confuse words with reality.[54] Furthermore, the method which analogy employs exhibits a joint dependency on empirical resources and on man's intellectual powers. In the phrase "Man is to God as Child is to Parent," the terms are derived from experience, and the relation of the terms is the product of reasoning. Both resources are necessary in the creation of the analogy. This argument form, along with argument from experience, and other forms in the *Rhetoric* function to combine reason with the knowledge of everyday affairs. The end product, if carefully constructed, should be sufficient to command the attention and belief of critical listeners.[55]

Whately's reliance on probable proofs, relative to the knowledge of the individual, does not imply that he "does not conceive of rhetoric as working on the public mind."[56] Quite the contrary, rhetoric's value derives from its use in correcting and preventing errors of thought or action on the part of the public mind. Whately, for instance, uses techniques from the *Rhetoric* in arguing social, religious, and educational issues.[57] His concern, as noted in the *Rhetoric,* was with the identification of that which is both *"conducive to the public good"* and morally defensible.[58]

Appeals to the passions are an integral part of the process of moving the public to action. Determining policies that are in the best interests of the public and convincing people of their value are actions dependent on man's intellectual powers. Once convinced, people must be moved to take appropriate action. In his 1810 *Prize Essay,* Whately, noting rhetoric had not lost entirely the influence it had enjoyed in the classical age, observed that "men still have passions to be excited, imaginations to be pleased, and hearts to be affected: and those who boast of their superior coolness of judgment . . . should remember that Caesar, who was on one occasion diverted from his settled resolution by the eloquence of Cicero, was the furthest of all men from being deficient in clearness of judgment, and firmness of character."[59] Contrary to Parrish's view, Whately did not ignore "the power of passion,"[60] but instead insisted that, because of its power, appeals to passion should be kept within the control of reason.

Man's moral faculty gives him a general sense of right and wrong. This moral quality helps restrain the passions and allows reason to remain in the dominant position. Whately constructed a complex set of interactions guiding the use of reason in influencing action. Because the mind is active, it can "will" itself to reason about any subject. Reason, once actuated, can indirectly influence the feelings by focusing thoughts on an object likely to arouse the passions. The feelings, having been aroused, directly influence the will, thus resulting in action.[61] The following diagram clarifies the interactions.

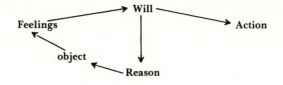

While indicating that one must convince the understanding before moving to the passions, the appeal to action requires the arousal of all three elements: reason, will and feelings. In this complex process, persuasion stands as an indispensable link between initial advocacy and subsequent action.

Whately's view of persuasion can be contrasted with that set forth by Campbell. While the communication of "lively and glowing ideas" is the driving force of persuasion for Campbell, this principle does not perform a similar function for Whately. Although he agreed that the copiousness of an address allows the mind more time to form "vivid" notions of an object, and thereby further excites the feelings, such detail was not regarded as a necessity. Argumentative discourse requires only that the claim be understood, and that can be achieved even though the mind possesses "inadequate notions" of the objects under discussion. In short, the mind does not require a vivid portrayal of an object before conviction is achieved.[62]

Once a speaker understands the complexity of the persuasive process and the role of the will and the passions in that process, he can ask himself an important question: "Is the audience convinced that the proposed action is necessary?" If the answer is "yes," he can move to the second stage of his address and illustrate "the expediency of the Means proposed." This, in turn, sets the stage for persuasion or *Exhortation,* the exciting of the passions "to adopt those Means, by representing the End as sufficiently desirable."[63] Thus, the appropriateness of exhortation depends on the audience's particular situation. A Christian minister, upon finding that his congregation is convinced of the necessity of obedience to God and believes that some means are more expedient than others, may begin with a purely exhortative stance, and by appealing to the passions, induce action in his listeners. Such discourse, however, must conform to certain principles. A speaker or writer, Whately asserted, must "keep on the side of what he believes to be truth, and, avoiding all sophistry, to aim only at setting forth that truth as strongly as possible . . . without any endeavour to gain applause for his own abilities."[64] Moreover, he advised the listener to "form his *judgment* according to the real and valid arguments urged, and to regulate his *feelings and sentiments* according to what the case justly calls for."[65]

Conclusion

The educational atmosphere at Oxford in the 1820s promoted the creation of two instructional treatises. Both the *Logic* and the *Rhetoric* began in unpublished manuscript form as outlines for the use of students and were redrafted to serve a wider audience of students and others who might profit from reading them. Their pragmatic, nonphilosophical nature was consistent with Whately's philosophy of realism. His remaining philosophical assumptions, categorized in terms of nominalism, relativism, and empiricism assured the primacy of language as an instrument of thinking, underlined the probable nature of most rhetorical proofs (including those supporting the truth of Christ's miracles), and secured the importance of knowledge drawn from observation and experience. Within this broad context, logic functions as a check on the consistency of reasoning while rhetoric focuses on the substantive relation between premises and conclusions. Taken together, the *techne* outlined by Whately produce good reasons sufficient for belief, whether the subject be Christian "truths," the transportation of prisoners, or any other social concern. With the moral faculty in firm control, reason could arouse passions to the extent necessary in moving a public, or a congregation, to action.

The net effect of the *techne* was to produce, as Aristotle would have desired, a *responsible rhetoric:* one geared to the free judgment of the measures promoted by the advocate. Whately's intellectual indebtedness to Aristotle cannot be denied. Both saw logic and rhetoric in utilitarian terms, and were concerned not only with matters of technique but also with the refinement of the ethical context in which arguments were advanced. Both saw argument as the central focus of a theory of communication (a fact far more important than Whately's nonavowal of the enthymeme as the chief vehicle for argument). Although they differed with regard to definitions, both affirmed the probable, contingent nature of rhetorical proofs. Their philosophical assumptions resulted in radically different views of the process of persuasion. Aristotle's view was organic in nature, with the modes of proof interrelated via language.[66] Whately, influenced by the faculty psychology of the eighteenth century, separated the functions of appeals to the head and to the heart. In essence, both approached the rhetorical art with a common-sense, realistic view of its potential for use and abuse.

Whately's acceptance of centuries of additions to and alterations of Aristotle's logic, and his desire to rekindle interest in its study culminate in a treatise which is a *neo-Aristotelian moral metalogic*. In his attempt to clarify the duty and function of logic, Whately set forth distinctions which move his treatment beyond the constraints imposed by Howell's dichotomizing of "old" and "modern" logics.[67] Rather than disparage one "logic" at the expense of another, Whately sought to define the powers and limits of both. Fully appreciating the necessity of observation (induction), he correctly perceived that the rules of such a process could not enjoy the same status as those of deduction. Moreover, he likewise understood the limited ability of a consistency-based logic to discover new knowledge. Finally, he realized that such a logic could promote truth only insofar as the initial premises on which a conclusion was based were "true." Given the **preponderance of** probable argument, the role of deduction was limited to insuring, in terms of consistency, that the conclusion "followed fairly" from the premises. Nor was his logic something the advocate used in its formal nature. Rather, it served the advocate as an aid to the proper ordering of reasons for belief and action.

The preceding commentary on Whately's logic and rhetoric alters the argument that Whately presented the "claims of the ancient system in its most authoritative form."[68] In a certain sense, he did, but not in the manner, nor for the reasons, suggested by Howell's analysis. Just as his adherence to Aristotle was tempered by his own philosophical position, his borrowing from eighteenth-century philosophy also was **tempered by assumptions more in tune with Reid than with Hume or Locke.** While agreeing with his recent predecessors (most notably, Campbell) that the province of rhetoric was the management of the materials of discourse, Whately nonetheless differed on a wide range of points. Rejecting Humean associationism in favor of Reid and Stewart's principles, Whately relegated Campbell's central concept ("vivacity") to a small role in the process of aiding persuasion. Furthermore, he sought to redress the balance between heretofore competing systems of "reasoning" by asserting the primacy of deduction as the only mode (a natural activity of the mind). Induction was not less needed, but could not claim the exalted status Campbell's mistaken analysis sought to present it with. Claiming Bacon too would regard the inductivists as mistaken, Whately disparaged attempts to totally supplant a method of reasoning with a method of observation. Rejecting Campbell's phenomenalism, Whately's naive realism led him to abjure speculative philosophy. As a result, his *Rhetoric* and *Logic* were concerned with pragmatic questions, not philosophical observations. While these differences are few, they are nonetheless significant in suggesting the distance between Campbell's *Rhetoric* and Whately's own perception of the arts of discourse.

Finally, one might be led to ask: Is Whately's perception relevant for a contemporary society? In a recent essay, Michael Leff observes that "for Whately, intersubjective agreement is not a valid ground for knowledge."[69] In the midst of the contemporary thesis that "rhetoric is epistemic," and in particular, that it is through rhetoric that social or public knowledge is created, Whately's views seem woefully inadequate, if not obsolete. Simply put, one consequence of Whately's analytic/rational approach is the disassociation of argument and self. An understanding of psychological variables and their effect on belief is important only insofar as such understanding is relevant to the management of the materials of discourse. The "manipulation" inherent in this perspective is tempered by one's moral faculty, hence it is not an attempt to move an audience through deceit or trickery. Whately was not insensitive to the power of party affiliation or deference to authority on the judgment of men. Hence, his system was designed to reduce such influence by an all-consuming attention to matters of rational judgment. That he did not perceive rhetoric in epistemic terms is not sufficient reason for neglecting the wisdom of his choices. *IF* we overlook the particular philosophical assumptions and concentrate on the *techne* themselves, there is much to recommend to the attention of contemporary students of rhetoric, and to its practitioners as well.

The value of Whately's rhetoric for contemporary rhetorical theorists can be clarified by an examination of two concepts of reason. The technical concept, as Paul Tillich defines it, stresses the cognitive aspects of man's powers.[70] Carried to the extreme, it results in doctrines such as those presented by A. J. Ayer and other logical positivists. Ontological reason, on the other hand, is defined as "the structure of the mind which enables it to grasp and to shape reality and is cognitive and aesthetic, theoretical and practical, detached and passionate, subjective and objective."[71] Whately's theory of rhetoric, because it stresses arguments which appeal to man's cognitive powers, relies on a technical concept of reason. The primary difficulty with such reliance, in Tillich's words, is that technical reason "dehumanizes man if it is separated from ontological reason."[72] Even though Whately recognizes the contingency in the world, his primary reliance on technical reason may have as its consequence the perpetuation of a manipulative attitude on the part of the communicator. A complete reliance on his doctrine, to the exclusion of other considerations of reason, dehumanizes man. The proper role of technical reason, as well as for the application of Whately's doctrines within more recent theories of discourse, is "only as an expression of ontological reason and as its companion."[73]

Whether rhetoric produces knowledge within an intersubjective realm or not, there will be recourse to standards underlying the rhetorical choices made. Whately's conception of "technical reason" produces a rhetoric of good reasons; it can rely on other mechanisms to produce a sense of "recognition" of the other in the interchange. Recourse to *techne* need not imply an abandonment of all interest in the other as a person. A person seeking recognition for self and other need ask no more than that the *techne* be fair and reasonable. Within this broad context, Whately's *responsible rhetoric* assures both parties to a dialogue that the reasons will be judiciously applied, and that the substantive relations between premises will be adequately tested. What more can one ask of the *techne* of his art?

Notes

An earlier version of this essay was presented at a program in honor of Everett Lee Hunt, Eastern Communication Association Convention, Boston, 1979.

1. Wayland Maxfield Parrish, "Whately and his *Rhetoric*," *Quarterly Journal of Speech,* 15 (1929), 58–79.
2. Wilbur Samuel Howell, *Eighteenth-Century British Logic and Rhetoric* (Princeton: Princeton University Press, 1971).
3. Douglas Ehninger, "Campbell, Blair and Whately: Old Friends in a New Light," *Western Speech,* 19 (1955), 263–69; Ehninger, "Campbell, Blair and Whately Revisited," *Southern Speech Journal,* 28 (1963), 169–82; Richard Whately, *Elements of Rhetoric,* ed. Douglas Ehninger (1846; rpt. Carbondale: Southern Illinois University Press, 1963). Future citations will be to this edition.
4. Ehninger, "Campbell, Blair and Whately: Old Friends in a New Light."
5. See Edward Copleston, *A Second Reply to the Edinburgh Review* (Oxford, 1810). For a general discussion of the educational climate at Oxford, see W. R. Ward, *Victorian Oxford* (London: Frank Cass, 1965).
6. Richard Whately, "What are the Arts, in the Cultivation of Which the Moderns have been less successful than the Ancients?" A Prize Essay recited in the Theatre, at Oxford (July 3, 1810), pp. 27–28.
7. Mark Pattison, "Oxford Studies," in *Oxford Essays,* contributed by Members of the University (London: Parker, 1855), p. 287. Arthur Prior also refers to Whately's *Logic* as a "common sense" treatise as it concentrates more on practical application than on theoretical issues. See Prior, *Logic and the Basis of Ethics* (Oxford: Clarendon Press, 1949), p. ix.
8. For a general discussion of the various "schools" of realism, see R. J. Hirst, "Realism," *Encyclopedia of Philosophy,* 1967. Whately's philosophical position is discussed in greater detail in R. E. McKerrow, "Whately on the Nature of Human Knowledge," *The Journal of The History of Ideas,* 42 (July-Aug., 1981), forthcoming.
9. See McKerrow, "Whately on the Nature of Human Knowledge."
10. Thomas Reid, *Essays on the Intellectual Powers of Man,* introd. Baruch Brody (1813–15; rpt. Cambridge: MIT Press, 1969), pp. 15–21, esp. p. 20. For an explication of Reid's epistemology in relation to rhetoric, see Eric Wm. Skopec, "Thomas Reid's Fundamental Rules of Eloquence," *Quarterly Journal of Speech,* 64 (1978), 400–408.
11. Richard Whately, *The Use and Abuse of Party Feeling in Matters of Religion, Being the Bampton Lectures for the Year 1822,* 4th ed. (London: Parker, 1859), p. 329. Hereafter cited as *Bampton Lectures.*
12. Whately, *Rhetoric,* p. 187.
13. Richard Whately, *The Judgment of Conscience and Other Sermons,* ed. E. Jane Whately (London: Longman, 1864), p. 9.

14. Richard Whately, "Instinct," in *Miscellaneous Lectures and Reviews* (London: Parker, 1861), p. 66. Whately's discussion of the process of generalizing from particulars is virtually identical to Aristotle's moderate realism stance, but differs in that Whately contends that classifications are based on the mind's purpose in knowing, and not on the intrinsic qualities of the objects themselves. Whately objects to Locke's conceptualism assumption that the "common terms" have meaning only because there is a corresponding concept or "idea" in the mind. See Whately, *Elements of Logic,* new ed., revised (Boston: James Munroe, 1857), pp. 138, 311. All future citations will be to this edition. For a general discussion of moderate realism and conceptualism, see A. D. Woozley, "Universals," *Encyclopedia of Philosophy,* 1967.
15. Whately, *Logic,* pp. 147–48.
16. Whately, *Logic,* p. 144.
17. Whately, *Logic,* pp. 144–45.
18. Whately, *Logic,* pp. 271.
19. Whately, *Logic,* pp. 271.
20. Whately, *Bampton Lectures,* p. 324; see Whately, *Logic,* pp. 333–35.
21. Whately, *Logic,* p. 327.
22. Ray E. McKerrow, "Probable Argument and Proof in Whately's Theory of Rhetoric," *Central States Speech Journal,* 26 (1975), 262.
23. Joseph Butler, *The Analogy of Religion,* introd. E. C. Mossner (New York: F. Ungar, 1961), p. 2.
24. Whately, *Bampton Lectures,* p. 77.
25. For a more detailed discussion of Whately's views on knowledge, see McKerrow, "Whately on the Nature of Human Knowledge."
26. E. Jane Whately, ed., *Miscellaneous Remains from the Commonplace Book of Richard Whately* (London: 1964), p. 168.
27. See E. Jane Whately, *Commonplace Book,* p. 82; Richard Whately, *Introductory Lessons on Mind* (Boston: James Munroe, 1859) pp. 7–9; Dugald Stewart, *The Collected Works of Dugald Stewart,* 11 vols., ed. Sir William Hamilton (1854–60; rpt. Westmead, England: Gregg, 1971), III, 14.
28. Mary Prior, "Whately, Richard," *Encyclopedia of Philosophy,* 1967.
29. John Stuart Mill, "Elements of Logic," *Westminster Review,* 9 (1828), 137–72. For further discussion of Whately's theory of logic, see Ray E. McKerrow, "Introduction," in Richard Whately, *Elements of Logic,* 2nd. ed. (1827; rpt. Delmar, New York: Scholars' Facsimiles & Reprints, 1975), pp. v-xiii; McKerrow, "Campbell and Whately on the Utility of Syllogistic Logic," *Western Speech Communication,* 40 (1976), 3–13.
30. G. E. M. Anscombe, "Aristotle," in *Three Philosophers,* ed. G. E. M. Anscombe and P. T. Geach (New York: Cornell University Press, 1961), p. 6.
31. See Henry Sturt, "Nominalism," *Encyclopedia Britannica,* 11th ed.; William Kneale and Martha Kneale, *The Development of Logic* (Oxford: Clarendon Press, 1962), pp. 79, 272; Morris Cohen and Ernest Nagel, *An Introduction to Logic and the Scientific Method* (New York: Harcourt, Brace, and World, 1934), pp. 87–91.
32. Ivo Thomas, "Logic: Interregnum," *Encyclopedia of Philosophy,* 1967.
33. McKerrow, "Campbell and Whately," 11–13.
34. Howell, *Rhetoric,* pp. 259–60.
35. Richard Whately, "Analytical Dialogues," unpublished MS. in Newman Collection, Batch 38, reel 6. For the history of the "Dialogues" and their relation to Whately's *Logic* and *Rhetoric,* see McKerrow, " 'Method of Composition': Whately's Earliest 'Rhetoric,' " *Philosophy and Rhetoric,* 11 (1978), 43–58.
36. Whately, *Logic,* p. 257.
37. McKerrow, "Campbell and Whately," 6–7.

38. Whately, *Logic,* p. 254; see Whately, "Bacon's Essays," *Miscellaneous Lectures and Reviews* (London: Parker, 1861), pp. 147–49.
39. John Stuart Mill, *System of Logic* (New York: Harper Bros., 1852), p. 142.
40. Whately, *Introductory Lessons on Mind,* p. 57.
41. The implications of this distinction are delineated in McKerrow, "Introd.," *Logic,* pp. x–xi.
42. Whately, "Analytical Dialogues." Quotations appear with the permission of the Fathers of the Birmingham Oratory.
43. Whately, *Logic,* p. 94.
44. Whately, *Rhetoric,* p. 43.
45. Whately, "Analytical Dialogues."
46. Edward Copleston, *The Examiner Examined or Logic Vindicated, Addressed to the Junior Students of the University of Oxford* (Oxford, 1809), p. 52.
47. Rhetoric also functions in a secondary role with respect to language use. The primary role of language is as a vehicle of thought; secondarily, it has the task of communicating thought. Logic is predicated on the first function, rhetoric on the second.
48. This argument is further developed in McKerrow, " 'Method of Composition,' " 46–48.
49. The concept of "psychological certitude" is incipient in Butler's *Analogy of Religion* and is fully developed in John Henry Newman's *Grammar of Assent.* Whately played a significant role in the development of the concept. See Thomas Vargish, *Newman: The Contemplation of Mind* (Oxford: Clarendon Press, 1970), pp. 16, 13; McKerrow, "Probable Argument and Proof," pp. 262–63.
50. Whately, *Rhetoric,* pp. 47, 53.
51. Richard Whately, "Historic Doubts Relative to Napoleon Bonaparte," in *Famous Pamphlets,* ed. Henry Morely (1819; rpt. London: George Routledge, 1886).
52. Whately, "Historic Doubts," p. 264. See pp. 259–64.
53. Whately, *Rhetoric,* pp. 85–108.
54. Whately, *Rhetoric,* p. 91. See Richard Whately, *Essays [Second Series] on Some of the Difficulties in the Writings of the Apostle Paul,* 5th ed., rev. and enlarged (London: B. Fellowes, 1845), pp. 274–75; Stewart, *Works,* III, 287–88, 324–25; Reid, *Essays on the Intellectual Powers of Man,* p. 486.
55. See McKerrow, "Probable Argument and Proof."
56. Parrish, Whately's *Elements of Rhetoric,* Parts I and II, Diss. Cornell University 1929, p. 40.
57. Ray E. McKerrow, "Richard Whately: Religious Controversialist of the Nineteenth Century,"*Prose Studies 1800–1900,* 2 (1979), 160–87.
58. Whately, *Rhetoric,* pp. 471–72.
59. Whately, *Prize Essay,* p. 26.
60. Parrish, Whately's *Elements of Rhetoric,* Parts I and II, p. 47.
61. Whately, *Rhetoric,* pp. 180–83. The philosophical rationale for this process is elaborated on more fully in McKerrow, "Whately on the Nature of Human Knowledge." See Whately, *Introductory Lessons on Mind,* pp. 33, 50.
62. Whately, *Rhetoric,* pp. 192–95.
63. Whately, *Rhetoric,* p. 176.
64. Whately, *Rhetoric,* p. 214.
65. Whately, *Rhetoric,* p. 214.
66. See William J. Grimaldi, *Studies in the Philosophy of Aristotle's Rhetoric* (Weisbaden: F. S. Verlag, 1972), pp. 8, 16–17.
67. Howell, *Rhetoric,* p. 707.
68. Howell, *Rhetoric,* p. 707.

69. Michael C. Leff, "In Search of Ariadne's Thread: A Review of Recent Literature on Rhetorical Theory," *Central States Speech Journal,* 29 (1978), 76.
70. Paul Tillich, *Systematic Theology,* 3 vols. (Chicago: University of Chicago Press, 1953–60), I, 72–75.
71. Tillich, *Systematic Theology,* I, 73.
72. Tillich, *Systematic Theology,* I, 73.
73. Tillich, *Systematic Theology,* I, 73. There are several parallels between the view expressed here and C. Jack Orr's discussion of "critical rationalism" as an alternative to current intersubjectivist theories. See Orr, "How Shall We Say: 'Reality is Socially Constructed Through Communication?' " *Central States Speech Journal,* 29 (1978), 263–74.

Perspectives on Judicial Reasoning

James L. Golden
Josina M. Makau

$\mathbf{I}$n what proved to be his valedictory essay, Douglas Ehninger in February, 1978, spoke on the theme: "Science, Philosophy, and Rhetoric—A Look Toward the Future." With fresh insights that had long characterized his productive career as a student of argument, he demonstrated convincingly the central role that rhetoric plays in the "doing" of science and philosophy. Because rhetoric has the power to generate knowledge which conforms to reality, Ehninger argued, it may be described as a genuinely "epistemic" field of study. He then challenged present scholars to strive for relevance by probing "contemporary trends and developments" rather than focusing on "the reconstruction of earlier doctrines." Only in this way, he concluded, will we have an opportunity to break "new ground" and bring "forth exciting results."[1]

Chaim Perelman and Stephen Toulmin, whose pioneering work in practical reasoning significantly influenced Ehninger's thinking,

JAMES L. GOLDEN *is Professor and Chairperson, Department of Communication, at Ohio State University.* JOSINA M. MAKAU *is Assistant Professor of Communication at Ohio State University.*

share his enthusiasm for the rhetorical study of argument. Like Ehninger, Toulmin and Perelman recognize the important role a "new" rhetoric can play in understanding the nature of reasoning in practical contexts. Joining Ehninger in a search for a paradigm of practical argument, these two scholars suggest that students of argument turn their attention to the legal context.

They suggest, for example, that unlike some kinds of discourse, legal discourse necessarily concerns itself with considerations of audience. And like all of rhetoric, the domain of legal argumentation is "that of the likely, the plausible, the probable, to the extent that the latter escapes mathematical certitude."[2]

The special promise law offers to the study of argumentation has led Stephen Toulmin to suggest that we "take as our model the discipline of jurisprudence."[3] Indeed, judicial decision-making adheres to rhetorical concern for audience, exists in the appropriate epistemic domain, and has as its most fundamental feature a preoccupation with reasonableness. Accordingly, E. Griffin-Collart recently observed of Perelman's work: "c'est dans le raisonnement juridique que M. Perelman a trouvé le meilleur modèle pour l'argumentation et il en a maintes fois recommendé l'étude aux philosophes."[4]

Because the United States Supreme Court represents the highest tribunal in this representative government, this body offers an "exemplar" for our discussion of a model of judicial reasoning. As society's final arbiter, Supreme Court Justices are expected to employ the "highest form of argument" possible in a practical context. By carefully examining how United States Supreme Court Justices reason, and by attending to relevant legal scholarship, students of argument can derive a justificatory model of reasoning to replace the mathematical model promulgated by a scientific concept of rationality.

The model of judicial reasoning presented in this paper seeks to fulfill the above objective through close analysis of fifty-two Supreme Court cases,[5] two Constitutional Law Case-Books,[6] and the writings of legal scholars. Our analysis of actual cases leads us to believe that Supreme Court Justices use a basic four-step process in their public and private deliberations, as well as in the opinions they write to explicate and justify their decisions. Though numerous variables influence the ultimate degree to which each Justice will focus on each of these four steps in any given case, we have found consistent adherence to the following pattern of reasoning: (1) examination of the facts in light of the legal statutes, rules, and precedents; (2) analysis of attitudes, beliefs, values, and needs of the composite audience; (3) invention of arguments, including a critical assessment of their strength or relevance; and (4) justification of reasons utilized in rendering the decision. The writings of legal scholars will be drawn upon as we extend the model's utility to a consideration of the standards of judgment applicable to judicial reasoning.

The first step of this process has two stages. First, the Justice must interpret the facts as presented by the participating litigants of the case. This hermeneutical process is highly complex; the Justices often have different perceptions of the facts. These different perceptions sometimes result in conflicting characterizations as in the landmark case, *Poe v. Ullman* (1961).[7] Describing the relevant facts for the majority opinion, Justice Frankfurter wrote:

> *Mrs. Doe, it is alleged, lives with her husband, they have no children; Mrs. Doe recently underwent a pregnancy which induced in her a critical physical illness—two weeks' unconsciousness and a total of nine weeks' acute sickness which left her with partial paralysis, marked impairment of speech, and emotional instability. Another pregnancy would be exceedingly perilous to her life. She, too, has consulted Dr. Buxton, who believes that the best and safest treatment for her is contraceptive advice.*

In contrast, Justice Douglas describes the facts in his dissent as follows:

> *One wife is pathetically ill, having delivered a stillborn fetus. If she becomes pregnant again, her life will be gravely jeopardized. This couple* have been unable *to get medical advice concerning the "best and safest" means to avoid pregnancy from their physician, plaintiff in No. 61, because if he gave it he would commit a crime. The use of contraceptive devices would also constitute a crime.* [emphasis added]

Justice Douglas's statement, "one wife is pathetically ill," seems intended to evoke immediate concern. This appeal to the audience's emotions contrasts sharply with the majority's less colorful account of Doe's condition. Yet this is only one of the important differences between the majority and minority characterizations of the facts.[8] What is important here is the fact that even in the first stage of the first step in judicial reasoning, Justices employ subtle rhetorical strategies.

Having characterized the facts, the Supreme Court Justice completes the first step in the reasoning process by addressing the question "What statutes, rules, or precedents apply to these data?" At the lowest level of our legal system, the term "rules" applies to general statements of "allowable or forbidden conduct,"[9] focusing primarily, though not exclusively, on "actions that individuals must or must not do."[10] When the rules are clear and the behavior of participating litigants is persuasively applicable to these rules, then the appropriate judicial decision is "simply that decision which follows from the application of . . . the rule to the legal facts of the case."[11]

At a higher level, however, these rules become more complex. Perhaps the most common rule at the highest level is precedent or *stare decisis. Black's Law Dictionary* defines this meta-rule as the doctrine that when a "court has once laid down a principle of law as applicable to a certain state of facts, it will adhere to the principle, and apply it to all future cases, where facts are essentially the same."[12] This rule serves as a warrant[13] in nearly every Constitutional Law case; to a large extent, precedent serves as a starting point from which all judicial reasoning proceeds. The Constitution, tradition, and the tacit agreement of the public combine to lend force to this basic rule of jurisprudence.[14]

It also is important to note that every member of the Court's audience recognizes and endorses the role precedent plays in promoting a high degree of probability, consistency, and predictability. As Justice Douglas put it: "Stare decisis provides some moorings so that men may trade and arrange their affairs with confidence." It "serves to take the capricious element out of law and give stability to a society. It is the strong tie which the future has to the past."[15] Precedents similarly provide argumentative credibility to the opinions Justices write. Use of *stare decisis* gives the Court's readers greater confidence in the Justices' impartiality. In short, precedents derive much of their strength from their power to create a sense of stability, coherence, and continuity for a legal community. The "settled meaning" precedents provide enables the Court's audience to predict the outcome of judicial decisions, and thus "the consequences of their actions."[16] At the same time, a secure body politic protects the Court from executive and legislative encroachment.

But if precedent, as a warrant, is the starting point, and to some degree, the core of judicial reasoning, its use is not without its limitations. Some of these limitations are grounded in the nature of law itself. As a dynamic, developing, and ongoing process, law is an "open texture" field of study which experiences constant growth.[17] An essential element of this field is its reliance on a steady "infusion of new ideas."[18] Precedent itself does not always permit of these ideas. In many cases, particular precedents prove to be overly static or situation-bound. In other cases, no precedent seems adequately analogous to the case at hand. Excellent examples of the latter problem are found in what legal scholars call "problems of the penumbra."[19] These are the areas of uncertainty resulting from such circumstances as the following: (1) more than one rule may apply in a given instance; (2) no standing rule or precedent is exactly applicable; (3) words within a particular statute may be subject to a wide variety of interpretations; or (4) the distinction between what a law is and what it ought to be is blurred.[20]

First Amendment cases offer a plethora of penumbra problems.

For example, though the Constitution *per se* does not specify a "right to privacy," many Supreme Court Justices believe that the First Amendment can be interpreted to protect such an interest. This interpretation has created a body of precedents, based primarily upon loose construction of the Constitution, protecting what Justices interpret as an individual's "right to privacy." When first confronted with this interpretation of the First Amendment, Justices faced excessive ambiguity in the relevant document and competing alternatives in litigative argumentation. As with the first half of step one in the judicial reasoning process, then, Justices facing penumbra and other such interests make choices, often framed in competing political constructs.[21]

Having worked as effectively as possible with the given facts and precedents in any case, the Justices move to the second step of their reasoning process, audience analysis. Because the Court faces a "real" audience, yet one whose joint expectations form an ideal of practical reasoning, this audience may be described as a composite of particular audiences. Different from a universal audience in its particularization, but similar to this ideal in its composition, this audience provides a substantive rhetorical challenge to the Court.

Accordingly, at the second step of their reasoning process, Justices analyze the needs and expectations of their audience. The Court faces eight different particular audiences,[22] all of whom come to the judicial opinion with different perceptions of the Court's function and with different sets of interests. Yet all these audiences form one particular audience comprised of a common set of *general* rules, predispositions, and expectations. The special expectations these audiences share "distinguish initiation from popularization."[23] This special composite audience made up of parties directly affected by the case, lawyers, Supreme Court Justices, lower court justices, legislators, administrators, legal scholars, and other educated members of the body politic create a group whose interests and shared expectations the Justices cannot ignore. When these shared expectations—such as of reasonable, predictable, impartial adjudication—are one compatible whole, step two of the judicial reasoning process is relatively simple. The Justices must simply take care to write well-reasoned decisions, grounded in precedent. But often the principal task of the second step in the judicial reasoning process is to balance the different expectations and interests of each particular audience with the incompatible expectations, interests, and perceptions of another group. For example, members of the composite audience often have different perceptions of the role presumption ought to play in Supreme Court adjudication; yet these different perceptions are based ultimately upon shared notions of the judicial function. A brief look at these differences and at the role they play in different types of cases will graphically illustrate the importance basic audience predispositions have in judicial reasoning.

Before the Supreme Court is able to render its judgment in any case, it must first characterize the participating litigants' interests and then determine who among them will carry the burden of proof. That is, whenever there is any degree of doubt regarding any question relevant to the Court's judgment, the Court must decide how to administer that doubt. Because this judgment of presumption has the effect of swaying any given case in favor of one of the participating litigants, the Court's judgment is expected to be made as carefully and as impartially as possible. The Court has many "loci" available to justify these judgments. Among them, perhaps the most general and commonly used "locus" is the uncontroverted desirability of judicial independence from the legislative and executive branches. The Court and its critics derive many warrants from this very general "locus."

Ironically, the most commonly accepted and most widely used of these derivations lead to incompatible judgments of justification on the question of litigative presumption. On the one hand, it is widely accepted that judicial independence permits the Court to serve as a bulwark against executive and legislative excesses and arbitrariness.[24] This interpretation of the judicial function leads, however, to the controversial view that the Court ought to apply strict scrutiny in its judgments of governmental behavior (which we will call nondeference to governmental agencies).[25] This controversial derivation from the general desirability of judicial independence serves as a warrant for the determination of presumption in many First Amendment and Fourteenth Amendment cases. In *Loving* v. *Virginia* (1967),[26] for example, Justice Warren writes for the majority:

> *At the very least, the equal protection clause demands that racial classifications . . . be subjected to the "most rigid scrutiny."*

This broad interpretation of the Court's powers differs sharply from the view that the Court's independence from the legislative and executive branches entails limited Court jurisdiction. Though most would accept such limited justiciability, the meaning and application of "non-legislative" and "non-executive" are highly controversial. This derivation of the desirability for judicial independence leads, for example, to deferential judgments of presumption (or the use of judicial self-restraint), such as those used in most recent economic regulation cases.[27] In *Nebbia* v. *New York* (1934),[28] for example, the Court held:

> *It does not lie with the courts to determine that the rule is unwise. With the wisdom of the policy adopted, with the adequacy or practicality of the law*

enacted to forward it, the courts are both incompetent and unauthorized to deal.

This brief discussion of judicial use of presumption in different types of cases illustrated how the composite audience's shared "locus"—that it is desirable to separate the three branches of government—may nonetheless lead to controversial predispositions toward judicial assertiveness.

Perhaps an even more difficult challenge is created when members of the composite audience come to the judicial decision with competing values. First Amendment cases, for example, often involve essential conflicts between fundamental American values: the value of unfettered debate vs. the need to maintain public order; the value of undaunted public inquiry vs. the individual's right to privacy. As the tide of public opinion flows in favor of heavy governmental security measures one decade, so it flows in favor of protecting citizenry from governmental invasions of privacy the next; as it moves from a concern for a real or imagined political menace one decade, so it becomes preoccupied with the need for an unfettered press the next.[29]

It would seem that if the Justices wish to accommodate the values of all their audiences, they must write opinions so abstract as to appeal to basic shared assumptions. But if they do so, they avoid resolving the conflicts essential in these difficult cases. Of course the Justices may also merely accede to the interests, values, and expectations of one audience at the cost of sacrificing the consent or approval of an opposing group. But this solution, too, poses long-term problems for the Court.

In recognizing the important role that the first two steps play in the gathering of data for argument construction, we are also constrained to observe that the balancing procedure which must take place between the interpretation of legal rules and the court's responsiveness to audience concerns is influenced by the type of Supreme Court case that is being adjudicated. We have found, for example, that since the early 1950's, economic regulation cases have generally produced little public controversy. The Court's inclination in such cases has, therefore, been to defer to the legislatures' rights to produce "reasonable" laws with respect to these types of interests. This practice of giving presumption to the rules and statutes of the legislative bodies is reinforced by the Justices' belief that their deference to the legislature will either be endorsed or largely ignored by the composite audience.[30] In contrast, cases dealing with fundamental human needs and rights, particularly those associated with civil rights issues and freedom of expression, are generally accompanied by strong audience commitments and values which force the Court to take seriously the conflicting public sentiments on relevant issues and often to reconstruct previous judicial rulings.[31]

When Justices have completed this task of providing essential data for deliberation and justification, they are ready to assume a more explicitly inventive role. They may now engage in the dual process of constructing and evaluating arguments. This, as we shall see, is perhaps the most difficult challenge in the deliberative process because of the tension that tends to exist between traditional rules and precedents on the one hand and prevailing audience opinions on the other. As we observed earlier, this perceptual problem carries its own burdens for the Justices. This problem becomes more complex as the Justices attempt to invent arguments based upon their perceptions.

Before proceeding to a discussion of this third step in the judicial reasoning process—namely, the invention of arguments—it is necessary first to acknowledge the Justices' creative function. There is a great body of testimony from legal scholars highlighting the need for instituting change in law by a creative act on the part of the judge. As we have seen, this creativity comes into play at the outset, as Justices characterize relevant facts and statutes. But this creativity becomes more apparent when rules and precedents are in conflict with expectations of the composite audience; or where no available rule is perceived as appropriate for the case under consideration; or perhaps even more often, where the composite audience is confused about its expectations as in many recent First Amendment cases.[32] This step may be seen as the "linkage" between the first two steps and the last:[33]

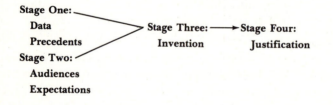

As the Justices invent arguments they must take these different perspectives into account.[34] And like all rhetors, Justices have access to what Aristotle called "all the available means of persuasion." In this sense, the Justice is like any other rhetor engaged in persuasion; by common consent rhetoric is essential in the very act of "doing law."[35] Yet jurisprudential reasoning is distinctive in its special relationship to the high expectations of the Court's composite audience. Judicial reasoning also is marked by a dependence on arguments based on examples and analogies.[36] Levi describes how these argument forms function in judicial reasoning. "From the standpoint of reasoning by example," he suggests, "the circumstances before the court are compared with a number of somewhat similar circumstances that have been classified in terms of opposing categories."[37]

As the example or analogy is a principal argumentative form of judicial invention, the chronological pattern is its basic structure. Pound lists three steps in the invention of a legal argument: (1) "finding the law," (2) "interpreting the rule," and (3) applying the rule "to the case in hand."[38] Similarly, Levi suggests a three-fold chronological sequence: (1) observation of similarity "between cases," (2) announcement of the relevant law "in the first case," and (3) application of the rule "to the second case."[39]

We have found a different chronological sequence in our study. Our look at First Amendment cases, economic regulation cases, property law cases and cases involving alleged racial discrimination indicates that the Court consistently employs a four-step decision-explicating procedure with varying emphases on each step: (1) characterization of the plaintiff's interest; (2) characterization of the government's purpose (as it relates to the alleged harm to the plaintiff's interest); (3) determination of governmental jurisdiction and of whether the "problem" actually exists; and (4) determination of whether there is a reasonable relation between the alleged problem and the means the government has chosen to alleviate the alleged problem.[40]

While in general agreement with Pound, Levi, and with our study, Benjamin Cardozo observed further that an analogical legal argument is developed against the background of history, tradition, and contemporary customs or mores.[41] Toulmin aptly summarizes the nature of the invention of jurisprudential arguments by analogy:

It would never be self-contradictory to say, "it was decided thus in a parallel case, but it ought not to be so decided in the present case." Rather, the historical record of past decisions creates standing presumption for the future. Critical comparisons with past rulings establish presumptive rules for future decisions in similar cases; and these rules are set aside, only when specific grounds can be advanced to rebut the presumptions so created.[42]

In sum, judicial argumentation fitting the "mould" described here would be both warrant-using and warrant-establishing in nature. For example, the Court's recent interpretation of step four of our model of analogical argument—whether there is a reasonable relation between the relevant problems and the means the government uses to solve these problems—in so-called benign discrimination cases employs the compelling state interest, less onerous alternative rule of one type of First Amendment case. Here the Court is warrant-using in the sense that it is drawing upon established rules. But the Court is warrant-establishing in the sense that it is creating rules for a new context, namely, cases involving governmental use of racial criteria for remedial purposes.

A vital part of step three in judicial reasoning is, of course, critical assessment of the arguments. As the reasoning unfolds, Justices and their critics use several tests to check the strength and relevance of judicial warrants and claims. The first test is the criterion of justice. So transcendent is justice that it has been called "the first virtue of social institutions;"[43] "the principal virtue, the source of all others;"[44] and the overriding end of law.[45]

Included in the notion of justice are the ideas of equity or equality and fairness. The leading precept of equity is that the judge is obligated to "treat like cases alike" and "different cases differently."[46] As Holmes expressed it, "Any legal standard . . . must be one which would apply to all men, not specially excepted, under the same circumstances."[47] To consider people in what appears to be the same situation as equals, then, is to avoid needless arbitrariness or partiality.

Among the most useful theories for understanding the nature and role the criterion of justice plays in evaluating the worth of judicial arguments are those of Chaim Perelman and John Rawls. The judge, Perelman argues, "is in the service of justice—the noblest of virtues." It is his task to determine the rules in a given situation and then apply them in a reasonable manner. Perelman's "rule of justice," which resembles Biblical "Golden Rule," Kant's Categorical Imperative, and Baier's Principle of Reversibility, supports the notion that "beings of one and the same essential category must be treated in the same way."[48] "Correctness," "reason," and "conscience," he further maintains, place a duty upon Justices to reject all forms of inequality, arbitrariness, and inhumanity, within the limits of their function.[49] According to Perelman, then, as the Justices invent arguments, they face the "rule of justice" as a criterion. This rule may serve them as they "keep watch in order that the law should be just."[50] But perhaps even more importantly, they must be aware that members of the composite audience are likely to come to the judicial decision with some version of this principle or rule.

Equally compelling as a tool for measuring the strength and relevance of judicial arguments is John Rawls's concept of "justice as fairness." Rawls, whose theory perhaps constitutes the most widely discussed in modern ethical theory, features a contract theory in which "free and equal beings with a liberty to choose" agree in an "initial situation" to a set of "principles of justice" presumed to be fair for all members of the group.[51] When specified rules are developed and approved, all participants are duty-bound to carry out the agreements. This prevents any persons covered by the contract from benefiting "from the cooperative efforts of others without doing" their "fair share."[52] Despite some possible philosophical weaknesses in Rawls's theory, Rawls proposes a compelling intuition; if a judicial argument is to be convincing, it must come down hard on the side of reasonableness rooted in initially agreed upon (or implicitly contracted) principles of fairness.

This use of justice as a criterion to assess arguments lends credence to the idea that judicial reasoning cannot limit itself to a consideration of the "is"; it must also come to grips with the "ought." Unless our judicial system deals effectively with the "ought," it runs the risk of losing "both the spirit and symbol of justice."[53]

A second test to be used in the critical assessment of judicial arguments is the requirement of structural integrity. In developing this criterion we are fully aware at the outset of the controversy generated by the legal positivists who tend to relate law to formal logic and the mathematical model. This view has been condemned by Holmes, Pound, and by many other contemporary scholars. The most recent and perhaps most persuasive contribution to this "attack" on legal positivism is Perelman's provocative essay, "The Rational and the Reasonable."[54] Here Perelman treats "rational" and "reasonable" as polar terms. A rational argument, Perelman argues, conforms "to the rules of logic" and "corresponds to mathematical reason" characterized by "a priori, self-evident and immutable truths."[55] A reasonable argument, on the other hand, is grounded in probability and "common sense," and achieves strength and relevance in accordance to the demands of the rhetorical situation.

Despite the usefulness of this distinction, it may be that, on strict construction, Perelman's distinction between the "rational" and the "reasonable" is more rigid than necessary. At some points, for example, certain aspects of the "rational" correspond closely to what may be described as the "reasonable."[56] For our purposes, some of the generally accepted rules of logic, which appropriately fall under the category of the "rational," have utility as a critical tool in evaluating the structural integrity of an argument. In this regard, we agree with Richard Wasserstrom, when he writes in *The Judicial Decision:*

> *It may indeed be true that the syllogism can neither furnish nor evaluate the content of propositions, but it does not follow that a procedure which seeks to use the syllogism to "test" the validity of arguments is thereby committed to employ any particular method for deriving the premises of these arguments. Courts cannot have used the syllogism to decide which premises to select; but this by itself does not show that they did not use the syllogism as a means for assessing the validity of arguments they formulated. . . . Many legal philosophers are surely mistaken if they infer the inherent arbitrariness of*

the judicial decision process from the limited utility of formal, deductive logic.[57]

Ray McKerrow supports Wasserstrom's view by arguing persuasively that arguments justify rather than verify. Rhetorical validity, he states, may be viewed as a kind of "pragmatic justification." In the Court's community of argument, fundamentals of logic serve, among other things, to determine "the constancy of . . . (the Court's) reasoning."[58] Thus, to evaluate the structural integrity of judicial arguments, we may employ formal principles pragmatically.

It is instructive to observe at this point, as the foregoing discussion strongly suggests, that in critically assessing arguments in judicial reasoning, rational methods occupy a central role. This emphasis on a rational base as the essence of a validity criterion enhances objectivity and increases the probability of making meaningful generalities. Moreover, it places judicial reasoning firmly within the philosophical approaches of Toulmin, Perelman, and Ehninger—all of whom, according to McKerrow, ground the operation of their respective criteria on an assurance of a rational, objective appraisal of arguments.[59]

The evaluative procedures outlined here further show that the critical assessment stage in the deliberative process in judicial reasoning is pluralistic in nature. For it makes use both of what McKerrow calls "arguments as process" which focus on "particular environments," and "arguments as product" which stress "definable structures."[60]

Both A. G. Guest and the well-known American legal scholar, Herbert Wechsler, share McKerrow's view that the denial of argument as verification does not deny the value of assessing the formal relationship between propositions. Logic, Guest argues, "acts as a kind of geography, explaining the directive force of propositions and their relationship one with another."[61] This includes, among other things, a consideration of whether the major premise of a rhetorical syllogism is acceptable to the composite audience, the minor premise contains proper syntax, and the conclusion is a logical result of the major and minor premises. In borrowing some of his ideas from logic, Wechsler introduces the notion of "neutral principles" consisting of standards which go beyond "the case at hand." A good argument, he maintains, "rests on reasons that in their generality and their neutrality transcend any immediate result that is involved."[62] These principles should be applied in a manner which conforms to the structure of logic, and they should be maintained until strong and compelling reasons for overturning them can be presented. McKerrow, Wasserstrom, Guest, and Wechsler suggest, then, that while formal logic, as a whole, with its stress on timeless principles and eternal truths, lies largely outside of the sphere of judicial reasoning, certain elements of logic—principally those dealing with structural form—give us a partial method for examining the integrity of an argument.

Nor is the structural integrity criterion limited to a concern for the logical form, internal consistency, and syntax of an argument. It is similarly concerned with the related problems of testing the quality of arguments from example and analogy, which are, as noted earlier, essential to judicial reasoning. In using this type of invention, the Justice has, as an end, the goal of ascertaining similarities and differences between the facts of a present case and the appropriate rules and precedents. When an analogy is used, therefore, it must be demonstrated that the general principle is appropriate for the particular case and for the judicial function that is being performed.

In our analysis thus far we have focused on the deliberative process as it develops along a three-step continuum: (1) examining relevant facts in relation to statutes, rules, and precedents which appear relevant; (2) analyzing the relevant expectations of the composite audience; and (3) creating and assessing arguments that will prove to be an adequate response. The final step in judicial reasoning is justificatory in nature. Because the Supreme Court is the highest appellate body in the United States and one of the most respected judicial bodies in the world,[63] and because this Court's decisions become precepts of American constitutional law, Supreme Court Justices are obliged to tell the composite audience how and why they reached their conclusions. To do otherwise is to deny the lower courts, administrators, and legislators guidelines they need to fulfill their functions. Though the Court's overriding authority, combined with a strong justification in defense of their decisions, "carry their own prima facie claim for acceptance" from the composite audience,[64] without adequate justification the Court's decisions could lose this authority.

Though always of considerable import, justification is particularly crucial when Justices use their creative power to overrule a precedent. The Court officially reversed itself eighteen times from 1860–1890 and thirty times from 1937–1949.[65] Even more prevalent was this practice during the era of the Warren Court. Cox has observed that "no other Anglo-American court has ever overturned so many precedents and made so much new law in so short a time as the Supreme Court under Chief Justice Warren."[66] Decisions with such far-reaching implications as those made by the Warren Court in such areas as First and Fourteenth Amendments require effective justification if they are to be convincing to all segments of the composite audience. In other words, while all decisions require careful justification and explication, Supreme Court reversals call for specially persuasive justifications; the Court must not only make clear why it decided as it did but also why it was compelled to reverse itself. And this difficult requirement necessarily calls into question the Court's overall integrity.[67]

Minority opinions also change the justificatory requirements of majority opinions. Canon 19 of the "Canons of the Judicial Ethics" cautions the Court:

> It is of high importance that judges constituting a court of last resort should use effort and self-restraint to promote solidarity of conclusion and the consequent influence of judicial opinion. . . . Except in case of conscientious difference of opinion on fundamental principle, dissenting opinions should be discouraged in courts of last resort.

Nonetheless, Justices often write minority concurring opinions and dissents which influence the invention of arguments by majority justices.[68] What is of most importance here, however, is the influence minority opinions have on the composite audience. If persuasive, these opinions compel the majority to provide especially convincing arguments for their decision.

It is significant to observe that this complex justification process enables Justices to reevaluate the arguments they already have created and tested during the first three stages of the reasoning process. As they write their opinion explicating and justifying their decision, Justices must phrase their arguments in such a way that they will, first of all, win the approval of the other Justices holding the majority view. If successful, they may even gain the support, or at least the respect, of those Justices who plan to author minority opinions. During the evolution of this step, the Justices interact freely with each other both orally and in writing. That considerable persuasion takes place in these encounters has been well documented. "I myself," observed Justice Jackson, "have changed my opinion after reading the opinions of other members of this Court. And I am as stubborn as most. But I sometimes wind up not voting the way I voted in Conference because the reasons of the majority didn't satisfy me."[69] Walter Murphy writes:

> It is almost trite to note that if a Justice is able to mass legal precedents and history to bolster an intellectually and morally defensible policy and can present his arguments in a convincing manner, he stands an excellent chance of picking up votes.[70]

Similarly, Joseph Tussman persuasively describes the value of this process:

> The tradition of dissenting opinions makes publicly apparent the conflicting strains within the Court, develops counter argument of great power, and pushes the Court into greater depth of analysis—to everyone's profit.[71]

At the same time, the Court stands to lose its persuasiveness if Justices do not adequately respond to each other's arguments. Concern for this problem led Robert McCloskey to observe:

> *The mystique of this venerable institution sometimes still inhibits plain talk. . . . The adversary relationship between concurrers and dissenters encouraged each side to argue as if the rightness of its own view is almost too obvious for discussion.*[72]

The important role that this aspect of judicial decision-making plays in shaping judicial arguments was largely overlooked by the authors of *The Brethren* who are inclined to regard these persuasive efforts among the Justices and the changes of opinions that ensue as signs of instability and weakness.[73] Far closer to the mark is the premise that judicial reasoning mandates one to work on justification through effective modification.[74]

Because justification is an all-encompassing step which embraces the entire judicial reasoning process, it may be useful to examine an actual Supreme Court case. This case illustrates how a majority of the Justices justified their decision on a complex and highly emotional issue.

In 1961, a group of plaintiffs—the Poes, Does, and their physician, Dr. Buxton—sought a Superior Court judgment declaring a Connecticut law banning the use of contraceptives unconstitutional.[75] The majority voted to dismiss the plea on the grounds of no demonstrable harm to the plaintiffs.

The justificatory arguments invented to defend the majority decision took only sixteen paragraphs; yet in those few paragraphs they adhered closely to the comprehensive pattern of judicial reasoning we have incorporated under our four-step plan. The majority opinion, authored by Justice Frankfurter, began with a summary of the facts. Then, armed with statements of law and relevant precedents, Frankfurter developed arguments with the interests and expectations of the composite audience in mind. The reasons presented were both theoretical and empirical, often based on examples and analogies. Additionally, they were buttressed by the citation of numerous authorities. Throughout, the arguments were tested with the criteria of justice as fairness and that of structural integrity. In the final paragraph, Frankfurter set forth the majority's basic intention, one which puts judicial reasoning in general and justification in particular in clear perspective. It read:

> *Justiciability is, of course, not a legal concept with a fixed content or susceptible of scientific verification. Its utilization is the resultant of many subtle pressures, including the appropriateness of the issues for decision by*

this Court and the actual hardship to the litigants of denying them the relief sought. Both these factors justify withholding adjudication of the constitutional issue raised under the circumstances and in the manner in which they are now before the Court.[76]

In arguing that their decision was justified, the majority were seeking to allay the potential disappointment of the litigants, to produce authoritative support for the decision as precedent, and to fulfill the expectations of legal experts. If successful in this argumentative endeavor, the majority hopefully would enhance the image of the Court as a disinterested, reasonable, and responsible tribunal.

This case is also particularly enlightening because of the minority opinions authored by Justices Harlan and Douglas. In their opinions, these minority Justices create a picture radically different from that created by Justice Frankfurter. And they suggest alternative interpretations of judicial responsibility to that offered by the majority. The dynamic created by the dialectic between the majority and minority opinions in this case is significantly different from the context created by judicial unanimity.

What is most significant, however, is the rhetorical nature of this final step in the judicial reasoning process. As were steps one, two, and three, the final step in this process is highly complex and, as *Poe* illustrated, intimately bound with the rhetorical situation unique to Supreme Court deliberation.

What conclusions, we may ask in summary, can we draw from these perspectives on judicial reasoning? We perceive five implications which warrant special consideration. First, each step of the judicial reasoning process—from characterization of the facts to justification of the decision—rests squarely in the domain of rhetoric. Audience plays a central role at every stage of the reasoning process; since judicial reasoning takes place always in the realm of the plausible, likely, or probable, it emphasizes pragmatic procedure. But unlike much rhetorical activity, judicial reasoning is influenced by the shared expectations of a highly rational composite audience. Members of this audience—though distinguished from one another by divergent, often competing values and interests—share the expectation that Supreme Court Justices will engage in the "highest level of argument"; these readers expect Supreme Court opinions to be predictable, internally consistent, and, above all, reasonable. A Court which violates these fundamental expectations risks loss of its authority.

From this concept of composite audience we derive a second important implication of this study. Though others have recognized the important role audience plays in legal argumentation, we believe the concept of composite audience discussed here may have special utility for students of argument. This concept provides the flexibility essential to practical contexts; the composite audience is, after all, a large *particular* audience. At the same time, the Supreme Court's composite audience encompasses the highest expectations and assumptions shared by all rational members of the Supreme Court audience. This audience offers theorists the practical material they have sought to "untangle the relationships among values grounded in self, society, and ideal audiences."[77] Further, these theorists may use this composite audience "to investigate the process by which values become salient in decision-making situations."[78]

But just as the composite audience influences Supreme Court decision-making, so is the audience itself influenced by Supreme Court opinions. Successful judicial argumentation *creates* audience perceptions and *shapes* audience opinions. From their characterizations of the facts to their creation of new rules, Justices expand knowledge. Further, Supreme Court decisions which are made at one point in history must withstand the challenges offered in later periods. This natural tension bestows on judicial decision-making a unique dynamic quality, contributing to its generation of new ideas and new perceptual frameworks. A third important implication of this study, then, is that the model of judicial reasoning which has evolved in the United States Supreme Court context offers compelling support to those who describe rhetoric as epistemic.

A fourth implication may be drawn from the special nature of the rhetorical context in which Supreme Court judicial reasoning occurs. To satisfy each aspect of their function, Supreme Court Justices must engage in all of the three principal rhetorical activities; no case is adequately adjudicated without careful deliberation, effective persuasion, and appropriate justification. Furthermore, the composite audience's special expectations of each of these steps offer paradigms for *every* aspect of argumentation. In short, Supreme Court judicial reasoning offers a complete model of argumentation.

The final, and perhaps most significant, implication of our study stems from the special nature of the third component of this complete model. Justification at the Supreme Court level appeals to the most refined intuitions of a rational audience seeking security and justice for its body politic. Responsive to the critical expectations of this audience, Supreme Court justificatory argumentation provides a practical manifestation of reasonableness; Supreme Court justificatory arguments epitomize good reasons. Perhaps most importantly, these arguments distinguish between "is" and "ought"; stress the primary, integrating virtue of justice; and highlight good reasons as viable and salutary means for producing wise decisions. As such, they offer persuasive evidence for Ehninger's hopeful claim that there is a moral dimension to argumentative validity.[79]

Notes

1. This lecture appears in James L. Golden, Goodwin F. Berquist, and William E. Coleman, *The Rhetoric of Western Thought,* 2nd ed. (Dubuque: Kendall/Hunt Publishing Company, 1978), pp. 323–30.
2. Chaim Perelman and L[ucie] Olbrechts–Tyteca, *The New Rhetoric: A Treatise on Argumentation,* trans. John Wilkinson and Purcell Weaver (South Bend: University of Notre Dame Press, 1971), p. 134.
3. Stephen Toulmin, *Uses of Argument* (Cambridge: Cambridge University Press, 1958), p. 7.
4. E. Griffin-Collart, from the Preface (Avant-Propos) to the *Revue Internationale de Philosophie, La Nouvelle Rhétorique: Essais en Hommage à Chaim Perelman,* 127–28 (1979), 3.
5. See Josina Makau, "The Judicial Opinion as a Rhetorical Performance," Diss., University of California, Berkeley 1979. Makau isolates reasoning patterns in forty years of precedents in four types of cases: First Amendment, economic regulation, property law, and racial discrimination cases.
6. Jesse Choper, Yale Kamisar, and William Lockhart, *Constitutional Law: Cases, Comments, and Questions* (St. Paul: American Casebook Series, West, 1975); and Gerald Gunther, *Cases and Materials on Constitutional Law* (Mineola: University Casebook Series, The Foundation Press, 1975).
7. *Poe v. Ullman; Doe v. Ullman;* and *Buxton vs. Ullman,* 367 U.S. 901, 81 S. Ct. Rp. 1752 (1961). Emphasis added. This case was particularly important because it directly addressed the question of justiciability.
8. For a thorough rhetorical analysis of this case see Makau, "Judicial Opinion," pp. 7–30.
9. Jerome Frank, *Courts on Trial* (Princeton: Princeton University Press, 1949), p. 262.
10. H. L. A. Hart, *The Concept of Law* (Oxford: Clarendon Press, 1961), p. 92.
11. Rolf Sartorius, "Hart's Concept of Law," in *More Essays in Legal Philosophy,* ed. Robert S. Summers (Oxford: Basil Blackwell, 1971), pp. 155–56.
12. *Black's Law Dictionary,* rev. 4th ed. (St. Paul: West, 1968), p. 1340.
13. See Stephen Toulmin, Richard Rieke, and Allan Janik, *An Introduction to Reasoning* (New York: Macmillan, 1979), pp. 203–27.
14. Renato Adler, "The Justices and the Journalists," Book Review, *New York Times,* 16 December 1979, p. 1.
15. William O. Douglas, "Stare Decisis," in *The Supreme Court: Views from the Inside,* ed. Alan F. Westin (New York: W. W. Norton, 1961).
16. Richard A. Wasserstrom, *The Judicial Decision* (Stanford: Stanford University Press, 1961), p. 61. See also Hart, "Positivism and the Separation of Law and Morals," *Harvard Law Review,* 71 (1958), 607.
17. Oliver W. Holmes has observed: "The law embraces the story of a nation's development through many centuries. . . . In order to know what it is, we must know what it has been, and what it needs to become. . . . (Law) is forever adopting new principles from life at one end, and it always retains old ones from history at the other" *(The Common Law* [Cambridge: Harvard University Press, 1963], pp. 5, 32). The term "open texture" comes from Hart, *The Concept of Law,* p. 24.
18. Edward H. Levi, *An Introduction to Legal Reasoning* (Chicago: University of Chicago Press, 1948), p. 4.
19. See, in particular, Hart's essay, "Positivism and the Separation of Law and Morals."
20. Hart, "Positivism," pp. 607–14.
21. See Gunther, *Cases,* pp. 468–1505 for extensive analyses of these so-called "penumbra" interests.

22. These audiences include the following: (1) participating litigants, (2) other Supreme Court Justices, (3) lower court Justices, (4) legislators, (5) administrators, (6) future Supreme Court Justices, (7) legal scholars, (8) and other educated members of the body politic.
23. Perelman, *New Rhetoric*, p. 100.
24. Madison wrote, for example: "Were the power of judging joined with the legislative, the life and liberty of the subject would be exposed to arbitrary control" *(The Federalist Papers*, No. 47). See also, Madison, *Fed. Paper*, No. 51 and Hamilton, *Fed. Paper*, No. 78. See also, Montesquieu, *Spirit of the Laws*, Bk. xi, Sect. 6 for a similar view.
25. In the modern Supreme Court, Justice Douglas was perhaps most noted for his application of this rule in many types of cases.
26. *Loving v. Virginia*, 388 U.S. 1, 87 S. Ct. 1817 (1967).
27. In the Modern Supreme Court, Justice Frankfurter was perhaps best known for his application of this rule in many types of cases.
28. *Nebbia v. New York*, 291 U.S. 502, 54 S. Ct. (1934); see also *Ferguson v. Skrupa*, 372 U.S. 229 (1963); *Wickard v. Filburn*, 317 U.S. 111 (1942).
29. See Makau, "Judicial Opinions," pp. 88–124, for a detailed discussion of this and similar problems related to First Amendment adjudication.
30. The following economic regulation cases supporting this claim are typical: *Nebbia v. New York*, 291 U.S. 502 (1934); *Williamson v. Lee Optical of Oklahoma*, 348 U.S. 483 (1955); *Railway Express Agency v. New York*, 366 U.S. 106 (1919); *Ferguson v. Skrupa*, 372 U.S. 726 (1963); and *Wickard v. Filburn*, 317 U.S. 111 (1942).
31. The following Supreme Court cases are illustrative of this point: *Louisiana v. United States*, 380 U.S. 145 (1965); *Bolling v. Sharpe*, 347 U.S. 497 (1954); *Brown v. Board of Education*, 347 U.S. 483 (1954); and *Loving v. Virginia*, 388 U.S. 1 (1967).
32. For a detailed discussion of the latter, see Makau, "Judicial Opinion," Chapter IV.
33. We are indebted to Professor Ray E. McKerrow for his suggestion of this diagram.
34. In describing the inventive aspects of the judicial function, most current legal scholars predictably reject the premise earlier set forth by legal positivists that law should be on the level of certainty exemplified by formal logic and mathematics. See, for example, Holmes, *The Common Law*, p. 5; and Henry Steele Commager, *The American Mind* (New Haven: Yale University Press, 1950), pp. 374–76. At the same time, however, many legal scholars are careful to limit the degree to which they feel comfortable with the Court's law-creating powers. See, for example, Herbert Wechsler's "Toward Neutral Principles of Constitutional Law," in *Principles, Politics, and Fundamental Law*, ed. H. Wechsler (Cambridge: Harvard University Press, 1961); and Joseph Tussman, *Government and the Mind* (New York: Oxford University Press, 1977).
35. Among those who have persuasively argued this point are Richard Rieke and Josina Makau. See Rieke, "Rhetorical Theory in American Legal Practice," Diss., The Ohio State University 1964.
36. See Levi, *An Introduction to Legal Reasoning*, p. 1.
37. Edward H. Levi, "The Nature of Judicial Reasoning," in *Law and Philosophy*, ed. Sidney Hook (New York: University of New York, 1964), p. 268. See also Makau, "Judicial Opinion," for a discussion of other argumentative strategies employed by the Court.
38. Roscoe Pound, *An Introduction to the Philosophy of Law* (New Haven: Yale University Press, 1922), p. 48.
39. Levi, *An Introduction to Legal Reasoning*, p. 2.
40. See Makau, "Judicial Opinion," for a detailed discussion of this procedure.
41. Benjamin Cardoro, *The Nature of the Judicial Process* (New Haven: Yale University Press, 1921), pp. 30–31.

42. Stephen Toulmin, *Human Understanding* (Princeton: Princeton University Press, 1972), p. 94.
43. John Rawls, *A Theory of Justice* (Cambridge: Harvard University Press, 1971), p. 3.
44. Chaim Perelman, *The Idea of Justice and the Problem of Argument* (London: Routledge and Kegan Paul, 1963).
45. This frequently repeated statement appears in such writings as these: Hart, *Concept of Law*, p. 155; Morris Ginsberg, *On Justice and Society* (New York: Cornell University Press, 1965), p. 66; and Perelman, *The Idea of Justice and the Problem of Argument*, pp. 7–16.
46. For an interesting discussion of this concept, see Tussman and TenBroek, "The Equal Protection of the Laws," *California Law Review*, 37 (1949), 341. Tussman and TenBroek graphically illustrate the complexities of this concept in constitutional adjudication.
47. Holmes, *The Common Law*, p. 88.
48. Perelman, *The Idea of Justice and the Problem of Argument*. In his book, *Justice*, Perelman observed, "To achieve his end, the philosopher must use a rational argumentation conforming to Kant's categorical imperative: His postulates and his reasoning must be valid for the whole of the human community" (New York: Random House, 1967), p. 82. In *The Idea of Justice*, Perelman further observed, "The just man will act in such a way as to conform to the duty laid upon him by the categorical imperative," p. 75.
49. Perelman, *The Idea of Justice*, p. 76.
50. Perelman, *The Idea of Justice*, p. 66.
51. Rawls, *A Theory of Justice*, pp. 12, 15, 31, 256.
52. Rawls, *A Theory of Justice*, p. 343.
53. Levi, "Nature of Judicial Reasoning," p. 279; also see Hart, "Positivism and the Separation of Law and Morals."
54. Chaim Perelman, "The Rational and the Reasonable," in *Rationality To-day*, ed. Theodore F. Geraets (Ottawa, Canada: The University of Ottawa Press, 1979), pp. 213–24.
55. Perelman, "Rational," pp. 213–14.
56. This point was emphasized by L. Dupré and K. Nielsen in their critiques of Perelman's presentation (Geraets, *Rationality To-day*, pp. 219–20). Perelman's responses to their questions suggest that he would prefer a looser construction of his distinction, thereby providing the flexibility we seek here.
57. Wasserstrom, *The Judicial Decision*, pp. 23–24.
58. Ray E. McKerrow, "Rhetorical Validity: An Analysis of Three Perspectives on the Justification of Rhetorical Argument," *Journal of the American Forensic Association*, 13 (1977), 131–41.
59. Ray E. McKerrow, "Rhetorical Validity."
60. These distinctions appear in Ray McKerrow, "Argument Communities: A Quest for Distinctions," *Proceedings of the Summer Conference on Argumentation*, eds. Jack Rhodes and Sara Newell (SCA, 1980), pp. 214–27. We concur with McKerrow's claim that "the opposition between process and product views of argument creates unnecessary difficulties in the creation of theory" (p. 214).
61. A. G. Guest, "Logic in the Law," in *Oxford Essays in Jurisprudence*, ed. A. G. Guest (Oxford: Oxford University Press, 1961), p. 27.
62. Herbert Wechsler, *Principles, Politics, and Fundamental Law*, p. 27.
63. See, for example, Wasserstrom, *Judicial Decisions*, p. 83.
64. William O. Douglas, "Stare Decisis," p. 133.
65. Archibald Cox, *The Role of the Supreme Court in American Government* (New York: Oxford University Press, 1976), p. 110.

66. Cox, *Role;* see also his volume, Archibald Cox, *The Warren Court* (Cambridge: Cambridge University Press, 1968).
67. See Murphy's *Elements of Judicial Strategy;* see also Robert McCloskey's *The Modern Supreme Court* (Cambridge: Harvard University Press, 1973).
68. See Murphy, *Elements,* for a detailed discussion of this procedure; see also Bob Woodward and Scott Armstrong, *The Brethren* (New York: Simon and Schuster, 1980).
69. Cited in Murphy, *Elements,* p. 44.
70. Murphy, *Elements,* p. 54.
71. Joseph Tussman, *The Supreme Court on Racial Discrimination* (New York: Oxford University Press, 1963), p. ix.
72. McCloskey, *Modern Court,* p. 275.
73. This is especially true in their strong attacks on the strategies of former Chief Justice Warren Burger. In critiquing *The Brethren,* Adler noted: "Now it must be obvious on a moment's reflection, that it is desirable—even essential to the judicial process—that the Justices be able sometimes to persuade one another, to change their minds." Adler, Book Review, *New York Times,* 16 December 1979, p. 26.
74. Stephen Toulmin, unpublished lecture delivered at The Ohio State University, Columbus, 22 Nov. 1974.
75. *Paul Poe et. al.* v. *Ullman, Doe* v. *Ullman,* and *Buxton* v. *Ullman* 367 U.S. 901, 81 S. Ct. Rp. 1752, 1961.
76. *Poe, Doe, Buxton;* for an extensive analysis of this case, see Makau, "Judicial Opinion," pp. 7–30.
77. Walter R. Fisher, "Toward a Logic of Good Reasons," *Quarterly Journal of Speech,* 64 (1978), 384.
78. Fisher, "Good Reasons."
79. Douglas Ehninger, "Validity as Moral Obligation," *Southern Speech Journal,* 33 (1968), 215–22.

INDEX

A

Absolutism, 71
Abstraction, 7–8
Academicae Quaestiones (Cicero), 117
Addison, Joseph, 123
Adjuncts, 110
Akenside, Mark, 123
Analogical inference, 93
Analogy, as argument from, 147–48; in judicial argument, 165
Anscombe, G. E. M., 143
Antecedents, 110
Antiphon, 99
Appearance-reality distinction, 8
Appropriateness, of argument, 98
Archaeology and discourse, 39
Argument, 61–62; from analogy, 147–48; appropriateness of, 98; from experience, 147; forms of, 97; rational, 167; reasonable, 167; steps in constructing legal, 159-65; from testimony, 147; validity of, 97–98; warrant-establishing, 85–86, 165–66, warrant-using, 85–86, 165–66
Argumentation, xix, 80–82, 97–99; legal, xxii–xxiii, 158–73
Argumentative demands, 87
Argumentum autem, 109
Argumentum rationem, 109
Aristotle, 11, 28, 29, 64, 78, 108, 111, 112, 123, 137, 138, 141–42, 143, 144, 150, 151
Arnold, Carroll, 50
Art of Delivering Written Language (Cockin), 124
Art/body of principles distinction, 27
Artificial signs, 127–28
Arts of discourse, 123, 143–49
Audience, xxii, 13, 29–44, 60; composite nature of, 161, 172–73
Austin, J. L., 89
Ayer, A. J., 152

B

Bacon, Francis, 123, 127–28, 144
Bampton Lectures (Whately), 142
Barthes, Roland, 3, 4

Bayly, Anselm, 122
Behavior theory, 129–32
Berger, Charles R., 10
Berkeley, George, 126
Berlo, David K., 16
Bevilacqua, Vincent, 71
Bitzer, Lloyd, F., 13, 38, 50, 52
Black, Edwin, 40–41
Black's Law Dictionary, 160
Blair, Hugh, 131
Boethius, 113, 114
Booth, Wayne, 50, 51–52
Boster, Frank, 11
Brethren, The, 171
Bryant, Donald, 24
Burden of proof, 162
Burgess, Parke, 40
Burgh, James, 122, 127, 128
Burke, Edmund, 122
Burke, Kenneth, 14, 25, 42
Butler, Joseph, 80, 81, 142

C

Campbell, George, 131, 142, 144, 149, 151
Cardozo, Benjamin, 165
Causes, 110
Cherwitz, Richard A., xviii, 69-84
Cicero, xix–xx, 107–16
Circumstances, types of in Cicero's *Topica,* 110
Classical theories of rhetoric, 130
Cockin, William, 122, 124
Coleridge, Samuel Taylor, 124
Common sense, 133, 139
Communication theory, 15–17
Comparatione maiorum, 110
Comparison, with equal events, 110; with events of less import, 110; with greater events, 110
Compendium (Aldrich), 143
Conceptualism, 140
Concretization, 7–8
Confirmatio, 112
Conjugata, 110
Conjugates, 110
Connective inference, 93
Consequents, 110

Grammar, 123–24
Grene, Marjorie, 51, 65
Grice, H. P., 95
Griffin-Collart, E., 158
Gronbeck, Bruce E., xix, xx, 85-106
Guest, A. G., 168
Gumb, Raymond, 96

H

Hall, Edward, 99
Harlan, John Marshall, 172
Hartley, David, 126
Hawkes, Terence, 3
Hegel, George, 71, 77
Hikins, James W., xviii, 69-84
Historic Doubts (Whately), 147
History of ideas, xvii, 26, 120
Hobbes, Thomas, 123, 126
Holmes, Oliver W., 166, 167
Howell, Wilbur Samuel, 137, 144
Hubbell, H. M., 108
Human nature, 128–29
Hume, David, 126, 127, 130, 131, 139, 142
Hungerland, Isabel, 95
Husserl, Edmund, 99
Hutcheson, Francis, 130
Hymes, Dell, 99

I

Idealism, 24–28, 41
Idealists and rhetoric, 37, 41
Ideologies, 53–54
Ideology, 26
Inductive inference, 93
Inference, as argumentative demand, 87; in Cicero's *Topica,* 109–15; classes: everyday, 87–90; as justificatory, 87; logical, 92–93; nature of in argument, 85–100; special-topical, 90–92
Inference, types of: analogical, 93; connective, 93; deductive, 93; definitive, 91; ethical, 90; extenuative, 91; inductive, 93; interpretive, 91; legal-regulative, 91; logical, 92–93; material, 89; perceptual, xix, 88; pragmatic, 89; procedural-constitutional, 92; semantic, 89
Inquiry, 53–61
Institutional rules, 95
Interactive motives, 43
Interpretative inference, 91
Intrinsic *loci,* 110, 116
Inventio, 108

Invention, 107–09; in judicial reasoning, 164–69, 170–71
Invention/disposition/style/memory/delivery view of rhetoric, 28

J

Jackson, Robert, 170
Johnstone, Henry, 50
Judicial Decision, The (Wasserstrom), 167
Judicial model of rhetoric, 158–71
Judicial reasoning, xxii–xxiii, 157–73; locus in, 162–66; persuasion in, 169–71; problems of the penumbra in, xvii, 160; rhetorical invention in, 164–69, 170–71
Judicial rhetoric, xxii, 157–73

K

Kames, Lord, Henry Home, 128
Kant, Immanuel, 71, 77, 78, 122, 125, 142, 166
Kaufer, David, 130
Kirkland, David, 33
Knowledge, public, 52; sources of, in Whately's theory of rhetoric, 142; tacit, 51, 56
Kuhn, Thomas, 9

L

Language, 8–9, 127–29
Langue, 2, 7, 12, 13
Latent structure, 3
Leach, Edmund, 3–4
Leader/follower relationship, 41–42
Leff, Michael, 151–52
Legal argument, steps in constructing, 159–65
Legal discourse, 157–73
Legal-regulative inference, 91
Lemert, James B., 16
Levi, Edward H., 164, 165
Lévi-Strauss, Claude, 2, 3, 4, 5, 12
Liska, Jo, 12, 16
Locke, John, 127, 139, 140
Lockean theory of ideas, 139
Loci, 109–15, 162; extrinsic types, 110; intrinsic types, 110
Locus, 108–13, 115; in judicial reasoning, 162–66
Logic, 123–24; 143–49; its relationship to rhetoric, 145–46
Logical coercion, 86–87
Logical inferences, types of, 92–93
Loving v. *Virginia,* 162

M

McCloskey, Robert, 171
McCroskey, James, 16
McGee, Michael Calvin, xvii-xviii, xvix, 23-48
McGuire, Michael, xvi-xvii, 1-22
McKerrow, Ray E., xxi, 137-56, 168
Macrorhetorical experience, 33–37
Makau, Josina, xxi-xxii, 157-77
Marx, Karl, 24, 26
Material inference, 89
Material rhetoric, defined, 37–44; and discourse, 39
Material theory of rhetoric, 23–48
Materialism, xvii, xviii, xvix, 24–26, 28–37
Maxim, 116
Maximal propositions, 113–15
May, William, 15
Mechanical models, 6, 9–11
Mertz, Robert J., 16
Microrhetorical experience, 31–32
Mill, John Stuart, xviii–xvix, 69–82, 133, 143
Miller, Gerald, 11
Mind, active and passive nature, 77–78; active powers, 139–40
Mind-body interaction, 125–27
Minorum, 110
Miron, Murry, 15
Modeling. *See* Theory building.
Models, criteria for, 4–5
Models of rhetoric, dramatistic, 14; judicial, 158–71; material, 28–37; mechanical, 12–15; molecular, 36–37; orthogonal, 34–37; statistical, 6, 9–12
Moderate realism, 140
Mohrmann, G. P., 131
Molecular model of rhetoric, 36–37
Montesquieu, C. de, 126
Moral faculty, 139–40, 148
Moral theory, 130
Motivation, theory of, 29–32
Murphy, Walter, 170

N

Natanson, Maurice, 24, 80
Natatio, 110
Natural signs, 127–29
Nebbia v. *New York,* 162
Newman, John, 80, 81
Nominalism, 140, 143, 150
Noumenal world, 78

O

Objectivism, 53–57
Objectivist/absolutist epistemology, 70–72
Objectivist epistemology, 53–56, 76–79
Occam's Razor, 32
Ochs, Donovan J., xix-xx, 107-18
On Liberty (Mill), xviii, xix, 69–82
Ontological reason, 152
Ontology, Polanyi's 57–58
Ortega, José y Gasset, 23, 41
Orthogonal model of rhetoric, 34–37
Osborn, Michael, xv–xxiii
Osgood, Charles, 15, 16
Overington, Michael A., 52

P

Parium, 110
Parole, 2, 7, 13
Parrish, Wayland Maxfield, 137, 148
Passmore, John, 74
Pattison, Mark, 138
Pentad: act, scene, agency, agent, purpose, 14
People, 44
Perception, 56–57, 127
Perceptual inference, xix, 88
Perelman, Chaim, xxii, 50, 52, 157–58, 166, 167, 168
Perrault, Charles, 122
Persona(e), 32, 33
Personal Knowledge (Polanyi), 51
Persuasion, in judicial reasoning, 169–71; scientific, 39, 50; in Whately's theory of rhetoric, 149
Peterfreund, Sheldon, 74
Phenomenal world, 78
Phenomenalism, 151
Philosophical epistemology, 72
Piaget, Jean, 2
Poe v. *Ullman,* 159
Poetry, 124
Polanyi, Michael, xviii, 49–65
Pound, Roscoe, 165, 167
Pragmatic inference, 89
Precedent, 160
Presumption, 162
Priestley, Joseph, 127
Prior, Mary, 143
Prize Essay (Whately), 138, 148
Probability, 141–42
Problems of the penumbra, in judicial reasoning, xvii, 160
Procedural-constitutional inference, 92
Pro Milone (Cicero), 112